D1568484

Understanding OCD

Understanding OCD

Skills to Control the Conscience and Outsmart Obsessive Compulsive Disorder

Leslie J. Shapiro
Foreword by Michael A. Jenike

 PRAEGER

AN IMPRINT OF ABC-CLIO, LLC
Santa Barbara, California • Denver, Colorado • Oxford, England

12-08-15
GB
$ 48.00

Library of Congress Cataloging-in-Publication Data

Shapiro, Leslie.
  Understanding OCD : skills to control the conscience and outsmart obsessive compulsive disorder / Leslie J. Shapiro ; foreword by Michael A. Jenike.
    pages cm
  Includes bibliographical references and index.
  ISBN 978-1-4408-3211-6 (hardback)—ISBN 978-1-4408-3212-3 (e-book) 1. Obsessive-compulsive disorder—Treatment. 2. Obsessive-compulsive disorder. I. Title.
  RC533.S53 2015
  616.85′227—dc23   2014041236

ISBN: 978-1-4408-3211-6
EISBN: 978-1-4408-3212-3

19 18 17 16 15   1 2 3 4 5

This book is also available on the World Wide Web as an eBook.
Visit www.abc-clio.com for details.

Praeger
An Imprint of ABC-CLIO, LLC

ABC-CLIO, LLC
130 Cremona Drive, P.O. Box 1911
Santa Barbara, California 93116-1911

This book is printed on acid-free paper (∞)

Manufactured in the United States of America

To Jerry, Sam, and Maxine

This book is all the lessons my patients taught me to teach.

Contents

Foreword

Leslie Shapiro has worked with me for over two decades treating some of the most disabled OCD patients in the world at the McLean Hospital OCD Institute outside Boston. We hired her because she was exceedingly well trained and experienced in the treatment of OCD, and we knew we were going to tackle some of the worst OCD cases extant in the first OCD residential facility in the United States. Leslie has become one of the most skilled and effective cognitive behavior therapists in the world. I was delighted when she told me she was going to write a book to share her vast experience and creative thoughts.

This book represents her decades of experience administering effective treatment for OCD. She has become our primary expert in the area of religious and moral OCD. She coined the term "moralosity" to describe a key facet of successful treatment of OCD patients. *Understanding OCD: Skills to Control the Conscience and Outsmart Obsessive Compulsive Disorder* addresses her unique observations not addressed by other researchers and OCD authors. *Understanding OCD: Skills to Control the Conscience and Outsmart Obsessive Compulsive Disorder* also provides a viable framework to facilitate healing for OCD patients, family members. Her advice and guidance will enormously benefit those who are caring for OCD patients and students.

This exciting book outlines the biologic basis of OCD and discusses how the illness hijacks the conscience. Most important, it discusses what caregivers, family members, and patients can do to control the illness so that they can lead more normal lives. Leslie's case examples bring the illness and those who suffer from it to life while clarifying what can be done to bring relief.

This remarkable book will be invaluable to those who are involved with OCD in any way. There is innovative material here that is not available in any other book on the subject. I highly recommend this book and am honored that Leslie has asked me to contribute this foreword.

Michael A. Jenike
Professor of Psychiatry, Harvard Medical School
Founder, OCD Program, Mass General Hospital
Founder and Director, OCD Institute, McLean Hospital

Acknowledgments

I am grateful to my mentor, Gail Steketee, who drew me in to working with OCD because of her grace, intelligence, skill, professional generosity, and for the patience she had while teaching me the real deal about what works in helping patients get better (plus she laughed at my jokes). I would like all of my patients, past and present, to know how much I admire their courage and strength during the course of treatment. Your journey of taking the "risk" of facing your obsessive fears by doing the opposite of what they demand, or even by doing nothing at all about them, often takes unprecedented bravery and courage. It is an honor to be with you during those agonizing moments, witnessing the process work, and then seeing the relief on your face when you experience the rewards of recovery! You begin living life on your, not the OCD's, terms. For those ambivalent about treatment, not one of the people who beat down the OCD has ever regretted it. I would like the many past and present colleagues at the OCD Institute to know how much I appreciate teaching me the things I need to do in order to do this work even better. Mike Jenike, who had the vision to get the OCDI up and running, knew that providing an environment specifically tailored to meet the clinical and emotional needs of OCD sufferers, as well as providing support to their loved ones, would vastly improve the quality of their lives. It has been a privilege to play a role in realizing that ideal. Thanks to Lisa Tener, my writing coach who I met at the incredible Harvard Medical School: Publishing Books, Memoirs & Other Creative Nonfiction course in 2012. Lisa was generous with her time and guidance, and who always knew there was a way to figure out how help me to get through the times when I was blocked or stressed. A shout out to Lorraine Giordano, my writing buddy, who I met through taking Lisa's Bring Your Book to Life course. Thank you to my friends Lisa Tieszen and David Adams for their genuine interest and support since I started talking about this project back some time ago. Thanks also to my parents and all my other kind family and friends who listened while I talked things through. Lastly, to my hero, Harlan, whose gentle soul belies the warrior in him who fought hard for his victory over OCD.

Part I

Hard-wired at Birth

1

Your Brain Has a Mind of Its Own

Having a Mental Illness and Societal Attitudes

Let's face it: The brain has a mind of its own. Having OCD (or any mental disorder) is not your mother's fault, and there is no one to blame for it except possibly the gene pools of your mother, your father, your grandparents, your great-grandparents—and so on. Having OCD is not a reflection of your character or a punishment for having done something wrong. You have OCD because of a glitch in your brain's neurocircuitry.[1]

People may socially stigmatize themselves or others for having a mental illness, but the truth is that most families are touched by some type of mental health issue. When we think about our extended families, we might recall someone who might have seemed different, have been depressed, have drunk too much, have looked high, have seemed "eccentric," or have experienced psychotic episodes. Even if you've never noticed any of these symptoms among your relations, it's likely that you really do know someone with a mental illness. That's because it's thought that 26 percent of people in the United States have a major mental illness.[2] And that figure is based only on the number of people who have sought help—many others are undiagnosed.

For people who have OCD, suffering social stigma would be enough to suffer. However, the guilt and shame people experience because of their horrific obsessions is another burden they must bear thanks to the disorder. OCD seems to turn what the sufferer finds most objectionable into obsessions, then vilifies the sufferer for having them. (Jacques, for example, loved playing with his grandson until he began to obsess about how easy it would be to drop him on the floor and cause brain damage.)

People who have OCD are naturally people of good conscience; otherwise, they would not be horrified by their thoughts. Because the disorder leads them to doubt their "goodness," they perform rituals to compensate for any "badness" and to prove that their obsessions are not intended. You can see that having compassion (and self-compassion if you are a sufferer) for people who have OCD, or any other mental disorder, is the most appropriate and humane response. There is no blame or shame for having it.

In Massachusetts, where I live, as well as in many other states, OCD has medical parity.[3] Since 1973, people with OCD have been protected under the Americans with Disability Act.[4] Simply stated, OCD is a medically defined health issue and thus is widely covered by health insurance. As previously mentioned, research and public health studies tell us that having a mental health issue is more common than we thought. Generous people with these disorders have given their time so that research could be conducted to better understand, develop, and make treatment available for those who suffer from the range of problems that interfere with living life to their full potential.

A future hope is that having a treated mental disorder will not be used against people in the workforce. Recently a former patient contacted me to relate how difficult applying to medical school has been because being honest about explaining that the time gap on her resume was spent getting treatment for and into recovery from OCD. Even though she feels proud of this accomplishment and would delight in being open about it, she knows that doing so will jeopardize her chances of admission. Instead, she is perceived as being vague and evasive by the faculty interviewers who determine whether she will have a future in medicine. She shakes her head at the irony: The mission of the medical profession is to heal, yet many of these healers have needed healing themselves—and are doubted because of it.

Having an Obsessive Conscience

In trying to understand why results of OCD treatment are so variable among people, I became aware that an obsessive sense of guilt might be a factor that accounts for cases that have been considered "treatment-resistant." Obsessive guilt seems to complicate the ability for sufferers to adhere to the essential factors of exposure and response prevention (ERP) treatment that normalize brain activity in the affected areas of OCD, because they feel that doing so is wrong.

Guilt and other moral emotions reside neuroanatomically adjacent to OCD. It is unclear whether there is a functional relationship between OCD and guilt, but they appear to interact. Several studies show a probable causal relationship, but there is no proof yet to validate this theory.[5]

If this turns out to be the case, however, it may mean that along with anxiety, OCD distress may be compounded by feelings of guilt when sufferers don't attend to the alleged danger (a necessary element of behavioral treatment). When they do—by ritualizing—they still won't get a sense of certainty that all is well, because even though there was no danger to begin with, the anxiety and guilt won't go away. In other words, there is no way to prove a negative.

Outlining the brain's functioning sets the stage for the heart of this book. Through clinical examples, readers will see that people who have OCD suffer not just from anxiety, but also from moral emotions brought on by scrupulosity, moral perfectionism, and feelings of obsessive guilt. It's plausible that a neurofunctional relationship exists between OCD and moral emotions and that it is often overlooked in treatment.

Obsessive conscientiousness, scrupulosity, moral perfectionism, and pathological guilt seem to be provoked when the neural dashboard sends out the same surplus of neurotransmitters under neutral circumstances. OCD sets off a false fire alarm in safe circumstances. And, just like wanting to check until there is no fire, people who experience these negative moral emotions just want to do the *right* thing to get rid of them! Typically, a series of complex compulsive behaviors is set in motion to track down what "wrong" there was to make "right."

Why We Have Moral Emotions

Moral emotions (e.g., guilt, shame, indignation, prosocial forms of pride, gratitude) are considered to play a crucial role in human evolution.[6] Over the millennia we have acquired the capacity for these prosocial emotions as a way to motivate behavior that helps us takes others' needs into consideration.[7] Altruism is a way in which prosocial behavior is expressed. Guilt seems to serve as a mediating emotion that promotes empathy, informs us when we have erred, and enables us to make reparation. Shame, on the other hand, reduces altruism, because it maintains a negative sense of self, causes a person to withdraw from social relationships, creates interpersonal distance, and increases social isolation.[8]

The relationship between moral emotions and social behavior has always been of interest to philosophers. More recent interest has been shown by an increase in clinical studies and is said to have become a "hot topic" in neuroscience, with the emergence of "social neuroscience" as a distinct academic discipline.[9]

Healthy functioning of a moral emotion system forms the basis for balancing selfish needs with concern for other people. An excess of guilt is often found to be a component of depression, posttraumatic stress disorder, OCD, and other psychiatric problems. A subtype of guilt that has been consistently reported in clinical populations as an exaggerated moral emotion is *omnipotent guilt* (also called *existential guilt*), which is what people might feel when they perceive themselves as being better off than unfortunate others.[10, 11] Another is *survivor guilt*, which people experience by surviving their loved ones after a natural catastrophic event, violence, or war.[12] Not knowing why some people are privileged when others aren't is a normal moral question. For many who have OCD, though, this becomes a symptom of obsessive omnipotent guilt, because there never will be a rational explanation for this state of humanity and—so far—there is no practical way to fix it. Feeling obliged to compensate for their participation in this injustice, these people ritualize by denying themselves pleasure or foregoing material items that aren't considered essentials for living.

Mind and Matter

The most sophisticated tool used for understanding how our brain works *is* our brain. Therein lies a bit of a conundrum as we try to use our limitations to push past our limitations. Scientists and researchers are challenged by pursuing discoveries that serve to surpass our limitations and advance our human condition (evolution). Neuroimaging (presented shortly hereafter) is one of many triumphant (and self-serving!) inventions sprung from the efforts of scientific minds to study and understand the human brain. These technical advances provide visual images of the specific brain activity and neural pathways involved in OCD, as well as many other brain-related and medical problems, which lead to improved treatments.

Neuroanatomically, OCD resides in the brain's frontal cortex—the area right behind the forehead and the right eye. The frontal cortex is the brain's "dashboard," signaling potential consequences from current actions, recognition of good and bad actions, the need to make judgments about appropriate and acceptable social behavior, cognitive connections from familiar and unfamiliar experiences, and the necessity of making moral decisions and judgment calls. Under normal circumstances, when these messages are sent, physiological responses are appropriately activated. With OCD, urgent messages are sent under circumstances in which nothing is wrong but that compel the person with OCD into action just to make sure. How does this happen?

Neurophysiologically, research shows that during an OCD episode, a specific neurocircuit gets stuck in an obsessive loop. Think of OCD as a prankster who pulls a fire alarm. Although there is no actual evidence of imminent danger, the orbital frontal cortex of the person who has OCD kicks into high alert and sets a circular gear in motion, compelling him or her to find the fire and put it out. The alarm starts in the frontal cortex with the cingulate gyrus and transmits to the striatum, on to the thalamus, then back to the frontal cortex.[13] Ridden with a sense of responsibility, the person checks everywhere for the fire, which only intensifies the obsessive need to be certain that all is safe. The problem is that no matter how hard you may try, there isn't any way to produce evidence of something's *not* being there. But when you have OCD, you try—all the time.

We are fortunate to have technological advances that give us literal *insight* into what our brain does under scientific research conditions. Functional magnetic resonance imaging (fMRI) has been used in many OCD studies to identify its neural pathways. The person lies in the core of the imaging machine and performs a cognitive task provided by the researcher. Imaging studies for OCD typically involve the person thinking, or listening to someone read a scenario, about his or her obsessive fear (e.g., not checking the stove before leaving the house, allowing it to burn down). That thinking activates changes in the person's brain blood flow, allowing the researcher to see the functional areas involved in the task. Ultimately, the data contribute to developing better treatments.

Another type of neuroimaging is structural magnetic resonance imaging (sMRI), which examines the physical structure of the brain and measures the volume of brain tissue. Research results show that OCD and many other psychiatric conditions are associated with either too large or too small amounts of tissue in specific areas of the brain.[14]

Positron emission tomography (PET) and single photon emission computed tomography (SPECT) measure brain functions such as blood flow, oxygen use, and metabolic activity to study brain abnormalities. Like a lighting rheostat, PET scans show specific areas of a person's brain that are turned up all the way when triggered by an obsession, then after exposure and response prevention (ERP) therapy those same areas are dimmer[15, 16, 17] (chapter 9 covers the essential aspects of ERP).

Neurofunctions Involved in Guilt/Morality/Altruism/Religion/Superstition

In support of the theory that guilt and OCD may have overlapping functions, several neuroimaging studies have demonstrated that guilt induction increased brain activity in nonclinical participants in the areas of interest identified in OCD. [18, 19, 20, 21, 22] Three fMRI studies located the areas of moral sentiments, moral cognition, and moral reasoning to be in the same regions.[23, 24, 25] Neuroimages of altruism,[26, 27, 28] religion,[29] and superstition[30] were also captured within the same brain areas of interest.

In closing, we have seen that clinical research and neuroimaging studies found OCD and the conscience-related regions of the brain to be adjacent and are likely to be interactive. I hope that presenting this literature helps the many people who have OCD and suffer from obsessive guilt find relief by learning that their symptoms are manifestations of a brain glitch, not a reflection on their character. An important step in recovery for sufferers, then, is to separate OCD symptoms from their true identities and live according to their true values and sense of self. It is okay to poke fun at obsessions. They are bullies who must be put in their place!

Notes

1. Except for OCD that results from strep throat in children, called Pediatric Auto-immune Neuropsychiatric Disorder Associated with Streptococcus (PANDAS).

2. National Institute of Mental Health, "The Numbers Count," National Institute of Mental Health, www.nimh.nih.gov/health/publications/the-numbers-count-mental-disorders-in-america/index.shtml.

3. National Association of Social Workers, "Behavioral Healthcare Parity," www.naswdc.org/practice/behavioral_health/behavioral.asp.

4. Edward N. Matisik, "The Americans with Disabilities Act and the Rehabilitation Act of 1973: Reasonable Accommodation for Employees with OCD" (Milford, CT: Obsessive–Compulsive Foundation, 1996).

5. Mancini and Gangemi, "Role of Responsibility and Fear of Guilt."

6. Ekman, "Basic Emotions."

7. Brune, "Evolutionary Psychology."

8. Oakley et al., eds., *Pathological Altruism*.

9. Cooper and Wallace, "Group Selection and the Evolution of Altruism."

10. Wright, *The Moral Animal*.

11. O'Connor et al., "Empathy-Based Pathogenic Guilt."

12. Rosas, "Beyond the Sociobiological Dilemma."

13. Tiger and McGuire, *God's Brain*.

14. Rauch and Baxter, "Neuroimaging of OCD."

15. Shin et al., "Activation of Anterior Paralimbic Structures."

16. Baxter et al., "Brain Mediation of Obsessive–Compulsive Disorder Symptoms."

17. Saxena et al., "Neuroimaging and Frontal–Subcortical Circuitry."

18. Shin et al., "Activation of Anterior Paralimbic Structures."

19. Basile and Mancini, "Eliciting Guilty Feelings."

20. Takahashi et al., "Brain Activation Associated with Evaluative Processes of Guilt and Embarrassment."

21. Zahn et al., "Neural Basis of Human Social Values."

22. Wagner et al., "Guilt-Specific Processing."

23. Zahn et al., "Neural Basis of Human Social Values."

24. Harrison et al., "Neural Correlates of Moral Sensitivity."

25. Wilson, "Relationship between Evolutionary and Psychological Definitions."

26. O'Connor, "Pathogenic Beliefs and Guilt."

27. Oakley et al., eds., *Pathological Altruism*.

28. Pulcu et al., "Role of Self-Blaming Moral Emotions."

29. Muramoto, "Role of the Medial Prefrontal Cortex."

30. Brugger and Viaud-Delmon, "Superstitiousness in Obsessive–Compulsive Disorder."

Bibliography

Basile, Barbara, and Francesco Mancini. "Eliciting Guilty Feelings: A Preliminary Study Differentiating Deontological and Altruistic Guilt." *Psychology* [Irvine] 2, no. 2 (2011).

Baxter, L. R. Jr., S. Saxena, A. L. Brody, R. F. Ackermann, M. Colgan, J. M. Schwartz, Z. Allen-Martinez, J. M. Fuster, and M. E. Phelps. "Brain Mediation of Obsessive-Compulsive Disorder Symptoms: Evidence from Functional Brain Imaging Studies in the Human and Nonhuman Primate." *Seminars in Clinical Neuropsychiatry* 1, no. 1 (1996): 32–47.

Brugger, P., and I. Viaud-Delmon. "Superstitiousness in Obsessive–Compulsive Disorder." *Dialogues in Clinical Neuroscience* 12, no. 2 (2010): 250–254.

Brune, M. "The Evolutionary Psychology of Obsessive–Compulsive Disorder: The Role of Cognitive Metarepresentation." *Perspectives in Biology and Medicine* 49, no. 3 (summer 2006): 317–329.

Cooper, Ben, and Chris Wallace. "Group Selection and the Evolution of Altruism." *Oxford Economic Papers* 56, no. 2 (2004): 307–330.

Ekman, Paul. "Basic Emotions." In *Handbook of Cognition and Emotion*, 45–60. Hoboken, NJ: John Wiley & Sons, 2005.

Harrison, B. J., J. Pujol, C. Soriano-Mas, et al. "Neural Correlates of Moral Sensitivity in Obsessive–Compulsive Disorder." *Archives of General Psychiatry* 69, no. 7 (2012): 741–749.

Mancini, F., and A. Gangemi. "The Role of Responsibility and Fear of Guilt in Hypothesis-Testing." *Journal of Behavior Therapy and Experimental Psychiatry* 37, no. 4 (2006): 333–346.

Muramoto Osamu. "The Role of the Medial Prefrontal Cortex in Human Religious Activity." *Medical Hypotheses* 62, no. 4 (2004): 479–485.

Oakley, Barbara, Ariel Knafo, Guruprasad Madhavan, and David Sloan Wilson, eds. *Pathological Altruism*. New York: Oxford University Press, 2011.

O'Connor, Lynn E. "Pathogenic Beliefs and Guilt in Human Evolution: Implications for Psychotherapy." In *Genes on the Couch: Explorations in Evolutionary Psychology*, eds. P. Gilbert and K. G. Mailey, 276–303. New York: Routledge, 2002.

O'Connor, Lynn E., Jack W. Berry, Thomas B. Lewis, and David J. Stiver. "Empathy-Based Pathogenic Guilt, Pathological Altruism, and Psychopathology." In *Pathological Altruism* eds. Barbara Oakley, Ariel Knafo, Guruprasad Madhavan, and David Sloan Wilson. New York: Oxford University Press, 2012.

Pulcu, E., R. Zahn, and R. Elliott. "The Role of Self-Blaming Moral Emotions in Major Depression and Their Impact on Social-Economical Decision Making." *Frontiers in Psychology* 4, no. 310 (2013): 310.

Rauch, S., and L. R. Baxter. "Neuroimaging of OCD and Related Disorders." In *Obsessive–Compulsive Disorders: Practical Management*, eds. L. Baer, M. A. Jenike, and W. E. Minichiello, 289–317. Boston: Mosby, 1998.

Rosas, Alejandro. "Beyond the Sociobiological Dilemma: Social Emotions and the Evolution of Morality." *Zygon* 42, no. 3 (2007): 685–699.

Saxena, S., A. L. Brody, J. M. Schwartz, and L. R. Baxter. "Neuroimaging and Frontal-Subcortical Circuitry in Obsessive–Compulsive Disorder." *British Journal of Psychiatry* 173 no. 35S (supplement) (1998): 26–37.

Shin, L. M., D. D. Dougherty, S. P. Orr, R. K. Pitman, M. Lasko, M. L. Macklin, N. M. Alpert, A. J. Fischman, and S. L. Rauch. "Activation of Anterior Paralimbic Structures During Guilt-Related Script-Driven Imagery." *Biological Psychiatry* 48, no. 1 (2000): 43–50.

Takahashi, Hidehiko, Noriaki Yahata, Michihiko Koeda, Tetsuya Matsuda, Kunihiko Asai, and Yoshiro Okubo. "Brain Activation Associated with Evaluative Processes of Guilt and Embarrassment: An fMRI Study." *NeuroImage* 23, no. 3 (2004): 967–974.

Tiger, Lionel, and Michael McGuire. *God's Brain*. Amherst, NY: Prometheus Books, 2010.

Wagner, Ullrich, Karim N'Diaye, Thomas Ethofer, and Patrik Vuilleumier. "Guilt-Specific Processing in the Prefrontal Cortex." *Cerebral Cortex* 21, no. 11 (2011): 2461–2470.

Wilson, David Sloan. "On the Relationship between Evolutionary and Psychological Definitions of Altruism and Selfishness." *Biology and Philosophy* 7, no. 1 (1992): 61–68.

Wright, R. *The Moral Animal: Why We Are the Way We Are*. New York: Vintage, 1994; reprint 1995.

Zahn, Roland, Jorge Moll, Mirella Paiva, Griselda Garrido, Frank Krueger, Edward D. Huey, and Jordan Grafman. "The Neural Basis of Human Social Values: Evidence from Functional MRI." *Cerebral Cortex* 19 (2009): 276–283.

2

Hypersurvival: Evolutionary Survival Instincts Gone Awry—Too Much of a Necessary Thing?

The essential human instinct is to stay alive. Every day we are challenged to meet physical, psychological, emotional, and safety needs to survive. Our hard-wired physical needs are food for nourishment, water for hydration, oxygen for breathing, sleep for recuperation, sunlight for rejuvenation, sex for procreation, and shelter for protection against the elements. Our instincts tell us when we are facing danger, and our reflexes jump into action to defend and protect our safety. Our basic personal psychological needs are met through self-care and having interpersonal relationships.

We are also born with instincts that prevent us from having to learn (the hard way) what is unsafe. According to Hampton, instinctive behavior is "native or inherited and not learned."[1] But how do we know or learn that something is not safe when we haven't had any previous experience with it?

Evolutionary biology explains that when we become afraid or are in danger, our brain activates our precaution system starting with the amygdala, which sets off a surge of adrenalin, causing our physiological functions to intensify, including rapid breathing and increased heart rate, providing an analgesic (numbing) effect for a higher threshold to pain.[2] The next instinct determines whether to fight or flee the danger.[3] Regardless of the behavioral decision to face the danger or to run away from it, the feared situation will be stored in the prefrontal cortex as a threat to be avoided in the future.

In OCD, the brain's precaution mechanism is set off in the absence of real threat or danger for which there is no quantifiable evidence. Even though people experience a real sense of threat during an episode, the true characteristic in OCD is *doubt*. And it is doubt that makes sufferers chase after a certainty that their obsessive fear is not real. Patients also describe the experience of obsessive fear and doubt as a bad *feeling* that stirs up guilt and that compels them to take every precaution to ensure that all is safe—just in case—to assuage any guilt of negligence.

Table 2.1 gives examples of normal instinctive behaviors that become OCD symptoms.

For Sally, driving became problematic, because she feared hitting someone with her car. Whenever she drove over bumps in the road, she imagined having hit someone. No matter how many times she drove back to check and make sure she had not caused a hit-and-run accident, she could never find any clues. When she got home, still bothered by nagging doubt, sometimes she would watch the news, or call the police station as other ways to check. Although accidents do happen, having thoughts or fears about them doesn't mean they *did* or *will* happen. Sally feels discouraged about her ability to come and go as she pleases, because doing so has become such an anxious and emotional ordeal.

Our survival does not depend on meeting our individual needs alone. It also depends on belonging to and cooperating with a group. Successful organizational systems help meet both the needs of the individual *and* the group.[4] Functional and social ritualistic behaviors within the group seem to foster cooperation and help set expectations needed for maintaining social order.[5]

The role of cooperative relationships (mating, group, family, kinship, and affiliation to the larger community) meets the essential preservation needs for procreation, producing food, and defending against threat. Our aptitudes for speech and language facilitate our ability to communicate our thoughts, feelings, and needs within and between groups. Our current technology (e.g., electronic media, smart phones, video chatting, videoconferencing) provides immediate contact with anyone at any time around the world, making it easy to maintain relationships with family, friends, and local, national, and

TABLE 2.1   Normal Instinctive Behaviors That Become OCD Symptoms

Normal Instincts	OCD
hygiene/grooming	contamination—washing/cleaning
safety/danger	fight-or-flight/checking
nesting	hoarding
existential fears and anxieties from uncertainty about death and afterlife, randomness of events, the need for control	superstitious, scrupulous, and hypermoral rituals intended to provide a sense of reason, order, and purpose

international communities. These communication skills provide the advantage of being able to learn from one another and foster personal growth, which, in turn, leads to developing functional improvements that benefit the entire community. Overall, striking a healthy balance between meeting personal and group needs seems to maintain a reasonable quality of life for all.

Societies thrive or die off depending on the functional or dysfunctional behaviors of the group. Counter to classifying OCD as the necessary right instincts, but with behavior having gone awry, Polemi and his colleagues examined the potential evolutionary advantages of OCD in hunting and gathering cultures. They found that certain compulsive behaviors may have succeeded in maintaining the functional requirements of the community.[6] Some examples are: compulsive checking, washing, counting, needing to confess, hoarding, and exactness, which may have helped promote hygiene, maintenance of the fire needed for cooking and heat, keeping track of food and other supplies, and maintenance of weapons for defense. But although these behaviors may have been advantageous for the group, they could also be seen as exhausting and detrimental to the individual.

Emotional needs are just as instinctive as the need for food, shelter, and safety. Experiencing and sharing love is a very powerful emotional need and could be considered instinctive. A few ways we demonstrate these feelings are by showing affection, playfulness, and support. Empathy and altruism foster interpersonal cooperation and enable appropriate social responses. We are, essentially, moral beings

Adaptive Moral Emotions

The human conscience may have been a trait developed for survival and preservation. The conscience processes positive and negative emotions during interpersonal interactions and moral events. Healthy guilt is one of the negative emotions necessary for social preservation, because it provides a positive social outcome. Unhealthy guilt is a negative emotion that has no functional purpose or any useful outcome, yet it seems so prevalent in humanity. Having OCD on top of an already guilty conscience causes an even more disproportionate amount of unhealthy guilt.

Empathy is the ability to put ourselves emotionally in the place of another so that we can understand that person's experience. Altruism, defined as the making of personal sacrifices on behalf of others, is a way of expressing empathy. These traits vary to a wide degree among us, as does also the degree to which we act on them. Unfortunately, we also experience fear, become emotionally threatened, and experience other negative emotions that cause us to act out our anger by being hurtful to others physically and emotionally. When this happens, there is a breakdown of trust in the relationship, and the reparation of love is difficult to achieve.

So why do we bother with all that? We bother because love feels good. We bother because, normally, we have a conscience that guides us toward right and good behavior. Our collective conscience has constructed social norms and taboos that constitute morality, and have organized codes of belief and behavior into religion and spirituality.

Accordingly, we have evolved to anticipate and work toward helping fulfilling others' needs. We may do so without any awareness of the hope that others will help us when we need it. We are both the benefactors and the beneficiaries of altruism. We also bother because of neurochemicals that produce good feelings that reinforce this good behavior. Everybody wins! We could leave it at that, but doing so might be a little naive.

As stated, people do experience a good feeling from performing altruistic acts. But here is the paradox: Unless there is a sense of personal satisfaction from performing an altruistic act, there does not seem to be any rational reason to do so. We feel satisfied knowing we helped someone without asking for anything in return, but is this really what is going on?

There are many theories about the competing role altruism plays for the individual and the group. On one hand, at the individual level, one theory states that there is no place for pure goodness and altruism, because instincts are selfish.[7] On the same hand, "[I]t seems, on evolutionary grounds, that altruism cannot exist, because species with this trait are expected to have gone extinct through the process of natural selection. (Selfishness increases biological fitness, and only the fittest survive.[8]) If pure altruists do exist, they would be selected out of existence by those competing to be at the top of the human "food chain."

The other hand is in favor of natural selection. Pure altruism, as defined by sacrificial acts made for the benefit of another without regard for the self, may only exist if *all* the members of a society are altruists.[9] It turns out that even though this is unrealistic, when a group consists of individuals willing to sacrifice themselves for the welfare of the group, the group may be more likely to survive than a group made up of selfish individuals who put their own interests first.[10]

Where are we in our current state of social evolution? Do we punish pure altruists, if they actually do exist? From a social adaptation perspective, pure altruism could be considered a weakness and be punished, while pure selfishness might be a strength and be rewarded. If evolution favors individual selection, the "survival of the fittest" individuals would fight each other to the death until the last few people standing perish because they cannot get along. They would fail to fulfill the physical, social, and emotional survival needs of the group and then, by folly, drive the whole human race into extinction. Having a healthy balance and moderation between the two is the moral of this and of almost every other discussion in this book.

We can say, then, that some of the "selfish" motives lurking beneath our seemingly noble and altruistic efforts are not unhealthy.[11] Although the words "selfish and "selfishness" are almost always perceived as bad, they can also express that which can also be regarded as personally functional and beneficial. When these words are used in these discussions, it is intended to mean self-survival and self-care (which also contributes to group survival) except when noted in the context of having self-centered motives.

Why is this important for our discussion? It is important because people with OCD are torn between the extremes of the selfish/altruistic dilemma. Knowing what a healthy balance is does not translate into rational behavior during an OCD episode.

With regard to natural selection, reciprocal altruism (RA) conceptualizes self-survival and social cooperation as a mutual self-service.[12] RA is seen as involving altruistic acts that promote personal future personal gains. It is fundamentally motivated by self-interest but is of practical benefit to *both* the individual and the group. So what appears to be altruism—personal sacrifice on behalf of others—is really just long-term self-survival. "Under certain conditions natural selection favors these altruistic behaviors because in the long run they benefit the organism performing them."[13]

Guilt in Social Contexts

The topic of cultural rituals in societies around the world is covered more in depth in chapter 3. The present goal is to discuss the adaptive purpose of social and cultural rules set by a community in order to maintain order. For example, it became necessary to construct rules to preserve members' safety and to proscribe impulsive sexual or violent behaviors that may be gratifying to the individual but that are harmful to the group. Legal systems punish those found guilty of violating the rules and provide justice to victims as best they can. In the best of all worlds, a humane society relies on a moral system that delivers punishment in proportion to the crime.

We know very well, though, that guilt is not limited to crime and justice alone. From a survival standpoint, healthy guilt is an emotion that keeps us safe from one another. From a psychological and evolutionary viewpoint, healthy guilt supports the function of reciprocal altruism (RA). When we were children, most of us were taught the Golden Rule: Do unto others as thou wouldst have them do unto you. Because almost all cultures have a version of this rule, it seems clear that we have an innate sense that this is the right way to behave.[14] (This will be explored more in the chapter on moralosity.)

The overall goal of this book is to highlight the differences between healthy and unhealthy guilt. This theme is woven throughout the book's related topics to help OCD sufferers be certain that obsessive guilt is *always* unhealthy—and that there are simple ways to tell the difference. Relevant examples will be provided.

Guilt has many definitions and will be more thoroughly explored in chapter 8. At this point, a few definitions of guilt will be provided to understand the role guilt plays in personal and social preservation. Healthy guilt has been classified in a few important ways. One is deontological guilt, which involves violating personal and moral values.[15] For example, Susan didn't prepare well for a test and cheated. She got away with it, but her conscience bothered her. Another is ontological guilt (also called altruistic guilt), experienced as the concern for others in interpersonal or societal situations.[16] Not intervening when witnessing a social injustice, such as bullying, might bring about ontological guilt. Of course there are times when it would not be safe to intervene; judgment is required in such situations. I remember being at the mall on a busy Saturday, witnessing a parent yelling at a young child for not being quiet enough. Would it have been too hard to ask whether they needed any help? But I was afraid of making the situation worse, fearing that I might be putting myself at risk. I felt ontologically guilty for not having done anything.

Healthy guilt is considered normal and always has a subjective sense of proportion. What you and someone else do in the same situation might be different. This is why it is so difficult for people who have OCD, who expect morality to have an absolute either–or right answer and who have an all-or-nothing way of acting in a world in which most moral decisions are relative to one's personal moral code.[17,18]

Morality and Religion

The same argument about whether altruism is a hard-wired selfish or altruistic trait can be made concerning morality and religion. Obviously, guilt would find its way into moral decisions and religious practice, because they involve matters of right/wrong and good/bad. People might experience healthy, unhealthy, or obsessive guilt depending on factors too numerous to cover here, but for our purpose, the important one would be having a predisposition toward anxiety.

Morality has been defined as psychological altruism toward unrelated people[19] and as a product of evolutionary pressures[20] to establish good behavior that benefits members of the group as well as the group itself. Morality keeps the social order.

The role of religion plays many parts. Because we are endowed with a conscience, whether through divine grace or through evolutionary adaptations, religion has helped organize how we communicate with a supreme omnipotent and omnipresent being who will either reward or punish us after we die for how we have lived our lives. Among other functions, religion provides a sacred space in which people can commune and experience the spirit of the divine.

The practice of normal religious rituals involves a prescribed order of steps that convey an act of faith and result in a feeling of well-being. This sense of well-being may be set off by higher levels of serotonin and reinforce their performance.[21]

Evolutionary biologists have yet to clearly identify religion as an evolutionary trait and characterize it as an expression of altruism.[22] One theory holds that including ever-watchful ancestors, spirits, and gods in the social realm, humans discovered an effective strategy for restraining selfishness and building more cooperative groups.[23] Another hypothesis posits that culturally determined patterns of behavior became organized into traditional religious practices that, passed down through generations, have given religions a vital evolutionary social function.[24] Sanderson's conclusion is that "there really is a religious module"—a bundle of highly specialized neurons and neuronal connections built by a set of genes—in the brain.[25] But this does not mean that all the features of religious belief and practice are evolved adaptations. Some features of religions are, in all likelihood, byproducts rather than adaptations.[26]

It may be somewhat obvious that OCD transforms the rituals designed for religious expression into symptoms (chapter 6 provides more detailed examples on this theme). Religion seems to be a common domain for the expression of obsessive–compulsive-like traits.[27] Rachman (1997) proposed that "people who are taught, or learn, that all their value laden thoughts are of significance will be more prone to obsessions—as in particular types of religious beliefs and instructions."[28] In one study, Catholics who had a high or moderate degree of religiosity scored higher on measures of OCD-related thoughts than less religious study participants.[29] Another study found that 42 percent of OCD outpatients had religious obsessions.[30]

In closing: Humanity seeks to know and understand its existence. Because of how we are designed, we have awareness of our mortality and experience existential anxiety about why we are here and what will happen to us when we are gone. We have created systems and structures to ensure our survival—first, by meeting our individual needs. We have been successful in preserving our survival through our innate ability to cooperate and maintain social relationships and to cope with actual and uncertain realities of our existence. OCD just takes it too far.

Notes

1. Hampton, "Can Evolutionary Psychology Learn from the Instinct Debate?": 57–74.

2. Veinante, Yalcin, and Barrot, "The Amygdala between Sensation and Affect": 1–9.

3. Maldonado, "Biology and Fear in Humans," www.articlesbase.com/health-articles/biology-and-fear-in-humans-2209833.html.

4. Cooper and Wallace, "Group Selection and the Evolution of Altruism": 307–330.

5. Ibid.

6. Polimeni, Reiss, and Sareen, "Could Obsessive–Compulsive Disorder Have Originated": 655–664. Read the entire article to learn more about this fascinating relationship between behaviors that seem advantageous to the group while being burdensome to the individual.

7. Rosas, "Beyond the Sociobiological Dilemma": 685–700.

8. Sesardic, "Recent Work on Human Altruism and Evolution": 128–157.

9. Wright, *The Moral Animal*.

10. Dawkins, *The Selfish Gene*.

11. Wilson, "On the Relationship between Evolutionary and Psychological Definitions": 61–68.

12. Trivers, "The Evolution of Reciprocal Altruism": 35–37.

13. Ibid., 35.

14. Holy Bible, Matthew 7:12.

15. Basile and Mancini, "Eliciting Guilty Feelings": 98–102.

16. Ibid.

17. Boyer and Liénard, "Ritual Behavior in Obsessive and Normal Individuals": 291–294.

18. Feygin, Swain, and Leckman, "The Normalcy of Neurosis": 854–864.

19. Cooper and Wallace, "Group Selection and the Evolution of Altruism": 1–21.

20. Moll et al., "The Neural Basis of Human Moral Cognition": 799–809.

21. Young and Young, "How to Increase Serotonin in the Human Brain": 394–399.

22. Sanderson, "Adaptation, Evolution, and Religion": 141–156.

23. Rossano, *Supernatural Selection*.

24. Lachmann, "Religion—An Evolutionary Adaptation": 1301–1307.

25. Sanderson, "Adaptation, Evolution, and Religion": 141–156.

26. Sica et al., "Culture and Psychopathology": 1001–1012.

27. Feygin, Swain, and Leckman, "The Normalcy of Neurosis": 854–864.

28. Rachman and de Silva, "Abnormal and Normal Obsessions": 233–248.

29. Sica et al., "Religiousness and Obsessive–Compulsive Cognitions and Symptoms": 813–823.

30. Tek and Ulug, "Religiosity and Religious Obsessions": 99–108.

Bibliography

Basile, Barbara, and Francesco Mancini. "Eliciting Guilty Feelings: A Preliminary Study Differentiating Deontological and Altruistic Guilt." *Psychology* [Irvine] 2, no. 2 (2011).

Boyer, Pascal, and Pierre Liénard. "Ritual Behavior in Obsessive and Normal Individuals: Moderating Anxiety and Reorganizing the Flow of Action." *Current Directions in Psychological Science* 17, no. 4 (2008): 291–294.

Cooper, Ben, and Chris Wallace. "Group Selection and the Evolution of Altruism." *Oxford Economic Papers* 56, no. 2 (2004): 307–330.

Dawkins, R. *The Selfish Gene*, 2nd ed. Oxford: Oxford University Press, 1989.

Feygin, Diana L., James E. Swain, and James F. Leckman. "The Normalcy of Neurosis: Evolutionary Origins of Obsessive–Compulsive Disorder and Related Behaviors." *Progress in Neuro-Psychopharmacology and Biological Psychiatry* 30, no. 5 (2006): 854–864.

Hampton, Simon J. "Can Evolutionary Psychology Learn from the Instinct Debate?" *History of the Human Sciences* 19, no. 4 (November 1, 2006): 57–74.

Lachmann, Peter J. "Religion—an Evolutionary Adaptation." *The FASEB Journal* 24, no. 5 (2010): 1301–1307.

Moll, Jorge, Roland Zahn, Ricardo de Oliveira-Souza, Frank Krueger, and Jordan Grafman. "The Neural Basis of Human Moral Cognition." *Nature Reviews Neuroscience* 6, no. 10 (2005): 799–809.

Polimeni, Joseph, Jeffrey P. Reiss, and Jitender Sareen. "Could Obsessive–Compulsive Disorder Have Originated as a Group-Selected Adaptive Trait in Traditional Societies?" *Medical Hypotheses* 65, no. 4 (2005): 655–664.

Rachman, S., and P. de Silva. "Abnormal and Normal Obsessions." *Behaviour Research and Therapy* 16, no. 4 (1978): 233–248.

Rosas, Alejandro. "Beyond the Sociobiological Dilemma: Social Emotions and the Evolution of Morality." *Zygon* 42, no. 3 (2007): 685–699.

Rossano, Matt J. *Supernatural Selection: How Religion Evolved*. New York: Oxford University Press, 2010.

Sanderson, Stephen K. "Adaptation, Evolution, and Religion." *Religion, Brain & Behavior* 38 (2008): 141–156.

Sesardic, Neven. "Recent Work on Human Altruism and Evolution." *Ethics* 106, no. 1 (1995): 128–157.

Sica, C., C. Novara, and E. Sanavio. "Religiousness and Obsessive–Compulsive Cognitions and Symptoms in an Italian Population." *Behaviour Research and Therapy* 40, no. 7 (2002): 813–823.

Sica, Claudio, Caterina Novara, and Ezio Sanavio. "Culture and Psychopathology: Superstition and Obsessive-Compulsive Cognitions and Symptoms in a Non-clinical Italian Sample." *Personality and Individual Differences* 32, no. 6 (2002): 1001–1012.

Tek, C., and B. Ulug. "Religiosity and Religious Obsessions in Obsessive–Compulsive Disorder." *Psychiatry Research* 104, no. 2 (2001): 99–108.

Trivers, R. L. "The Evolution of Reciprocal Altruism." *Quarterly Review of Biology* 46 (1971): 35–37.

Veinante, Pierre, Ipek Yalcin, and Michel Barrot. "The Amygdala between Sensation and Affect: A Role in Pain." *Journal of Molecular Psychiatry* 1, no. 9 (2013): 1–9.

Wilson, David Sloan. "On the Relationship between Evolutionary and Psychological Definitions of Altruism and Selfishness." *Biology and Philosophy* 7, no. 1 (1992): 61–68.

Wright, R. *The Moral Animal: Why We Are the Way We Are*. New York: Vintage, 1995.

Young, Simon N., and Simon N. Young. "How to Increase Serotonin in the Human Brain without Drugs." *Journal of Neuroscience* 32, no. 6 (2007): 394–399.

3

All Walks of Life: Global Prevalence and the Universal Culture of Rituals

This chapter reports how much OCD there is in the world and what it looks like. We continue with the theme of examining adaptive personal and social functioning in the face of uncertainty and how OCD changes it into excessive fear and the need for control.[1]

Every culture has norms for social order and cohesion that vary from place to place and every culture has people with OCD. Cultural rituals are recognized by behaviors that have no practical outcome, that are done out of social obligation, and that are typically performed at a specially designated place and time.[2]

Global Prevalence of OCD

OCD is a nondiscriminatory disorder: It affects all walks of life all over the globe. The first topic to be covered in this chapter is what the rate of OCD is in the United States and around the world. You will see that you are not alone!

Here in the United States, the Epidemiological Catchment Area reports that 2.3 percent of the population will experience an episode of OCD at some point in their life (lifetime prevalence), and 1.2 percent will have an episode in any given year (twelve-month rate).[3] These same rates were found in other research studies conducted in the United States on how many people suffer with OCD.[4,5] It is considered the fourth most common psychiatric illness in the United States.[6]

It turns out that the rate of OCD around the world is relatively the same (see Table 3.1). The World Health Organization (WHO) determined that

TABLE 3.1 Prevalence of Religious OCD Symptoms around the World

Prevalence of Religious OCD Symptoms around the World	Number of Patients	Percent of Patients with Religious Symptoms
United Kingdom[1]	41	5
United States[2, 3, 4, 5, 6, 7, 8]	24–425	5–38
Costa Rica[9]	26	10
India[10, 11, 12]	82–410	4–31
Japan[13]	343	8
Turkey[14, 15, 16, 17, 18]	45–141	11–42
Egypt[19]	90	60
Bahrain[20]	50	40
Saudi Arabia[21]	32	50
Israel[22, 23]	28–34	41–93

Source: Data from David Greenberg and Jonathan Huppert, "Scrupulosity: A Unique Subtype of Obsessive–Compulsive Disorder," *Current Psychiatry Reports* 12 (2010): 282–289.

Prevalence of Religious Obsessions from Other Study Samples		
Singapore[24]	20	7
India[25, 26]	13–70	22–23
France[27]	36	4
Spain[28]	36	1.4
Belgium[29]	36	1.3

Prevalence of OCD Symptoms from Cultural Study Samples		
Turkey[30]	3,012	3
Turkey[31]	45	42
Canada[32]	3258	3
Israel[33]	562	3.6
Qatar[34]	2,080	3.5
Iran[35]	293	9
Iran[36]	25,180	1.8

1. J. H. Dowson, "The Phenomenology of Severe Obsessive–Compulsive Neurosis," *British Journal of Psychiatry* 131 (1977).

2. S. E. Swedo et al., "Obsessive–Compulsive Disorder in Children and Adolescents: Clinical phenomenology of 70 consecutive cases," *Archives of General Psychiatry* 46 (1989).

3. M. A. Riddle et al., "Obsessive Compulsive Disorder in Children and Adolescents: Phenomenology and Family History," *Journal of the American Academy of Child Adolescent Psychiatry* 29 (1990).

4. J. L. Eisen et al., "Patterns of Remission and Relapse in Obsessive–Compulsive Disorder," *Journal of Clinical Psychiatry* 60 (1999).

5. E. B. Foa & M. J. Kozak, "*DSM–IV* Field Trial: Obsessive–Compulsive Disorder," *The American Journal of Psychiatry* 152, no. 4 (1995).

6. A. Pinto et al., "The Brown Longitudinal Obsessive Compulsive Study: Clinical Features and Symptoms of the Sample at Intake," *Journal of Clinical Psychiatry* 67 (2006).

7. A. M. Garcia et al., "Phenomenology of Early Childhood Onset Obsessive Compulsive Disorder," *Journal of Psychopathology and Behavioral Assessment* 31 (2009).

8. D. A. Chavira et al., "A Comparative Study of Obsessive–Compulsive Disorder in Costa Rica and the United States," *Depression and Anxiety* 25 (2008).

9. Ibid.

10. S. Akhtar et al., "A Phenomenological Analysis of Symptoms in Obsessive-Compulsive Neurosis," *British Journal of Psychiatry* 127 (1975).

11. S. Khanna, P. N. Rajendra, and S. M. Channabasavanna, "Sociodemographic Variables in Obsessive Compulsive Neurosis in India," *International Journal of Social Psychiatry* 32, no. 3 (1986).

12. T. S. Jaisoorya et al., "Obsessive–Compulsive Disorder with and without Tic Disorder: A Comparative Study from India," *CNS Spectrums* 13 (2008).

13. H. Matsunaga et al., "Symptom Structure in Japanese Patients with Obsessive–Compulsive Disorder," *American Journal of Psychiatry* 165 (2008).

14. A. Eğrilmez et al., "Phenomenology of Obsessions in a Turkish Series of OCD Patients," *Psychopathology* 30, no. 2 (1997).

15. Cenk Tek and Berna Ulug, "Religiosity and Religious Obsessions in Obsessive–Compulsive Disorder," *Psychiatry Research* 104, no. 2 (2001).

16. R. Tükel et al., "Gender-Related Differences among Turkish Patients with Obsessive–Compulsive Disorder," *Comprehensive Psychiatry* 45, no. 5 (2004).

17. F, Karadağ et al., "OCD Symptoms in a Sample of Turkish Patients: A Phenomenological Picture," *Depression and Anxiety* 23, no. 3 (2006).

18. L. Besiroglu, S. Karaca, and I. Keskin, "Scrupulosity and Obsessive Compulsive Disorder: The Cognitive Perspective in Islamic Sources," *Journal of Religion and Health* 7 (2012).

19. A. Okasha et al., "Prevalence of Obsessive Compulsive Symptoms (OCS) in a Sample of Egyptian Adolescents," *Encephale* 27, no. 1 (2001).

20. A. Shooka, M. K. al-Haddad, and A. Raees, "OCD in Bahrain: A Phenomenological Profile," *International Journal of Social Psychiatry* 44, no. 2 (1998).

21. O. M. Mahgoub and H. B. Abdel-Hafeiz, "Pattern of Obsessive–Compulsive Disorder in Eastern Saudi Arabia," *British Journal of Psychiatry* 158 (1991).

22. D. Greenberg and G. Shefler, "Obsessive Compulsive Disorder in Ultra-Orthodox Jewish Patients: A Comparison of Religious and Non-Religious Symptoms," *Psychology and Psychotherapy* 75, no. Pt 2 (2002).

23. D. Greenberg and E. Witztum, "The Influence of Cultural Factors on Obsessive Compulsive Disorder: Religious Symptoms in a Religious Society," *Israel Journal of Psychiatry and Related Sciences* 31, no. 3 (1994).

24. B. H. Chia, "A Singapore Study of Obsessive Compulsive Disorder," *Singapore Medical Journal* 37, no. 4 (1996).

25. D. Mataix-Cols et al., "Obsessive–Compulsive Symptom Dimensions as Predictors of Compliance with and Response to Behaviour Therapy: Results from a Controlled Trial," *Psychotherapy and Psychosomatics* 71, no. 5 (2002).

(Continued)

TABLE 3.1   (Continued)

26. Y. C. Reddy et al., "A Follow-Up Study of Juvenile Obsessive–Compulsive Disorder from India.," *Acta Psychiatrica Scandinavica* 107, no. 6 (2003).

27. M. A. Fullana et al., "Obsessive–Compulsive Symptom Dimensions in the General Population: Results from an Epidemiological Study in Six European Countries," *Journal of Affective Disorders* 124 (2010).

28. Ibid.

29. Ibid.

30. A. S. Çilli et al., "Twelve-Month Prevalence of Obsessive–Compulsive Disorder in Konya, Turkey," *Comprehensive Psychiatry* 45, no. 5 (2004).

31. C. Tek and B. Ulug, "Religiosity and Religious Obsessions in Obsessive–Compulsive Disorder," *Psychiatry Research* 104, no. 2 (2001).

32. J. L. Kolada, R. C. Bland, and S. C. Newman, "Obsessive–Compulsive Disorder," *Acta Psychiatrica Scandinavica* 89 (1994).

33. A. H. Zohar et al., "An Epidemiological Study of Obsessive–Compulsive Disorder and Related Disorders in Israeli Adolescents," *Journal of the American Academy of Child Adolescent Psychiatry* 31, no. 6 (1992).

34. Suhaila Ghuloum, Abdulbari Bener, and Mohammed Tamim Abou-Salch, "Prevalence of Mental Disorders in Adult Population Attending Primary Health Care Setting Qatari Population," *Journal of the Pakistan Medical Association* 61, no. 3 (2011).

35. F. Assarian, H. Biqam, and A. Asqarnejad, "An Epidemiological Study of Obsessive–Compulsive Disorder among High School Students and Its Relationship with Religious Attitudes," *Archives of Iranian Medicine* 9, no. 2 (2006).

36. M. R. Mohammadi et al., "Prevalence of Obsessive–Compulsive Disorder in Iran," *BMC Psychiatry* 4 (2004).

OCD is the tenth-highest cause of disability and the eleventh leading mental health problem in the world, and that it accounted for 2.5 percent of total years people have lived with a disability.[7] Although whether you have OCD doesn't depend on where you live, getting treatment for OCD is easier in some parts of the world than in others.

Other results of the study found that China, Korea, Southeast Asia, Australia, New Zealand, and Japan had the least prevalence of OCD. A higher incidence was found in India, Pakistan, Afghanistan, Bangladesh, Thailand, Indonesia, followed by western Europe and North America. A higher occurrence of OCD was found in Russia, Eastern Europe, the Middle East, Africa, and South and Central America. Argentina and Uruguay were found to have the highest rates of OCD.[8]

An anecdotal finding came from an island fishing community of about 5,000 people in Pakistan.[9] Of the roughly 1,500 people identified with OCD, 56 percent were women, and 50 percent were under age 25. Their most common obsessions were contamination, pathological doubt, religious thoughts, the need for symmetry, and the fear of losing things. Checking, arranging, washing, counting, and ordering were the predominant compulsions.[10]

Another Pakistan study, conducted in Peshawar, found that the types of obsessions the people in their study had were influence by their social and religious background.[11] The themes of obsessions and compulsions of the 50 patients were religious (60 percent), contamination (28 percent), and safety (20 percent).[12]

In the first study of its kind, Himle and colleagues used the National Survey of American Life to study the relationship between OCD and religious faith among African Americans and black Caribbeans.[13] They found that low participation in religious practice, especially for Baptists as compared to Catholics, indicated higher OCD severity owing to the place of worship's being a highly triggering and emotional environment for those with religious and "bad thought" obsessions.[14]

Neurobiology of Cultural and Superstitious Rituals

A brief note on the neurobiology of superstitious behavior and OCD rituals is in order here, because they share the same neural pathways. The neuroactivity in the basal ganglia related to the conscience and morality is also involved in cultural rituals and follows the same cingulate-striato-thalamic circuit as OCD.[15,16] Activation of superstitious belief is also found in the basal ganglia and has connections with the orbito-frontal cortex and the hippocampus.[17]

Liénard and Boyer describe ritualized behavior as a neurocognitive model for organizing the flow of action, characterized by stereotypy, rigidity in performance, a feeling of compulsion, and specific themes, in particular the potential danger from contamination, predation, and social hazard.[18] They report that ritualized behavior is not limited to OCD and is part of normal living, but that OCD rituals are selective behaviors based on the human vigilance/precaution systems.[19]

According to Tambiah, components of cultural rituals are words and actions characterized by formality and scrupulous adherence to the prescribed rules and order, washing/purification, orientation to thresholds and boundaries, and special colors.[20] "These features typify, but they also define a psychiatric illness, obsessive–compulsive disorder. . . ."[21]

Cultural Practices or OCD Rituals?

Because we are conscious beings, we are aware of our mortality. Death is our deepest and darkest anxiety. Consciously or unconsciously, we worry about when we will die, how we will die, and what happens after we die. We are also anxious about things we don't know or understand, and over circumstances for which we have no control: weather, death, sickness, scarcity, aggression, natural disasters/acts of God, unexpected personal tragedy, and so forth. Cultural rituals help us cope with these uncertainties, with the unknown, and with the uncontrollable forces that affect our existence.

In chapter 2, we reviewed how reciprocal altruism is our best attribute for providing collective support. Our personal behavior in response to these fears will vary in how well we cope (or not cope) with crises. The norms for how we take responsibility for our actions are largely shaped by the culture in which we live. If there is any chance that by some personal effort we can influence the outcome of these forces, then we will act in ways that convey our humility and seek mercy, all to allay our anxieties. OCD, however, belies these normative practices meant to sustain our personal and group spirit. Any chance of being responsible for harm compels the sufferer to make ritualistic good-faith efforts to appeal to the real or imagined supernatural force that controls the relationship between cause and effect. The emotions of fear, guilt, and anxiety are normal in the face of the unknown, but OCD provokes these emotions even in the absence of verifiable danger. Culturally accepted rituals and superstitious behaviors are magnified by the disorder.

Fear of death also causes a fear of living. Rational thinking can determine a reasonable level of risk in a given situation. In chapter 1, we learned that at the very site in the brain where these determinations are made, OCD exaggerates *any* risk as certain danger, to be avoided (public transportation, eating a food item that fell on the floor, using a public restroom). The irony with OCD is that when a *real* negative event happens, people with OCD handle it the same way as others without OCD do. For example, during the 2009 swine flu outbreak, an ABC News website headline read "Swine Flu: Handwashers Blasé for Now." A patient from the OCDI was interviewed for this story. Her response? "'I'm very germ conscious, but I'm not at all phased by the news,' she told ABCNews. com. 'It hasn't caused me any angst and doesn't prevent me from doing what I would normally do.' Typically Mary Ellen washes her hands after touching a doorknob or shaking a hand. 'If we approach the elevator, I let my husband push the button,' she said. 'I don't expect people to open doors for me, but I don't open a door if I don't have to.'"[22]

In a similar fashion, when someone undergoing treatment in the program has suffered a loss through death, he or she has never blamed himself or herself for a ritual he or she did or did not perform. The response has always been appropriate grief, and plans for dealing with it are set in motion.

The arts provide a format through which creative people express their most intimate, yet universally felt emotions. Artists have their unique styles, but their works are also influenced by the style of their culture. Unfortunately, creativity is an often inaccessible coping resource for sufferers, because OCD demands that its rigid irrational rules for functioning. "A heavy and suspicious sense of guilt generally impoverishes all affective life; it smothers creative forces and casts a shadow over life as a whole. What concerns us here is that it produces a fearful and evasive style of religion, separating religion for the actual culture around it."[23] The creative process does not flow freely when obsessions and anxiety compete for, and overcome, the person's mind and emotions. Rituals are calling to be performed, not creative acts.

In their ethnographic study on life cycle transition rituals, Dulaney and Fiske found the same OCD patterns in twenty traditional cultures as identified in industrialized countries.[24] Cultures included in the study were Bimin-Kuskusmin and Umeda (Papua New Guinea), Trobriand (Melanesia), Tambaran Cult (Ilahita Arapesh of Sepik River region), Aboriginals (Arnhem Land, Australia), Sherpas (Nepal), Gujjars (Uttar Pradesh), Chukchee Shamans (Siberia), Merina Kingship (Madagascar), Moose (Burkina Faso), Maasai Warrior (Africa), Desana (Vauper Territory, Columbia), Mapuche (Central Chile), and Zuni and Mescalero Apache (New Mexico).[25] Table 3.2 reflects their findings.

TABLE 3.2   OCD Patterns in 20 Traditional Cultures

Obsessions

Arranging people/things symmetrically or in precise spatial configuration

Attention to threshold or entrance

Concern with anything regarded as polluting, dirty, unclean, impure

Concern/disgust with bodily wastes or secretions

Fear of harming self or others

Having violent or horrific images

Fear of blurting out obscenities or insults/acting on criminal impulses

Forbidden aggressive/perverse sexual thoughts, images, or impulses

Fear that something terrible will happen

Lucky or unlucky numbers

Intrusive nonsense sounds, words, or music

Numbers that have special significance

Colors that have special significance

Scrupulosity

Compulsions

Ordering or arranging things so that they are in their "proper" place

Taking special measures to prevent harm to self or others

Repeating actions

Frequently repeating actions, hand washing/personal hygiene to remove contact with contaminants

Stereotypical hoarding

Source: Data from Siri Dulaney and Alan Page Fiske, "Cultural Rituals and Obsessive–Compulsive Disorder: Is There a Common Psychological Mechanism?" *Ethos* 22, no. 3 (1994): 243–283.

Following are a few related examples from people in my practice:

- My papers, mail, desk items have to be "squared up" and perfect to ward off bad luck.
- I'm afraid my mother will be assaulted if I have a bad thought while going down the stairs and I don't repeat my steps.
- Someone I love will have an accident if I see red or black and don't fix it until I have a "white" (pure) thought.
- I must strip down naked before entering my house, then go straight to the mudroom and take a shower so I don't bring outside germs inside and cause my family to become sick.
- I should not watch movies or television shows with violence, because they might influence my actions.
- Touching, tapping, and counting until I feel right help bad things from happening.

Superstition or OCD?

Superstition is a universal coping mechanism invented for influencing that which is beyond our control or to placate the forces that may have control over our fate. Jahoda defines superstition as "[u]nreasoning awe or fear of something unknown, mysterious or imaginary; a tenet, scruple, habit, etc. founded on fear. . . ." [26] Between cultures, superstitious beliefs and behaviors may appear different, but they fulfill the same human need to ward off harm, maintain order, and appeal for good luck safety.

Some popular good luck superstitions are crossing one's fingers, picking up a penny or a pin, finding a four-leafed clover, having a ladybug land on you, throwing rice (now bird seed, rose pedals, and the like) at weddings, wishing upon a star (with the right thought), knocking on wood, hanging a horseshoe right-side-up, and saying "God bless you" to a sneeze. Common bad luck superstitions are the number 13, stepping on cracks, opening umbrellas in the house, breaking a mirror, the evil eye, walking under a ladder, and having a black cat cross your path.

Athletes are particularly superstitious. They wear lucky clothes, carry lucky objects, and eat or don't eat certain food before a game. Baseball batters and pitchers are notoriously ritualistic as they ready themselves by velcroing their gloves, stomping on the dirt, adjusting their hats, and performing who knows what kind of mental rituals. Webster's encyclopedia of superstitions describes other athletes' and coaches' superstitious behaviors, such as runners' using the same winning shoes until they are too broken-down to wear, players' never tying laces on gear until on the field, being the last person to leave the locker room before a game, and carrying three pennies while playing golf. Webster also reported that a survey conducted in New Zealand found that 21 percent of men wore "lucky" underpants while playing sports.[27]

As previously notes, OCD is an extension of ordinary social and cultural norms and behaviors. It might not be surprising that research has shown a significant correlation with superstitiousness and obsessional thoughts and compulsive checking in people with OCD.[28] OCD sufferers often ask how to tell the difference between normal and compulsive behavior. There is often some legitimate confusion about this if the onset of OCD was at a very young age, or if a parent with OCD set the household rules. Other times OCD is so severe that people lose sight of what was normal behavior before the onset of the OCD episode.

A clear way to tell the difference between accepted cultural or superstitious rituals and compulsive behaviors is to ask: Am I practicing this behavior the same way as others, or am I making up fear-based rules that go beyond the simplicity of the norm? Does the ritual involve specified steps that have a beginning and an end, or is it performed until it feels right? Do I think the behavior is a little silly but do it anyway, or do I feel compelled to do it? Am I doing it for luck, or acting on feelings of anxiety or guilt that it is my responsibility to do whatever I can to prevent something bad from happening? Of course there is a range of belief about the validity of superstitious rituals. Most people could skip them if they were challenged to do so, but some will always adhere to them "just in case." Some superstitions have become acts of politeness, such as saying "God bless you" when someone sneezes.

Symbolic Cognitive Expressions

What might be bad/unlucky/triggering for some can be lucky/good/neutralizing for others, depending on the context. Table 3.3 gives a sample from some patients' hierarchies.

Emotional contamination is another symptom based on superstitious or magical associations between two unrelated events. Typically, emotional contamination results from being somewhere, handling items/objects, or negative interpersonal interactions with specific people that triggers off a strong OCD response. One patient had emotional contamination from an event that occurred when he was in college in New Mexico. Over time, his distress over anything related to the college and the town in which it was situated to the entire state. Seeking a geographical cure, he moved across the country, ever vigilant about license plates, television shows/films, and any material related to the college, city, and state of New Mexico.

Though-action fusion (TAF) is an OCD cognitive construct described as a belief that thoughts cause actions.[29] People fear that the consequences of their obsessions are set in motion just by virtue of having them. It's not that people

TABLE 3.3   Symbolic Cognitive Expressions

Common Colors

Red = sex, blood

Green = envy

Black = death, evil

Orange = hell, hellfire

White = purity, goodness, holiness

Common Letters

D = devil

S + a = Satan

F = f***

H = Hell (bad)
H = heaven (good)

I = intercourse

Common Numbers

666 (and its multiples; add it up = 18 and its multiples)

13 = bad luck (not just obsessive; hotels skip this floor number)
4 = 1 + 3 (13)

3 = The Trinity

Odd numbers = bad luck
Even numbers = good luck

Other Common Symbolic Obsessions

Birthdates of loved ones

Dates/anniversaries of important events

The same three numbers on digital clocks (e.g., 1:11) = hold breath = bad luck

Crossing thresholds

---

with OCD don't have neutral or positive thoughts, but there is a cognitive bias toward the negative because obsessions get sufferers' attention. When asked about the power of normal thoughts affecting reality, people are dismissive. They say they *know* that it doesn't make sense.

On the flip side, two versions of thought–action fusion among "rational" thinkers are chain mail and the lottery. Chain mail is a product of a collective and superstitious social conscience with a cognitive bias toward the positive. It has specific rules to follow for setting positive results in motion. The lottery has an even less chance than the probability of any of the obsessive fears of happening. And yet lucky numbers are played every day for the chance that those lucky numbers will win a lot of money. Have you engaged in either of these opportunities "just in case"? Interestingly, they both have an element of guilt based on whether you participate or not. Chain mail warns you that if you don't follow the rules, you will break the chain and ruin your chance for the promised outcome. With the lottery, you may suffer guilt from buying a losing ticket and wasting money.

In closing, human nature fears uncertainty and a lack of control over circumstances. Cultural rituals and superstitions provide a way of appealing to the cosmic forces to look down on us with good favor. They give us an illusion of control when there is none—just in case there is.

Notes

1. Polimeni et al., "Could Obsessive–Compulsive Disorder Have Originated."
2. Ibid.
3. Torres et al., "Obsessive–Compulsive Disorder."
4. Karno et al., "The Epidemiology of Obsessive–Compulsive Disorder."
5. Torres et al., "Obsessive–Compulsive Disorder."
6. Karno et al., "The Epidemiology of Obsessive–Compulsive Disorder."
7. Ayuso-Mateos, "Global Burden of Obsessive–Compulsive Disorder."
8. Ibid.
9. Muhammad Gadit, "Obsessive–Compulsive Disorder."
10. Ibid.
11. Nazar et al., "Frequency of Religious Themes."
12. Ibid.
13. Himle et al., "The Relationship between Obsessive-Compulsive Disorder and Religious Faith."
14. Ibid.
15. Rapoport and Fiske, "The New Biology of Obsessive–Compulsive Disorder."
16. Rauch and Baxter, "Neuroimaging of OCD and Related Disorders."
17. Brugger and Viaud-Delmon, "Superstitiousness in Obsessive-Compulsive Disorder."
18. Liénard and Boyer, "Whence Collective Rituals?"
19. Boyer and Liénard, "Ritual Behavior in Obsessive and Normal Individuals."
20. Tambiah, "The Magical Power of Words."
21. Wallace, *Religion*.
22. ABC News, "2 Billion Infected?" http://abcnews.go.com/Health/SwineFlu/story?id=7523338&page=1.
23. Vergote, *Guilt and Desire*, 74.
24. Dulaney and Fiske, "Cultural Rituals and Obsessive–Compulsive Disorder."
25. Ibid.
26. Jahoda, *The Psychology of Superstition*.
27. Webster, *The Encyclopedia of Superstitions*.
28. Veale, "Friday the 13th and Obsessive Compulsive Disorder."
29. Obsessive–Compulsive Cognitions Working Group, "Cognitive Assessment of Obsessive–Compulsive Disorder."

Bibliography

Akhtar, S, N. N. Wig, V. K. Varma, D. Pershad, and S. K. Verma. "A Phenomenological Analysis of Symptoms in Obsessive–Compulsive Neurosis." *British Journal of Psychiatry* 127 (Oct 1975): 342–348.

Assarian, F., H. Biqam, and A. Asqarnejad. "An Epidemiological Study of Obsessive-Compulsive Disorder among High School Students and Its Relationship with Religious Attitudes." *Archives of Iranian Medicine* 9, no. 2 (2006): 104–107.

Ayuso-Mateos, Jose Luis. "Global Burden of Obsessive–Compulsive Disorder in the Year 2000" (2004).

Besiroglu, L., S. Karaca, and I. Keskin. "Scrupulosity and Obsessive Compulsive Disorder: The Cognitive Perspective in Islamic Sources." *Journal of Religion and Health* 7 (2012): 7.

Boyer, Pascal, and Pierre Liénard. "Ritual Behavior in Obsessive and Normal Individuals: Moderating Anxiety and Reorganizing the Flow of Action." *Current Directions in Psychological Science* 17, no. 4 (2008): 291–294.

Brugger, P., and I. Viaud-Delmon. "Superstitiousness in Obsessive–Compulsive Disorder." *Dialogues in Clinical Neurosciences* 12, no. 2 (2010): 250–254.

Chavira, D. A., Griselda Garrido, M. Bagnarello, et al. "A Comparative Study of Obsessive–Compulsive Disorder in Costa Rica and the United States." *Depression and Anxiety* 25 (2008): 609–619.

Chia, B. H. "A Singapore Study of Obsessive Compulsive Disorder." *Singapore Medical Journal* 37, no. 4 (1996): 402–406.

Çilli, A. S., M. Telcioglu, R. Aşkin, N. Kaya, S. Bodur, and R. Kucur. "Twelve-Month Prevalence of Obsessive–Compulsive Disorder in Konya, Turkey." *Comprehensive Psychiatry* 45, no. 5 (2004): 367–374.

Dowson, J. H. "The Phenomenology of Severe Obsessive–Compulsive Neurosis." *British Journal of Psychiatry* 131 (1977): 75–78.

Dulaney, Siri, and Alan Page Fiske. "Cultural Rituals and Obsessive–Compulsive Disorder: Is There a Common Psychological Mechanism?" *Ethos* 22, no. 3 (1994): 243–283.

Eğrilmez, A., L. Gülseren, S. Gülseren, and S. Kültür. "Phenomenology of Obsessions in a Turkish Series of OCD Patients." *Psychopathology* 30, no. 2 (1997): 106–110.

Eisen, J. L., W. K. Goodman, M. B. Keller, et al. "Patterns of Remission and Relapse in Obsessive–Compulsive Disorder." *Journal of Clinical Psychiatry* 60 (1999): 346–351.

Foa, E. B., and M. J. Kozak. "*DSM-IV* Field Trial: Obsessive–Compulsive Disorder." *The American Journal of Psychiatry* 152, no. 4 (1995): 654.

Fullana, M. A., G. Vilagut, S. Rojas-Farreras, D. Mataix-Cols, R. de Graaf, K. Demyttenaere, J. M. Haro, et al. "Obsessive–Compulsive Symptom Dimensions in the General Population: Results from an Epidemiological Study in Six European Countries." *Journal of Affective Disorders* 124 (2010): 291–299.

Gadit, Amin A. Muhammad. "Obsessive–Compulsive Disorder (OCD): Is This Disorder Under-recognized?". *Journal of Pakistan Medical Association* (2012).

Garcia, A. M., J. B. Freeman, M. B. Himle, et al. "Phenomenology of Early Childhood Onset Obsessive Compulsive Disorder." *Journal of Psychopathology and Behavioral Assessment* 31 (2009): 104–111.

Ghuloum, Suhaila, Abdulbari Bener, and Mohammed Tamim Abou-Salch. "Prevalence of Mental Disorders in Adult Population Attending Primary Health Care Setting Qatari Population." *Journal of Pakistan Medical Association* 61, no. 3 (2011): 216–221.

Greenberg, D., and G. Shefler. "Obsessive Compulsive Disorder in Ultra-Orthodox Jewish Patients: A Comparison of Religious and Non-Religious Symptoms." *Psychology and Psychotherapy* 75, no. 2 (2002): 123–130.

Greenberg, D., and E. Witztum. "The Influence of Cultural Factors on Obsessive Compulsive Disorder: Religious Symptoms in a Religious Society." *Israel Journal of Psychiatry and Related Sciences* 31, no. 3 (1994): 211–220.

Himle, Joseph A., Linda M. Chatters, Robert Joseph Taylor, and Ann Nguyen. "The Relationship between Obsessive–Compulsive Disorder and Religious Faith: Clinical Characteristics and Implications for Treatment." *Psychology of Religion and Spirituality* (2011).

Jahoda, Gustav. *The Psychology of Superstition*. London: Penguin, 1969.

Jaisoorya, T. S., D. P. Reddy, S. Srinath, et al. "Obsessive–Compulsive Disorder with and without Tic Disorder: A Comparative Study from India." *CNS Spectrums* 13 (2008): 705–711.

Karadağ, F., N. K. Oguzhanoglu, O. Ozdel, F. C. Ateşci, and T. Amuk. "OCD Symptoms in a Sample of Turkish Patients: A Phenomenological Picture." *Depression and Anxiety* 23, no. 3 (2006): 145–152.

Karno, M., Golding, J.M., Sorenson, S.B., Burnam, A. "The Epidemiology of Obsessive–Compulsive Disorder in Five U.S. Communities." *Archives of General Psychiatry* 45, no. 12 (1988): 1094–1099.

Khanna, S., P. N. Rajendra, and S. M. Channabasavanna. "Sociodemographic Variables in Obsessive Compulsive Neurosis in India." *International Journal of Social Psychiatry* 32, no. 3 (1986): 47–54.

Kolada, J. L., R. C. Bland, and S. C. Newman. "Obsessive–Compulsive Disorder." *Acta Psychiatrica Scandinavica* 89 (1994): 24–35.

Liénard, Pierre, and Pascal Boyer. "Whence Collective Rituals? A Cultural Selection Model of Ritualized Behavior." *American Anthropologist* 108, no. 4 (2006): 814–827.

Mahgoub, O. M., and H. B. Abdel-Hafeiz. "Pattern of Obsessive–Compulsive Disorder in Eastern Saudi Arabia." *British Journal of Psychiatry* 158 (1991): 840–842.

Mataix-Cols, D., I. M. Marks, J. H. Greist, K. A. Kobak, and L. Baer. "Obsessive–Compulsive Symptom Dimensions as Predictors of Compliance with and Response to Behaviour Therapy: Results from a Controlled Trial." *Psychotherapy and Psychosomatics* 71, no. 5 (2002): 255–262.

Matsunaga, H., K. Maebayashi, K. Hayashida, et al. "Symptom Structure in Japanese Patients with Obsessive–Compulsive Disorder." *American Joournal of Psychiatry* 165 (2008): 251–253.

Mohammadi, M. R., A. Ghanizadeh, M. Rahgozar, A. A. Noorbala, H. Davidian, H. M. Afzali, H. R. Naghavi, et al. "Prevalence of Obsessive–Compulsive Disorder in Iran." *BMC Psychiatry* 4 (2004): 2.

Nazar, Zahid, Mian Mukhtar ul Haq, and Mohammad Idrees. "Frequency of Religious Themes in Obsessive Compulsive Disorder." *Journal of Postgraduate Medical Institute* 25 (2011): 35–39.

Obsessive Compulsive Cognitions Working Group. "Cognitive Assessment of Obsessive–Compulsive Disorder." *Behaviour Research and Therapy* 35, no. 7 (1997): 667–681.

Okasha, A., K. Ragheb, A. H. Attia, A. Seif el Dawla, T. Okasha, and R. Ismail. "Prevalence of Obsessive Compulsive Symptoms (OCS) in a Sample of Egyptian Adolescents." *Encephale* 27, no. 1 (2001): 8–14.

Pinto, A, M. C. Mancebo, J. L. Eisen, et al. "The Brown Longitudinal Obsessive Compulsive Study: Clinical Features and Symptoms of the Sample at Intake." *Journal of Clinical Psychiatry* 67 (2006): 703–711.

Polimeni, Joseph, Jeffrey P. Reiss, and Jitender Sareen. "Could Obsessive–Compulsive Disorder Have Originated as a Group-Selected Adaptive Trait in Traditional Societies?" *Medical Hypotheses* 65, no. 4 (2005): 655–664.

Rapoport, J. L., and A. Fiske. "The New Biology of Obsessive–Compulsive Disorder: Implications for Evolutionary Psychology." *Perspectives in Biology and Medicine* 41, no. 2 (1998): 159–175.

Rauch, S., and L. R. Baxter. "Neuroimaging of OCD and Related Disorders." In *Obsessive-Compulsive Disorders: Practical Management*, eds. L. Baer, M. A. Jenike, and W. E. Minichiello, 289–317. St. Louis: Mosby, 1998.

Reddy, Y. C., S. Srinath, H. M. Prakash, S. C. Girimaji, S. P. Sheshadri, S. Khanna, and D. K. Subbakrishna. "A Follow-up Study of Juvenile Obsessive–Compulsive Disorder from India." *Acta Psychiatr Scand* 107, no. 6 (2003): 457–464.

Riddle, M. A., L. Scahill, R. A. King, et al. "Obsessive Compulsive Disorder in Children and Adolescents: Phenomenology and Family History." *Journal of the American Academy of Child and Adolescent Psychiatry* 29 (1990): 766–772.

Shooka, A., M. K. al-Haddad, and A. Raees. "OCD in Bahrain: A Phenomenological Profile." *International Journal of Social Psychiatry* 44, no. 2 (1998): 147–154.

Swedo, S. E., J. L. Rapoport, H. Leonard, M. Lenane, and D. Cheslow. "Obsessive-Compulsive Disorder in Children and Adolescents: Clinical Phenomenology of 70 Consecutive Cases." *Archives of General Psychiatry* 46 (1989): 335–341.

Tambiah, S. J. "The Magical Power of Words." *Man* 3, no. 2 (1968): 175–208.

Tek, Cenk, and Berna Ulug. "Religiosity and Religious Obsessions in Obsessive–Compulsive Disorder." *Psychiatry Research* 104, no. 2 (2001): 99–108.

Torres, A. R., M. J. Prince, P. E. Bebbington, D. Bhugra, T. S. Brugha, M. Farrell, R. Jenkins, et al. "Obsessive-Compulsive Disorder: Prevalence, Comorbidity, Impact, and Help-Seeking in the British National Psychiatric Morbidity Survey of 2000." *American Journal of Psychiatry* 163, no. 11 (2006): 1978–1985.

Tükel, R., A. Polat, A. Genç, O. Bozkurt, and H. Atli. "Gender-Related Differences among Turkish Patients with Obsessive-Compulsive Disorder." *Comprehensive Psychiatry* 45, no. 5 (2004): 362–366.

Veale, D. "Friday the 13th and Obsessive Compulsive Disorder." *BMJ* 311, no. 7011 (1995): 963–964.

Vergote, Antoine. *Guilt and Desire: Religious Attitudes and Their Pathological Derivatives.* Translated by M. H. Wood. New Haven, CT: Yale University Press, 1978.

Wallace, Anthony F. C. *Religion: An Anthropological View.* New York: Random House, 1966.

Webster, Richard. *The Encyclopedia of Superstitions*. Woodbury, MN: Llewellyn Publications, 2008.

Zohar, A. H., G. Ratzoni, D. L. Pauls, A. Apter, A. Bleich, S. Kron, M. Rappaport, A. Weizman, and D. J. Cohen. "An Epidemiological Study of Obsessive–Compulsive Disorder and Related Disorders in Israeli Adolescents." *Journal of the American Academy of Child and Adolescent Psychiatry* 31, no. 6 (1992): 1057–1061.

4

We *All* Have "Bad" Thoughts

We said that there are essentially no "bad" thoughts, but that the reaction to them determines order from disorder. The difference between a thought being a normal passing intrusion and an obsession is a matter of brain chemistry. OCD causes a disproportionate anxiety or emotional reaction to the *same* thoughts and feelings that everyone else has. Typical reactions are behavioral, but some are mental. We know that obsessions are intrusive thoughts, images, or impulses that provoke anxiety. They are the *very* thoughts you are not "supposed" to have, and in places where you are not "supposed" to have them. You have these thoughts *because* you don't want them. One way to know the difference for yourself in Blake's situation is the extent to which you might or might not want to be around children and playgrounds.

It was such a nice day out, so Blake decided to eat lunch at the nearby playground. While watching the children running around, he noticed a particularly cute little girl with pig-tails bouncing up and down, and got a warm and fuzzy feeling. If you don't have OCD, this is a pleasant experience. For Blake, however, his OCD changed that pleasurable feeling into an obsessive nightmare. He suddenly thought, "What if I'm a pedophile?" He then had a sudden surge of anxiety. With his heart pounding and his thoughts racing, threw away his half-eaten sandwich, collected his things, and fled back to the office. That physiological and emotional experience now became a conditioned response and is assumed to indicate that something must be terribly wrong. Who *wouldn't* feel that way? Who *wouldn't* feel immoral, guilty, and maybe even risky?

Obsessions always have a kernel of reality to them (there are pedophiles in the world), but cannot be verified: What's the difference between me and a pedophile? How do I know I am *not* one? Having these thought might mean I *am* one! Trying to reassure yourself won't work, because there is no way to definitely proof either way. You can never prove you have *not* done something, no matter how hard you try. And when you have OCD, you try all the time.

Negative emotions can also trigger obsessions. When we are angry, we tend to have "bad" thoughts about the person or "wish" bad things for others. When we are lonely, we might curse others' social lives.

Those who have intrusive "bad" thoughts (and don't we all?)—be they violent, sexual, or blasphemous—feel guilty for having them. Typically, sufferers with these obsessions will punish themselves as atonement for having them. They won't let themselves enjoy leisure activities such as reading or watching television and instead will mentally chastise themselves in isolation.

Most of us do not intend to cause harm or hurt others. When we do, inevitably, we try to make some form of restitution directly to the person when we can (apologize, recompense financially, offer to do a favor, etc.), make restitution in an indirect way when we can't (make a donation, do volunteer work, etc.), and in circumstances in which there may not be *anything* we can do, feel our sorrow and firmly intend to do better next time. At some point, letting go of the guilt is the healthy end to the process. When we persist in prolonged and disproportionate self-criticism, we maintain unhealthy guilt

The problem with OCD, however, is that it invades any random and benign situation. OCD deceives the sufferer into feeling an impending sense of threat or risk (when there is none) and that certainty is imperative for the sake of preventing potential harm.

What do you think it would be like to constantly have these thoughts going on all the time:

- What if I snap and kill my wife?
- What if I really left the stove on?
- What if I left the stove on and didn't care?
- What if I am really evil?
- What if I am possessed by the Devil?
- What if I am going insane?
- What if I am insane?
- What if I get stuck in a permanent brain loop of obsessive doubt?
- How do I know that's already happening?
- What if I am already stuck in a permanent state of fear?
- What if I feel confused forever?
- What if I don't know anything any longer?
- What if I'm trapped like this forever?
- What if this isn't OCD?

What if . . . what if . . . what if . . . I . . . I . . . I . . . . The unending obsessive doubt causes the person to withdraw and isolate until he or she feels he or she has things figured out. Doing so increases the sense of urgency and risk, and the self becomes the sole focus, which in turn prevents the person from doing what would help the most: shifting the focus outward by engaging in social and community events.

While Dave is brushing his teeth, he is bombarded by: "How do you know Alice [his daughter] is safe at school right now?" His heart is pounding and racing, and he can't think about anything else. What should Dave do? What would you do? Dave puts down his toothbrush and calls the school. Mr. Ames takes his call and tells Dave that there has been no report of Alice missing the bus or going to the nurse, and as far as the school knows everything is fine. Dave is not satisfied with this answer, and he asks Mr. Ames some reassuring questions. Mr. Ames is a little irritated, because he feels Dave doesn't believe him or is questioning his judgment. Mr. Ames reassures Dave that should anything happen, he will be notified. This forced end to the conversation leaves Dave still uncertain and distressed. After all, isn't he responsible for his daughter's welfare? Mr. Ames never actually went to go check to see that Alice was safe, so how could he be sure that she's okay? Sweaty and heart still pounding, Dave thinks about jumping into his car and driving to Alice's school to lay his own eyes on Alice just to be sure she's safe. Instead of finishing getting ready for work, he believes going to check on her is the only way he can allay his distress. He will be missing an important meeting at work, though. Now he has more anxiety, fear, and guilt: Neither option is good, but he must do the *right* thing. Feeling stuck in not knowing what the *right* decision is, he thinks, "I know I'm being ridiculous, but why should I take the chance in case something *is* wrong? But then I will feel like a fool if I see her going about her day and that I missed the meeting for nothing. How do I decide what to do? Someone just tell me what to do!" Dave continues to grapple with what to do. The thing is, though, this is a false moral dilemma. There is no real need to make a choice, because there is no real threat or risk. What's going on is Dave's brain is having a brain glitch that fires warning shots against nothing.

An interesting study was conducted in 1978 that reported that 80 percent of students, research workers, nurses, clinicians, and the like had either intrusive, unacceptable thoughts or impulses that were similar to clinical obsessions.[1] One of their conclusions was that normal and abnormal obsessions are similar in form and content, differing in frequency and intensity and in their feared consequences, and that there was no qualitative difference between normal and clinical thoughts and obsessions.

Table 4.1 depicts the results of a similar study of intrusive thoughts experienced by a nonclinical sample.

TABLE 4.1 Normal Intrusive Thoughts

	Item	Female %	Male %	OCD Category[1, 2]
1.	driving into a window	13	16	aggressive/harming
2.	running car off the road	64	56	aggressive/harming
3.	hitting animals or people with car	46	54	aggressive/harming
4.	swerving into traffic	55	52	aggressive/harming
5.	smashing into objects	27	40	aggressive/harming
6.	slitting wrist/throat	20	22	aggressive/harming
7.	cutting off finger	19	16	aggressive/harming
8.	jumping off a high place	39	46	aggressive/harming
9.	fatally pushing a stranger	17	34	aggressive/harming
10.	fatally pushing a friend	9	22	aggressive/harming
11.	jumping in front of a train/car	25	29	aggressive/harming
12.	pushing stranger in front of a train/car	8	20	aggressive/harming
13.	pushing family in front of a train/car	5	14	aggressive/harming
14.	hurting strangers	18	48	aggressive/harming
15.	insulting strangers	50	59	aggressive/harming
16.	bumping into people	37	43	aggressive/harming
17.	insulting authority figure	34	48	aggressive/harming
18.	insulting family	59	55	aggressive/harming
19.	hurting family	42	50	aggressive/harming
20.	choking a family member	10	22	aggressive/harming
21.	stabbing a family member	6	11	aggressive/harming
22.	accidentally leaving the heat/stove on	79	66	aggressive/harming
23.	leaving home unlocked, finding an intruder inside	77	69	aggressive/harming
24.	leaving taps on, finding home flooded	28	24	aggressive/harming
25.	swearing in public	30	34	aggressive/harming
26.	breaking wind in public	31	49	aggressive/harming
27.	throwing something	28	26	aggressive/harming
28.	causing a public scene	47	43	aggressive/harming
29.	scratching car paint	26	43	aggressive/harming
30.	breaking a window	26	43	aggressive/harming
31.	wrecking something	32	33	aggressive/harming

	Item	Female %	Male %	OCD Category[1,2]
32.	shoplifting	27	33	*aggressive/harming*
33.	grabbing money	21	39	*aggressive/harming*
34.	holding up bank	6	32	*aggressive/harming*
35.	having sex with an unacceptable person	48	63	*sexual*
36.	having sex with an authority figure	38	63	*sexual*
37.	finding fly/blouse undone	27	40	*sexual*
38.	kissing an authority figure	37	44	*sexual*
39.	exposing self	9	21	*sexual*
40.	acting against sexual preference	19	20	*sexual*
41.	seeing authority figures naked	42	54	*sexual*
42.	seeing strangers naked	51	80	*sexual*
43.	having sex in public	49	78	*sexual*
44.	performing a disgusting sex act	43	52	*sexual*
45.	catching a sexually transmitted disease	60	43	*contamination*
46.	contamination from doors	35	24	*contamination*
47.	contamination from phones	28	18	*contamination*
48.	getting a fatal disease from strangers	22	19	*contamination*
49.	giving a fatal disease to strangers	25	17	*contamination*
50.	giving everything away	52	43	*contamination*
51.	removing all dust from the floor	35	24	*contamination*
52.	removing dust from unseen places	41	29	*contamination*

[1] The column on the right indicates the corresponding OCD symptom category on the Y-BOCS symptom checklist. (See www.stlocd.org/handouts/YBOC-Symptom-Checklist.pdf.)
[2] W. K. Goodman, L. H. Price, S. A. Rasmussen, C. Mazure, R. L. Fleishman, C. L. Hill, G. R. Heninger, & D. S. Charney, "The Yale–Brown Obsessive Compulsive Scale," *Archives of General Psychiatry* 46 (1989): 1012–1016.

Source: Purdon C. & Clark D. "Obsessive Intrusive Thoughts in Nonclinical Subjects. Part 1: Content and Relation with Depressive, Anxious and Obsessional Symptoms." *Behaviour Research and Therapy* 31 (1992): 713–720. Used by permission.

Cognitive Considerations

Insight: The Range

People often wonder whether their thoughts make sense. With OCD, there is always a kernel of truth, but there may be a range of insight into the level of belief in them. Figure 4.1 illustrates the spectrum of insight, from rational to delusional.

Rational thoughts make sense. Insight is considered and rated at 95–100 percent. People will understand the logic and thinking involved in the ideas. People who have this level of insight don't have problems assessing how realistic their thoughts and beliefs are and have good judgment in making decisions.

Worry thoughts are normal, insightful, and controllable but can be somewhat preoccupying. Some people believe that a state of worry means they are "on top" of things in a somewhat superstitious way: "If I think about all the worst-case scenarios, then I'll be prepared." In getting ready for public speaking, you might try to anticipate what could go wrong as a way to be ready for eventualities. There is nothing wrong with that strategy until the worrying interferes with you confidence and you start to "psych yourself out."

Ruminations are more intense than worry thoughts, are preoccupying, and interfere with your ability to concentrate or focus. Persistent worry thoughts and ruminations about "real life" concerns (money, health, making good judgments and decisions) may be indicative of Generalized Anxiety Disorder (GAD). Other symptoms of GAD might include fatigue, irritability, problems falling or staying asleep, sleep that is often restless and unsatisfying, restlessness, and often becoming startled very easily. Physical problems may consist of muscle tension, shakiness, headaches, and digestive problems. Ruminations can cause paralysis in decision making as the anxiety begins to override the ability to make the "right" decision. A good course of cognitive-behavior therapy will help reduce these symptoms.

Obsessions are always negative "taboo" thoughts that spike anxiety and cannot be controlled. Someone with OCD who has excellent insight will say he or she knows that the thoughts are irrational and that they need not to be pushed away. Someone who has good insight believes this about 80–95 percent. Fair insight means that the person believes that the thoughts are realistic and are less flexible to change. The person is less willing to take the rational risk by

Rational / Worry / Rumination / Obsessions / Overvalued Ideas / Delusions

FIGURE 4.1   Range of insight into thoughts.

doing the opposite of the obsession, which is what exposure therapy entails (more discussion later on treatment).

Overvalued ideation (OVI) is poor insight. The person can agree that how you describe the excessiveness of his or her beliefs makes sense but cannot do this on his or her own. According to Foa et al., "[P]atients who were extremely certain that their feared consequences would occur evidenced poorer outcome [with exposure/response therapy] than patients with mild or moderate certainty, despite the reduction of such certainty at post-test." A high-functioning attorney with whom I have worked for many years will not forgo excessive checking in his practice because he fears uncertainty can and will lead to catastrophic outcomes for his clients. His work takes three times longer than his colleagues, and he is always behind. The intention of therapy is not to cause carelessness, but to accept that perfection is an ideal, not a goal. Achieving that "right" feeling is transitory and does not actually produce a better product.

Delusional beliefs have zero insight, yet the person fully believes they are realistic. Common delusions are beliefs such as that a conspiracy (a national or international intelligence organization, a spy ring, a secret cabal, etc.) is out to get you because you have special information or power, or that you are the Messiah sent by God to save the world. (One might wonder, though, whether we would recognize a messiah or simply prescribe medication for him.)

Thought Suppression: Why It Doesn't Work

The white bear phenomenon was an experiment designed by Daniel Wegner that challenged people not to have a thought.[2] The effort put into not having a thought is an action that makes you keep having it. A watered-down way of understanding the experience of obsessions is by remembering when you've had an annoying jingle or sitcom theme song stuck in your head. You might have initially noticed it, groaned to yourself about it, and tried to get rid of it, yet it didn't go away. After a while, you might start deliberately singing it to yourself as a way to dismiss it. Either way, it ran its course and probably didn't interfere with what you were doing.[3]

If you looked at the list of intrusive thoughts earlier in the chapter, you saw that they are similar for people with and without OCD. The main difference in the experience of having them is that with OCD, they cause physiological symptoms of anxiety and are emotionally more upsetting. Many people feel guilty for having them and feel the need to prove they are not wanted. The problem with trying to get rid of them is the rebound effect; the thoughts get stronger. This process has been captured by neurophysiological images taken while nonclinical study participants were instructed to suppress unwanted thoughts. The images showed increased activity in the anterior cingulated cortex and the dorsolateral prefrontal cortex areas of the brain. As such, the effort you put into not having a thought makes you have it.

State/Trait Anxiety and Guilt

Our emotions naturally react to feared or negative (and positive) situations that occur in reality. Some people experience anxiety or guilt situationally (state) or chronically (trait). State anxiety and guilt are emotional conditions we experience to an external cue in the environment, such as seeing a neighborhood house on fire. That is a scary event, and we are relieved when we realize we will not be personally affected by it. We feel badly for our neighbors and want to help them, but we know the situation was out of our hands and might be considered an "act of God." After the fire is out, our fear and emotions calm down. Having low-state anxiety or guilt will prompt appropriate empathy, making us want to help our neighbor—but we won't necessarily feel more vulnerable to fire or responsible for its occurring.

OCD treatment for people with high-state anxiety or guilt can still be successful, but they may not achieve the same results as someone with low-state anxiety or guilt. This should be a consideration for why a treatment response may seem less robust than expected for symptoms that typically appear to be more straightforward.

Someone with high trait anxiety and guilt is more prone to consistently feel on edge or at fault in daily life. If your levels of trait guilt and anxiety are high, your state level will be even higher in triggering situations. In the aftermath of a house afire, you might have varying degrees of anxiety or guilt about many aspects of the consequences of the fire.

Someone who has OCD experiences trait anxiety or guilt at a higher than "normal" level. He or she might somehow feel that there was something he or she could have known or done to prevent or minimize the fire. He or she may develop a sudden obsessive concern about fire and perform safety and checking rituals. Treatment will be more challenging in these cases. Assessing level of obsessive guilt and addressing it as another symptom of the disorder has been helpful when this emotional aspect is recognized as a clinical interference.

Notes

1. Rachman and de Silva, "Abnormal and Normal Obsessions": 233–248.
2. Wegner, *White Bears and Other Unwanted Thoughts*, vii.
3. Mitchell et al., "Separating Sustained from Transient Aspects": 292–297.

Bibliography

Foa, Edna B., Jonathan S. Abramowitz, Martin E. Franklin, and Michael J. Kozak. "Feared Consequences, Fixity of Belief, and Treatment Outcome in Patients with Obsessive-Compulsive Disorder." *Behavior Therapy* 30, no. 4 (1999): 717–24.

Mitchell, Jason P., Todd F. Heatherton, William M. Kelley, Carrie L. Wyland, Daniel M. Wegner, and C. Neil Macrae. "Separating Sustained from Transient Aspects of Cognitive Control during Thought Suppression." *Psychological Science* 18, no. 4 (2007): 292–297.

Rachman, S., and P. de Silva. "Abnormal and Normal Obsessions." *Behaviour Research and Therapy* 16, no. 4 (1978): 233–248.

Wegner, Daniel M. *White Bears and Other Unwanted Thoughts: Suppression, Obsession, and the Psychology of Mental Control.* New York: The Guilford Press, 1994.

5

In Good Company: A Who's Who of Obsessive Conscience

If you suffer from an obsessive conscience, you are in good company![1] In chapter 3 we learned that OCD is a nondiscriminatory disorder that prevails across all cultures and societies. In a similar fashion, this chapter shows that OCD also does not care about position or station in society. Saints, historical figures, people of letters, and other notables whose lives were recorded for posterity now serve as examples of people who struggled with OCD and who made their mark in the world not because of it but, in spite of it.

Although we are fortunate to gain access and insight into many illustrious lives, these historical accounts are essentially limited to Western culture, most notably in Europe. This may be accounted for by the excellent archival preservation methods used by the Catholic Church in the 17th to 18th centuries. Oral accounts of OCD from traditional cultures may have been lost to time. Nevertheless, it is to be hoped that in the near future, documented examples from all parts of the world will be made available online by the many organizations that have already electronically scanned rare and out-of-print historical and literary documents, many of which were used as sources for this chapter.

Scrupulous and well-preserved record-keeping by Catholic clergy portrayed an increasing moderate religious attitude just prior to the Age of Enlightenment (mid-17th century to early 18th century). This more accepting attitude is shown by the sudden and numerous accounts of religious figures whose practices came to be understood as excessive, obsessive, and compulsive. The documentation at that time seemed to recognize that people suffering from scruples were experiencing more a problem the mind than a special religious calling. This shift in attitude made it possible for these accounts to be written with impunity, as they likely would have been accused of heresy during the Middle Ages.

It is clear from both the psychological and religious standpoints that the many religious figures cited below became saints in spite of, not because of, their OCD scrupulosity. These OCD sufferers are included in this chapter as a review of the history and the presence of OCD over the centuries. Descriptions of the extent of their devotion to overcome their scruples is provided in chapter 6, which is fully devoted to subject of scrupulosity. Readers will understand that the religious figures mentioned in this chapter who suffered from scrupulosity set out to rid themselves of it to better serve God and humanity.[2]

Commentaries on the Early Role of Scruples in Confession[3]

Acts of confession give license to scrupulosity. Scrupulous Catholic penitents typically confessed unsinful minute details, *just in case* they mattered, because they were never sure their confessions were done properly. John Aho has written about the history of confession in his book *Confession and Bookkeeping*.[4] This chapter cites his work (except for the portion on Climacus) up until the chapter portion that begins discussing the saints. Some of the religious and historical figures who shaped how the sacrament of confession was to be conducted appear to have had scrupulosity themselves.

According to Paden (as cited in Aho 2005), confession was the first recognized Catholic ritual in the fifth century.[5] Its origin was attributed to the Syrian monk Saint John Cassian, (AD 360–435), also known as John the Ascetic (quoted in Aho 2005) whose prescription for performing the sacrament was very strict:

> [W]e should . . . constantly search all the inner chambers of our hearts . . . with the closest investigations lest . . . some beast furtively insinuate itself 'into the secret recesses of the heart' . . . just as the miller meticulously examines the quality of grain before admitting it to the store . . . . [E]ach believer in an effort to rid themselves of their own noxiousness, must scrutinize their untoward desires and thoughts, enumerate them in writing, and divulge them daily to the abbot.[6]

John Climacus (525–606) was a Christian monk who lived in a Sinai desert monastery. He wrote the virtues by which ascetic monks should live in their striving toward God in *The Ladder of Divine Ascent*.[7] Sympathetic to those afflicted with scruples, he advised, "No one in the face of blasphemous thoughts need think that the guilt lies within him, for the Lord is the Knower of hearts and He is aware that such words and thoughts do not come from us but from our foes."

Watkins (as cited in Aho, 2005) quoted Saint Donatus (592–651), bishop of Besancon, as being of the same strict mind of Cassius: "Confession must be always rendered assiduously and with unceasing zeal, alike of thought, of the idle word, every hour, every moment. . . . Accordingly not even little matters of thought are to be neglected from confession, because it is written, 'he who neglects little things, falls little by little.'"[8]

About 500 years later, in his *Steps of Humility*, St. Bernard of Clairvaux (1090–1153) (as cited in Aho, 2005), reformed the practice of confession after seeing the devastating effect it had on some adherents, stating that the literal form of confession was *simulata confessio*, "exaggerated guilt."[9]

Haering (as cited in Aho, 2005) noted that the French poet Alain de Lille (*c.* 1116/1117–1202/1203) suggested to those who had an overly precise conscience "not always to descend to minutiae, for truly a searching after the unknown can give occasion for sin because he who blows his nose too much brings forth blood."[10] Raymund de Pennafort (1175–1275) (as cited in Aho, 2005) was a spiritual physician who said that overzealousness in presenting one's complaints to the spiritual physician "is not speaking the truth" . . . but is "admitting falsely for the sake of humility. 'As Augustine says, 'if it was not a sin before confession, it is now.'"[11]

Jean de Charlier de Gerson, (1363–1429) (as cited in Aho, 2005) wrote in *Instructio contra scrupulosam conscientiam*, "[I]f a scrupulous man were to confess all those things that have been written for confessions, he well might keep a confessor in his purse."[12]

Saints

- Francis of Assisi (1181–1226), born into the family of a prosperous silk merchant, went to war in 1204 to defend his town of Assisi in war with Umbria. While in the war, he experienced a vision that resulted in his surrender of his luxurious worldly possessions, and committed himself to serve God as a poor and humble servant, thenceforth leading a life of poverty. He did not have scrupulosity, but his advice for a scrupulous penitent was "not to take any notice of those things which caused him such heavy scruples, and not to plague himself by confessing then, and thus get rid of the confusion, which is the consequence of entering into those explanations to several confessors."[13]
- Angela Foligno (1248–1309), after having found her sins to be unacceptable, led a life devoted to increasing her perfection and an existential pursuit of the unknown. Her "Book of Visions and Instructions" is a 70-chapter first-hand account of her conversion as dictated to her Franciscan confessor, Father Arnold of Foligno.[14]

- Catherine of Genoa (1447–1510), as recorded in Friedrich von Hügel's *The Mystical Element of Religion*, received Communion with unusual frequency for a lay person due to what is described as "remarkable mental and at times almost pathological experiences."[15]
- Ignatius of Loyola (1491–1556) wrote of his own suffering: "After I have trodden a cross formed by two straws, or after I have thought, said, or done some other thing, there comes to me from 'without' a thought that I have sinned, and on the other hand it seems to me that I have not sinned; nevertheless I feel some uneasiness on the subject, inasmuch as I doubt and yet do not doubt."[16]

  Sometime later, he advised a young Jesuit, "Humble yourself and trust that Divine Providence will rule and guide you by means of your superior. . . . [I]f you have true humility and submissiveness, your scruples will not cause you so much trouble. Pride is the fuel they feed on, and it is pride that places more reliance on one's own judgment and less on the judgment of others whom we trust."[17]

- Mary Magdalene de Pazzi (1566–1609) considered her ecstasies to be evidence of her weakness rather than a reward for her holiness. She believed she received them from God because she was too weak and unworthy to become holy otherwise.[18]
- Marguerite-Marie (1647–1690) is said to have conducted her examination of conscience so rigorously that "it threw her into agitation and fear, so much did she dread bringing the slightest stain to holy communion. . . . [S]he condemned all the sins that she could not see in herself, of which she thought she was guilty."[19]
- Veronica Giuliani (b. 1660–1727) suffered from a combination of scrupulosity and eating disorders. She repeatedly confessed the same sins and, in a culture in which thinness reflected holiness, fasted herself into a state of emaciation.[20]
- Alphonsus Maria de'Liguori (1696–1787) was a lawyer who went into an emotional crisis after having lost his first case after eight years in practice.

  He thought his mistake would be ascribed not to oversight but to deliberate deceit. He felt as if his career was ruined, and left the court almost beside himself, saying: "World, I know you now. Courts, you shall never see me more." For three days he refused all food. Then the storm subsided, and he began to see that his humiliation had been sent him by God to break down his pride and wean him from the world. . . . On 28 August, 1723, the young advocate had gone to perform a favourite act of charity by visiting the sick in the Hospital for Incurables. Suddenly he found himself surrounded by a mysterious light; the house seemed to rock, and an interior voice said: "Leave the world and give thyself to Me."[21]

Scrupulous Anonymous, a monthly newsletter since 1997, was founded on the suffering, scruples, religious guilt, recovery, and teachings of St. Ligouri (see the section on resources for more information). Father Santa, who publishes the newsletter now has a weekly live call-in radio show on Radio Maria USA.[22]

- Thérèse of Lisieux (b. 1873–1897) said, "[C]hildish pleasure seemed sinful to me, and I had so many scruples that I had to go to Confession . . . . [I heard] one lady said I had beautiful hair; another asked . . . who was that pretty little girl. Such remarks, the more flattering because I was not meant to hear them, gave me a feeling of pleasure which showed plainly that I was full of self-love."[23]

Religious Figures

- Notable women such as Julian of Norwich (1342–1416), Catherine of Siena (1347–1380), and Catherine of Genoa (1447–1510) all seem to have suffered from similar combinations of scrupulosity and perfectionism.[24]
- Margery Kempe (1373–1438) is said to have written the first confessional autobiography about the sins she feared having committed after confession, over which she returned repeatedly to the confessional.[25]
- Erasmus (1466–1536) exhibited excessive fear of germs and sickness and regularly requested that the church holy water and baptismal water be changed.[26]
- Giovanni Battista Scaramelli (1687–1752) gave advice on how to overcome obsessions and compulsions that sounded similar to what is now behavior therapy.[27]
- Richard Baxter (1615–1691), a British clergyman, was something of a celebrity healer for people with melancholy, a term which in his day encompassed obsessions and compulsions. He published advice for sufferers.[28]
- John Bunyan (1628–1688) describes his struggle with obsessive blasphemous thoughts in autobiography, *Grace Abounding to the Chief of Sinners.*[29] He was so obsessed with the idea of his own lack of judgment about salvation that he compulsively reread the scripture, which only worsened his mental state. He experienced the double bind that plagues scrupulosity sufferers: Though he knew that prayer was the only way he could approach Christ, he could not pray, because doing so would compound his guilt.[30]
- John Moore (1646–1714), Anglican bishop, pointed out that trying to suppress distressing thoughts can make them worse:

  I come now to the last case I proposed to speak to, which doth relate to these unhappy persons, who have naughty, and sometimes blasphemous thoughts start in their minds, while they are exercised in the worship of God, which makes them ready to charge themselves with the sin against the Holy Ghost, to pronounce their condition to be without hopes of remedy, and to fear that God hath utterly cast them off . . .

- Because these frightful thoughts do for the most part proceed from the disorder and indisposition of the body. . . .
- Because they are mostly good people, who are exercised with them.
- Because it is not in the power of those disconsolate Christians, whom these bad thoughts so vex and torment, with all their endeavours to stifle and suppress them. Nay often the more they struggle with them, the more they increase . . . .[31]

• Hannah Allen (b. 1683–?) wrote an autobiographical account of her struggle with obsessive blasphemous thoughts:

[T]he enemy of my soul . . . cast in horrible blasphemous thoughts and injections into my mind, insomuch that I was seldom free day or night, unless when deep sleep was upon me. . . . I was persuaded I had sinned the unpardonable sin. . . . I would often in my thoughts wish I might change conditions with the vilest persons I could think of, concluding there was hope from them though not for me. . . .[32]

Historical Notables

• Robert Boyle (1627) is considered the first chemist due to his having established precise methodology for scientific experimentation using the elements. Boyle also suffered from scrupulosity. "That Scrupulousnes [sic] of Conscience is no duty of Command of Christianity; and tho it be oftentimes a good signe, yet 'tis really an Infirmity or distemper of the mind."[33] Even though his scientific work was so well respected, in 1680 he declined to become the president of the Royal Society of London for Improving Natural Knowledge owing to his scruples against taking oaths.

• John Locke (b. 1632) is known as the father of liberal philosophy and originator of the concept of the *social contract* that recognized human rights as being naturally endowed upon people, instead of bestowed by the English monarchy. Locke's writings reflect an OCD dichotomous thinking style:

I might doubt whether it were best to read . . . or send you my own naked thoughts. To those a thousand other scruples, as considerable, might be added, which would still beget others, in every one of which there would be, no doubt, still a better and a worse. . . .[34]

• Samuel Johnson (1709), a devout Anglican, regarded his distress as a dangerous compound of "imagination" and the kind of obsessive guilt that threatens sanity. In his prayer of January 23, 1758, he said:

LORD, who wouldst that all men should be saved, and who knowest that without thy grace we can do nothing acceptable to thee, have mercy upon me, enable me to break the chain of my sins, to reject sensuality in thought, and to overcome and suppress vain scruples.[35]

In a collection of his essays by Murphy, he was observed

> . . . reviewing every year of his life, and severely censuring himself, for not keeping resolutions, which morbid melancholy, and other bodily infirmities, rendered impracticable. We see him for every little defect imposing on himself voluntary penance, going through the day with only one cup of tea without milk, and to the last, amidst paroxysms and remissions of illness, forming plans of study and resolutions to amend his life. Many of his scruples may be called weaknesses; but they are the weaknesses of a good, a pious, and most excellent man.[36]

Modern/Popular Cultural Figures

When you Google "people with OCD," several lists appear listing celebrities and other well-known people. It's unclear how reliable these lists are—they describe some behaviors that may be explained by personality traits without indicating a diagnosable disorder. The following list includes people who have self-disclosed having OCD or who seem to clearly meet the criteria: [37]

- Nikola Tesla (July 10, 1856–January 7, 1943) Nikola Tesla, an inventor, physicist, and mechanical and electrical engineer, is known for his work in electricity and magnetism. His OCD involved contamination fears, and he is said to have hated touching round objects, to have disliked hair other than his own, and to have found jewelry repulsive. He used the number 3 and its multiples when performing functional tasks. It was reported that before he ate, he estimated the mass of his food, used 18 napkins, and would not eat alone with a woman.
- Howard Hughes's (1905–1976) OCD was portrayed in the 2004 feature film *The Aviator*. The film depicts Hughes' obsessive drive for innovation, engineering perfection, and large lifestyle. As the movie depicts, by the late 1950s, he had begun hoarding his urine and compelling his staff to wear gloves. He became completely nonfunctional as his life became debilitated by untreated OCD.
- Stanley Kubrick (July 26, 1928–March 7, 1999) is an *avant garde* film director and producer considered among the greatest of the 20th century. Jon Ronson's 1998 documentary film *Stanley Kubrick's Boxes* reveals the obsessive detail and precise cataloging Kubrick employed when collecting material for movie ideas and projects.[38] Pictures, newspaper clippings,

film outtakes, notes, and fan letters were used as research for his films. It is unclear whether Kubrick had OCD—his meticulous hoarding behavior may have been part of his creative genius.

- Marc Summers was one of the first celebrities to out himself as having OCD. He hosted the children's game show *Double Dare* and had several other television roles. His book about his experience with OCD is titled *Everything in its Place: My Trials and Triumphs with Obsessive Compulsive Disorder.*[39]

- Howie Mandel has also been public about having OCD. It is said he invented the "fist bump" as a way of avoiding shaking hands with contestants on *Deal or No Deal* as the game show's host. He also wrote a memoir about having OCD in his book, *Here's the Deal: Don't Touch Me.*[40]

Other celebrities said to have OCD, to name a few, are Leonardo DiCaprio (who played Howard Hughes in *The Aviator*), Justin Timberlake, Megan Fox, Cameron Diaz, and Howard Stern (www.OCDtypes.com).

It is safe to say that people who have OCD are in good company. It is more common than people think and is an equal-opportunity disorder. Because it is widely inherited, it can be considered a force of nature, not something that people can just "get over."

Notes

1. *A Short History of OCD* (www.ocdhistory.net/) has been an invaluable resource for discovery of information directly related to this book's topics.

2. The concept of God in this book represents creativity, love, vitality, and acceptance. God may be experienced as religious, spiritual, or reverence toward that which is greater than ourselves. OCD is the antithesis of creativity, because it demands adherence to rules based on fear and absolutes. People who have OCD are as creative as those without OCD, but they are gripped with fear and doubt about their abilities to do the "right" and "good" thing.

3. The following examples cited from here until the section "Religious Figures" are borrowed largely from Aho, *Confession and Bookkeeping*, which adeptly captures the history of scrupulosity in Catholicism.

4. Aho, *Confession and Bookeeping*, 81–94.

5. Ibid.

6. Ibid., p. 26.

7. St. John Climacus, "*The Ladder of Divine Ascent*," 79.

8. Aho, *Confession and Bookkeeping*, 26–27.

9. Ibid., 26.

10. Ibid., 27.

11. Ibid., 26.

12. Ibid., 27.

13. Candide, *The Life of St. Francis of Assisi*, 345.

14. Foligno, *The Book of Divine Consolation of the Blessed Angela of Foligno*, 104.

15. Von Hugel Baron, *The Mystical Elements of Religion*. London: J. M. Dent and Sons (1908): 335.

16. O'Flaherty, *How to Cure Scruples*, 6.

17. Letter from Ignatius Loyola to Fr. Juan Marin, *Monumenta Ignatiana*, Selected Letters of St. Ignatius of Loyola. Matriti, Typis G. Lopez del Horno 1904. http://www.archive.org/details/monumentaignati05ignagoog.

18. Fabrini, *The Complete Works of Saint Mary Magdalen De' Pazzi*.

19. Languet, "La Vie De Marguerite-Marie," 315.

20. Filippo Maria Salvatori (1740–1820). *The Lives of S. Veronica Giuliani, Capuchin Nun: And, of the Blessed Battista Varani of the Order of S. Clare. Saints and Servants of God*; Series 2. London: R. Washbourne (1874): 335.

21. Knights of Columbus Committee on War Activities, *The Catholic Encyclopedia*.

22. http://mission.liguori.org/newsletters/scrupanon.htm.

23. St. Thérèse of Lisieux, *L'histoire D'un Ame*, 46.

24. Delemeau, *Sin and Fear*, 320–321.

25. Butler-Bowdon, ed., *The Book of Margery Kempe*, 191–194.

26. Huizinga, *Erasmus and the Age of Reformation*.

27. Scaramelli, *The Directorium Asceticum*.

28. Delemeau, *Sin and Fear*, 103–104.

29. Bunyan, *Grace Abounding to the Chief of Sinners*, 14.

30. Sneep and Zinck, "Spiritual and Psychic Transformation": 156–164.

31. Hunter and Macalpine, *Three Hundred Years of Psychiatry*, 252–253.

32. Allen, *A Narrative of God's Gracious Dealings with That Choice Christian*, 3–4.

33. Baldwin, "Michael Hunter": 4.

34. King, ed., *Excerpts from the Life and Letters of John Locke*, 110–116.

35. Boswell et al., *The Life of Samuel Johnson*, 139.

36. Murphy, *An Essay on the Life and Genius of Samuel Johnson*, 136.

37. www.disabled-world.com/artman/publish/famous-ocd.shtml.

38. Ronson, "Stanley Kubrick's Boxes."

39. Summers and Hollander, *Everything in Its Place*.

40. Mandel and Young, *Here's the Deal, Don't Touch Me*.

Bibliography

Aho, James. *Confession and Bookkeeping: The Religious, Moral, and Rhetorical Roots of Modern Accounting*. New York: State University of New York Press, 2005.

Allen, Hannah. *A Narrative of God's Gracious Dealings with That Choice Christian*. London: John Wallis, 1683.

Baldwin, Martha. "Michael Hunter: Robert Boyle (1627–91): Scrupulosity and Science." *Isis* 93, no. 2 (2002): 277–279.

Boswell, James, John Wilson Crocker, and John Wright. *The Life of Samuel Johnson: Including His Tour to the Hebrides* Vol. 7. London: Henry G. Bohn, 1859.

Bunyan, John. *Grace Abounding to the Chief of Sinners*, unabridged. London: IndoEuropean Publishing, 2010.

Butler-Bowdon, W., ed. *The Book of Margery Kempe: A Modern Version of the Earliest Known Autobiography in English, A.D. 1436*: Devin–Adair Company, 1944.

Candide, Challipe. *The Life of St. Francis of Assisi.* London: D. & J. Sadlier & Company, 1899.

Delemeau, Jean. *Sin and Fear: The Emergence of a Western Guilt Culture 13th–18th Centuries* [Le péché et la peur. La culpabilisation en Occident, XIIIe-XVIIIe siècles]. New York: St. Martin's Press, 1989.

Fabrini, Rev. Placido. *The Complete Works of Saint Mary Magdalen De' Pazzi Carmelite and Mystic (1566–1607).* Philadelphia: Rev. Antonio Isoleri, Miss. Ap., 1900.

Foligno, Angela. *The Book of Divine Consolation of the Blessed Angela of Foligno.* London: Chatto and Windus, 1909.

Huizinga, Johan. *Erasmus and the Age of Reformation.* London: Harper Torchbook, 1957/1924.

Hunter, Richard, and Ida Macalpine. *Three Hundred Years of Psychiatry, 1535–1860.* London: Oxford University Press, 1963.

King, Lord, ed. *Excerpts from the Life and Letters of John Locke.* London: George Bell & Sons, 1884.

Knights of Columbus Committee on War Activities. *The Catholic Encyclopedia: An International Work of Reference on the Constitution, Doctrine, Discipline, and History of the Catholic Church.* New Haven, CT: The Encyclopedia Press, Inc., 1913.

Languet, J. J. "La Vie De Marguerite-Marie." Translated by Eric Nicholson. In *Sin and Fear: The Emergence of a Western Guilt Culture, 13th–18th Centuries*, ed. Jean Delemeau, p. 677. New York: St. Martin's Press, 1990.

Mandel, Howie, and Josh Young. *Here's the Deal, Don't Touch Me*, 1st ed. New York: Bantam Books, 2009.

Murphy, Arthur. *An Essay on the Life and Genius of Samuel Johnson: Ll.D.* London: Printed for T. Longman, B. White and Son, B. Law, J. Dodsley, H. Baldwin, and 32 others, 1792. http://quod.lib.umich.edu/e/ecco/004855149.0001.000/1:3?rgn=div1.

O'Flaherty, V. M., SJ. *How to Cure Scruples.* Milwaukee, WI: The Bruce Publishing Co., 1966.

Ronson, Jon. "Stanley Kubrick's Boxes." 48 minutes. World of Wonder; Broadcast by Channel 4 http://www.channel4.com/more4/documentaries/doc-feature.jsp?id=215. United Kingdom, 2008.

St. John Climacus. "The Ladder of Divine Ascent." New York: Harper & Brothers, 1959.

St. Thérèse of Lisieux. "L'histoire D'un Ame (the Story of a Soul)." London: Burns, Oates, & Washbourne, 1922.

Scaramelli, John Baptist. *The Directorium Asceticum, or Guide to the Spiritual Life*, 8th ed. London: Burns, Oates, & Washburn, 1924/1754.

Sneep, John, and Arlette Zinck. "Spiritual and Psychic Transformation: Understanding the Psychological Dimensions of John Bunyan's Mental Illness and Healing." *Journal of Psychology and Christianity* 24, no. 2 (2005): 156–164.

Summers, Marc, and Eric Hollander. *Everything in Its Place : My Trial and Triumphs with Obsessive Compulsive Disorder.* New York: J.P. Tarcher/Putnam, 1999.

Van Ornum, William. *A Thousand Frightening Fantasies: Understanding and Healing Scrupulosity and Obsessive–Compulsive Disorder.* New York: Crossroad Pub., 1997.

Von Hugel Baron, Friedrich. *The Mystical Elements of Religion,*

Part II

The Exploited
Conscience

6

Scrupulosity: It's Not Religious

[A] scruple can be cured only by refusing to examine it for guilt.
—*St. Ignatius of Loyola from* How to Cure Scruples[1]

The opposite of a scrupulous person is not an unscrupulous person, but a person of faith.[2]

Scrupulosity is *not* a religious problem, nor is it a virtue. If you suffer from scrupulosity, you may feel as if your soul is contaminated. It isn't because God is not involved in scrupulosity. On the other hand, it may always be contaminated if your expectation is achieving religious perfection. Being scrupulous does not make you a better person or even prove that you are a good person, just as your intrusive unwanted thoughts do not make you a sinful or a bad person. Scrupulosity is not a test from God. It is a product of your brain chemistry. It interferes with the quality of your life, relationships, work, and sense of spirit/faith. That your OCD symptoms cause you distress means that you care about all these things. If you did not care, you would not suffer from scruples, but perhaps rather from destructive personality issues.

Historical theological writings describe the dual theological and psychological nature of scrupulosity. These writings explain how scrupulosity was recognized as a psychological problem that went beyond the tenets of religious beliefs and practices. St. Ignatius of Loyola, who suffered from scrupulosity, described it as "an inclination in devout people to go too far in the right direction, to be too cautious, too safe, too sure about pleasing God and too anxious to be certain that they have not sinned."[3] Loyola clarified that normal fear of sin leads to reflection upon whether a sin was committed in error. For the scrupulous, this kind of reflection is problematic, because obsessive anxiety, doubt, and fear about having committed a sin becomes misinterpreted as guilt of sin. Accordingly, scrupulosity is considered more difficult to treat than other types of OCD (e.g., washing, checking).

As a behavior therapist, I was surprised to find that one of the best books I have read on the obsessive conscience was written from the psychoanalytic tradition. In *Guilt and Desire*, Antoine Vergote describes the profound extent to which the psyche in patients with OCD is affected by their obsessions. He uses the term "legalism" to characterize the rigid adherence of the scrupulous to the letter of the religious law rather than to the spirit of the law:

> Religious guilt reverts to legalism so that the individual can assure himself that his behavior and actions receive God's sanction. He compensates for impurity and imperfection by multiplying the prescriptions accompanying his actions; every action that is allowed becomes a duty and hence a formal religious act.[4]

Because scrupulosity sufferers fear they are sinning just by having their obsessions, they atone for them typically by excessively praying, confessing, and, especially, denying themselves pleasure. When people with scrupulosity feel pleasure, there is often a superstitious-like reflex to stop it because they think there will be a price to pay. It also provides a ritualistic way of atoning for sins committed unknowingly. Vergote describes a scrupulous person as someone who "defers all pleasures because if they are not directly warranted by God he fears he may fail to acknowledge the master provider of all life's gifts and that God may consequently withdraw his benevolent providence."[5] The scrupulous lose sight of where healthy religious expression ends and their scrupulosity begins and wonder: When is *not* performing a compulsion *not a sin*?

Examples of Scrupulous Obsessions

1. If I have a blasphemous thought, I have sinned.
2. If I have a blasphemous thought, I must atone for it.
3. I am responsible for my blasphemous thoughts.
4. I must say my prayers perfectly for them to be valid.
5. If I am not sure that I confessed thoroughly, I must do it again to be sure.
6. If I have a distracting thought during prayers, I must start over.
7. If I'm unsure about being responsible enough, I must go over the scenario until I am sure that I have been.
8. If I think I made a mistake, especially when other people were involved, I should find out by any means possible.
9. I always try to be sure that I have atoned for my sins so that I won't die with a stain on my soul.
10. Not only do I feel sinful when I think I have acted irresponsibly, I feel guilty when I have sinned by omission.
11. People who suffer are more righteous.
12. Suffering will secure me a place in heaven.

13. I feel uneasy when I am not worrying.
14. Experiencing pleasure is difficult, because I fear that I am likely to sin.
15. I must pray to protect the person about whom I had a bad thought.
16. Ignoring a blasphemous thought is wrong.
17. I must try as hard as I can to resolve the blasphemous thoughts or images, or else I am sinful.
18. Even if having the blasphemous thought is "normal," if I don't try as hard as I can to resolve it, I am sinful.
19. Having these thought makes me a sinner/bad person.
20. Not only should I be perfect in my actions, I should also be perfect in *preventing* harm.
21. The thoughts I have about harming someone are realistic and mean I must do something to prevent it.
22. I can never be sure that God won't punish me, so I must be perfect.
23. Having the bad thoughts is as bad as having enacted them.
24. Feeling angry is sinful.
25. I am scared that my bad thoughts are influenced by evil. Therefore, I must think good thoughts.
26. Not performing a ritual in the face of bad thoughts is sinful.
27. God will punish me if I don't perform a ritual to undo the bad thought.
28. Undergoing behavior therapy for religious OCD is blasphemous.
29. Having an evil thoughts means that I am evil.
30. It is disturbing when I can't seem to know whether I really mean to have these bad thoughts.
31. If I haven't said something correctly, I have lied and thus sinned.

Not surprisingly, scrupulosity takes "cleanliness is next to godliness" to figurative and literal levels of the extreme.[6, 7, 8] Religiously faithful OCD patients go beyond the normal prescribed rules for achieving spiritual cleanliness and compulsively clean their soul and physical space perfectly before presenting themselves to God for prayer. OCD has turned these religious guidelines into something other than what was intended.

What follows are examples of normal traditional preparations and performances of common religious rituals and daily lifestyle practices that are meant to bring the faithful closer to God. The religions exemplified here have been selected because they have been the most common types I have treated in my clinical practice and at the OCD Institute.

Case material will follow in the subsequent portion of the chapter. If your particular religious faith has not been represented in these examples, please understand that it is not the particular content of obsessions or what ritualistic behavior you perform that matters. Instead, the lesson is that OCD is the doubting disease, and it strikes what is most sacred and valued to the faithful individuals. Regardless of your faith, treatment will *always* consist of "doing the opposite" of the obsession while resisting compulsive urges to respond to it with mental or physical rituals.

Normal Religious Practice

Use of Water

Water can safely be called the most-used actual and symbolic element for cleansing the soul and the surrounding physical space for prayer and for other religious purposes. How these ritual cleansing practices become problematic for Christian, Muslim, Jewish, and Hindu patients are described in the section on scrupulosity that follows. Luckily, no one resorts to purifying with fire![9]

Ritual Purification

In Christianity, water is used in baptism to clean the soul of original sin and for entering into the faith. Catholics, Eastern Orthodox, Lutherans, Methodists, Presbyterians, and Congregational Reformers continue to baptize infants.

Like all practicing Catholics entering church, Luke dips his fingers in holy water and makes the sign of the cross to bless and renew himself. He then sits in a pew and waits for Mass to begin.

In Islam, *wudu* is the ritual performed before the five daily prayers that purify the body and spirit before presenting oneself to Allah. Salima performs the four *fard* (obligatory) acts and follows the specific order in which they are to be performed. She knows that water is to be used efficiently and is not to be wasted. If she skips one of the steps, she goes back and repeats it, then completes the successive acts.[10] Salima performs *ghusl* (a higher form of purification) after sexual activity and menstruation.[11]

Jewish laws requires hand washing before the three daily prayers if a person has touched areas of the body normally covered by clothing, used the bathroom, or scratched the hair. Leah covers her entire hand up to the wrist with water. When water is unavailable, Leah wipes her hands on a cloth or any other available substance.

Jewish women who have scrupulosity are both blessed and cursed by their reproductive abilities. The mikvah, or ritual bath, purifies women seven days after their menstrual cycle has ended so that marital relations can be resumed. Every month, Leah checks her vaginal area twice a day during those seven clean days to make there is no evidence of blood. She is then ready to prepare for (*chafifah*) entering the mikvah. The ritual water must be free from foreign matter so that its purity is maintained for others.

Washing and purification rituals are common in Hinduism, which uses 14 different baths for varying circumstances.[12] The Ganges River is considered the most important site of ritual purification. Rani's prayers will vary according to place, time, and occasion. She chants the popular hymns *Agamar-ana Sūktam* and *Puru-a Sūktam*. Rani performs the Hindu predawn bathing and prayer rituals that ready her to recite: If she doesn't, the *Kurma Purana* says she will be impure and unable to recite her mantras (*japa*), make prayer offerings (*homa*), or perform deity worship. If she eats without having bathed, she is said to be "eating only filth, for everything [s]he touches becomes as impure as [s]he."[13]

Sexual issues are also problematic for many faithful. There is nothing in the Bible that specifically addresses "autosexuality" (masturbation), but many religions have prohibitions against it. Historically, "spilling" semen was considered sinful in many Judeo-Christian faiths because it subverted potential procreation.

Paul lived a secular life and became a Jehovah's Witness when he got married. He suffers with obsessive guilt about having masturbated in the past as well having "fornicated" by having had sex outside of marriage. He washes compulsively when he has intrusive thoughts about these past behaviors.

Some men who have OCD have anxiety about having nocturnal emissions (wet dreams) while sleeping, which is especially problematic, because nocturnal emissions happen unintentionally and unpredictably. Ibrahim, a Muslim, lives in dread of waking up from having had a wet dream, as Islam considers semen to be impure. When this happens, he is obligated to wash everything that had contact with his semen. He also performs *ghusl*, a more thorough cleansing ritual than *wudu*, because he is considered to be in a *junub* state of impurity. Sexual intercourse and menstrual bleeding are other conditions that create the state of *junub*.[14]

Cleanliness and Hand Washing before Meals

The act of washing the hands in Judaism brings holiness into the mundane. If a meal is served with bread, observant Jews wash their hands. Leah pours water out from a cup or glass first twice over her right hand and then twice over her left hand, repeating this sequence three times. She takes care that her unwashed hands do not touch the water before the washing. She recites a blessing while she washing: "Blessed art Thou, O Lord our God, King of the Universe, who has sanctified us with Thy commandments and has commanded us concerning the washing of the hands." She then dries her hands with a towel, after which she can eat. Leah keeps a cup of water and a basin at her bedside so that she can wash her hands immediately on waking and pour out the "nail water" (*netillas yadayim*—water used to rinse the dirt out from under fingernails) so that it doesn't come into contact with food or drink.[15]

Food/Dietary

Islamic dietary laws (*halal*) are given in the Qur'an. The animals Salima eats must be alive until they are (ritually) slaughtered. She does not eat swine/pork and its by-products, carnivorous animals, birds of prey, foods containing ingredients such as gelatin, enzymes, emulsifiers, and flavors that are questionable because the origin of the ingredients is unknown, as well as any foods contaminated with any of the above products. She does not drink alcohol, its consumption being prohibited in Islam.

Jewish kosher (*kashrut*) laws are said to have begun around 1275 BC after God revealed the Ten Commandments to Moses atop Mt. Sinai.[16] Like Salima with Islamic law, Leah adheres to Jewish law that declares what animals are considered acceptable to eat and how they are to be slaughtered. She does not eat animals whose hooves are fully cloven (cows, goats, and sheep), nonpredatory birds, or fish that have scales and internal bones. She does not eat meat and dairy products together, and she waits between three to six hours before eating one after having eaten the other.

To identify kosher and pareve (neutral) foods in supermarkets, Leah looks for grocery items marked with symbols that indicate that they are safe to be brought into and consumed in the kosher home.

Rules are also established for managing the kitchen, storing food, and meal preparation in order to maintain a kosher household. Utensils, pots, pans, cooking surfaces, plates, flatware, dishwashers, dishpans, and sponges are to be kept separate and cannot be used if they have touched meat and dairy products, kosher and nonkosher food, and if heat has been conducted until they have been cleaned.

Cows are sacred for Hindus, and like most Hindus, Rani is a vegetarian. According to an ancient Hindu story, the original cow, Mother Surabhi, was one of the treasures churned from the cosmic ocean. The five products of the cow (*pancha-gavya*)—milk, curd, ghee (clarified butter), urine, and dung—are considered sacramental.[17]

Since the Great Depression, Mormons have embraced a strong ethic of economic self-reliance and have been encouraged to keep at least a three-month supply of food in storage in case of emergencies. Lisa has dutifully secured this food supply in case the need arises. Lisa also follows the health and dietary tenets prescribed in *The Word of Wisdom*, a code of health that Mormons believe God revealed to Joseph Smith in 1833. It contains a list of healthy foods people are encouraged to eat, with an emphasis on plant-based whole foods. Vices, such as alcohol, tobacco, tea, coffee, and illegal drugs, are prohibited.

Fasting

Catholics fast involves the taking of the Eucharist. To receive the Eucharist, Luke abstains from food and drink, except for water and medicine, for at least the hour before receiving Holy Communion. During the season of Lent, Luke fasts on Ash Wednesday and Good Friday. Luke can eat a light breakfast, lunch, or dinner, but only one full meal for the day. Luke practices this spiritual exercise to commemorate the day Christ suffered, to be in control of his physical desires, to do penance for sins, and to be open God's grace. Luke is also challenging temptations against the deadly sin of gluttony, and is in spiritual connection with the poor.

The holy month of Ramadan is a mandatory fasting period that commemorates the period when the Qur'an was first revealed to the Prophet Muhammad. Salima begins her fast before sunrise and eats only after sunset. She abstains from eating, drinking, swallowing, smoking, use of profane language, and sexual intercourse during the daylight hours.

Yom Kippur, the Day of Atonement, is a "high holiday" on which Jews fast from sunset to sunset. There are six other holy day fasting days on which the fasting lasts from sunrise to sundown. With the exception of medicine or other products taken by mouth for medical reasons, the faithful do not ingest anything. Leah is vigilant about not swallowing.

Rani, a Hindu, fasts on particular occasions such as new Moon days and special festivals, as well as to the god of the day. Fasting is considered a means of self-discipline and body and soul purification, a way to enhance concentration during meditation or worship, a social act of empathizing with the hungry, and an act of sacrifice. Rani fasts according to the 24-hour traditional practice and abstains from all food and drink, although observers may occasionally drink milk or water.

Mormons fast on the first Sunday of each month. Individuals, families, and congregations may also hold fasts as desired. Lisa follows the fasting rules and abstains from food and drink for two consecutive meals. After her fast, she joins her fellow Mormons in a mindful "fast and testimony meeting" ritual that brings Mormons closer to God. She and her family also fast as a way to appeal to God for help with a specific concern. In Lisa's case, she appealed to God to heal her uncle from cancer.

Religious Observance

Prayer

There are many common aspects of prayer among religions: mindset, posture, the wearing of special articles of clothing/artifacts, and music. Most religious prayers have a prescribed set of ordered steps that are considered acts of faith in the tradition of the religion. Some religions make relevant adaptations that address new issues that arise out of contemporary and cultural changes; some traditions are kept consistent, being timeless. This chapter portion reflects the types of practices that become the subject of scrupulousness in OCD and that will be more specifically addressed in the chapter on treatment (chapter 9).

Until Vatican II (1962), Luke's Catholic Mass services were conducted in Latin. Luke was uneasy when Mass was said in English, but he adjusted. He adhered to the Catholic tenet of praying to God for help with humility and reverence. Trusting in God is also an important act of faith, and Luke tried to remain open to how God might answer his prayers, not presuming that what he asked for would necessarily be delivered in the way he expected.

Salima performs the five Muslim daily prayers in Arabic facing Mecca (*qiblah*). The prayers are said at dawn (*Salat al-Fajr*), midday (*Salat al-Zuhr*), afternoon (*Salat al-ʿAsr*), dusk (*Salat al-Maghrib*), and at night (*Salat al-ʿIsha*).[18] She recites the units (*rakʿah*) of each prayer in the proper ordered, sequential steps (*tartib*), and with physical fluidity (*muwalat*).[19]

Jewish prayers are chanted in Hebrew. Leah performs the three formal daily prayers, as well as other situational prayers conducted throughout the day (before rising, eating, etc.). The prayers are conducted in the morning (*shacharit*), in the afternoon (*minchah*), and at night (*arvith* or *maariv*). She makes an effort to have the proper "concentration" or "intent" (*kavanah*) to communicate with God in a mindful and reverent manner. [20]

Hindu prayers can be broadly classified into mental (*Prārthana*) and physical (*Kāyika Prārthana*).[21] There are prayers for every action, event, circumstance, and situation. Rani prays when waking up, going to sleep, bathing, eating, studying, traveling, bestowing a name, giving birth, witnessing death, witnessing marriage, taking medicine, and undergoing major life events.[22] She prays to petition, praise, worship, confess, seek comfort, and emotionally vent to a particular deity.

Mormons are instructed to be sincere and devote one's attention to God while praying. Mormons conduct personal, family, and community prayers. According to the Mormon prophets, "To make our prayers meaningful, we must pray with sincerity and 'with all the energy of heart' (Moroni 7:48). We must be careful to avoid 'vain repetitions' when we pray (see Matthew 6:7)."[23] The four steps of Mormon prayers are to address God, thank Him, ask Him, and close with the name of Jesus Christ.[24]

Rites of Celebration and Festivals

Religious holidays and ceremonies are moments in time to take special notice of life, passage of time, and important events, feeling reverence for spiritual and material gifts that have been bestowed upon us. Some religions mark the passing of seasons, moments in the life cycle, important moments in the history of the religion, and so forth. By nature, these celebrations are meant to be festive and fun, a time to feel appreciation, to share love, and perhaps to forget about troubles for a while. We may feel generous and make donations to charities or social causes during these events.

Confession, Forgiveness, and Atonement

One of the ultimate ironies reported by scrupulous Catholics is that when they were children, they made up sins to confess, so to perform the duty of this sacrament. Even though they had trouble identifying mortal or venial sins they committed, they "lied," because having nothing to confess seemed untruthful.

Also referred to as penance, the first step of confession is the "examination of conscience." The penitent reflects on any commission of mortal or venial sins that stand in the way of God's grace. The directive is to be sorry for the sins and to make a heartfelt commitment to avoid repeating them. Ultimately, there is no expectation of perfection on the penitent's behalf. Being contrite and having the intention to resist those temptations is sufficient for entering the confessional.

The next step is entering the confessional, a small enclosed space divided by a wall, which has a space for a meshed screen that ensures privacy and some anonymity to the penitent. The person expresses his or her contrition and confesses what sins he or she committed, after which the priest assigns the appropriate penance. The person leaves the confessional relieved, knowing what to do and how to seek God's grace and forgiveness. If a serious sin was forgotten, it will be included in the next confession.

Confession begins with making the sign of the cross and saying, "In the name of the Father, and of the Son, and of the Holy Spirit. My last confession was _____ (days, weeks, months, years) ago." The priest may then read a passage from Holy Scripture. The person begins confessing the sins that are most the most serious, and when he or she is finished says, "I am sorry for these and all the sins of my past life." Confession ends with the priest and penitent making the sign of the cross while absolution is granted. If the priest closes by saying, "Give thanks to the Lord for He is good," the penitent answers, "For His mercy endures forever." The priest will have given the appropriate penance, which the person will then carry out.

Islam's practice of confession, atonement, and forgiveness are not structured rituals, but rather are central themes in prayer and deeds. At least 70 sins are identified in the Qur'an, and specific words define them. There are 14 verses in the Qur'an on the subject of atonement (*tawba*), the first of which is from a saying of Allah: "If you show your almsgiving, it is a blessing, but if you give it to the poor secretly, it will be better for you, and He will atone for your evil deeds" (Qur'an, Sura 2:271).[25]

In Judaism, Yom Kippur is the Day of Atonement. From sundown to sundown, Jews reflect over the past year for when they had *missed the mark* (made moral mistakes), which is the Jewish meaning of sin. Fasting, going to the Temple and praying therein, and apologizing are the usual practices conducted during this holiday. By doing so, Jews hope to be inscribed into the Book of Life for the next year.

Jews seek forgiveness from those whom they have wronged over the past year. When possible, the person apologizes to make amends for his or her wrongdoing. If forgiveness is not received, the person apologizes again. Forgiveness will be sought by apologizing a third time. If forgiveness is still not granted, the person seeking forgiveness will have sufficiently sought forgiveness, and the responsibility for making amends now lies with the person wronged.

Precision/Perfectionism

Vergote states that perfectionism is a constant obsessional theme and that sufferers "wear themselves out because they feel compelled to accomplish every task to perfection; then, because they never achieve that goal, they find themselves in a constant state of uneasiness and dissatisfaction."[26]

It is unclear how precise or perfect religious rituals need to be to be considered properly performed. Becuase religious prayer is considered sacred, having a proper mindset for their performance is said to be of utmost importance for many religions. What constitutes a proper mindset and knowing when you have it are vague and subjective states of consciousness, ranging from casual to formal. Most people know it when they feel it and are able to engage in this spiritual practice. For the scrupulous, though, it is easy to see how achieving the proper mindset would almost preclude the ability to feel ready to practice acts of faith at all. Even if the perfect mindset were achieved for prayer, the OCD would demand that other religious rituals be precisely and perfectly performed.

Another consideration for proper mindset is the occurrence of intrusive thoughts. Some religions proscribe having intrusive thoughts at all, while some specify the prohibition of their occurrence during prayer. No one can control what and when thoughts occur. With OCD, intrusive obsessions are always inappropriate and occur with a vengeance when the sufferer tries to suppress them. Participating in any aspect of religion will provoke obsessions and some people will consider them to be sinful acts. This often causes excessive time spent mentally ritualizing to have a "good" thought that "undoes" the bad one.

Some religions require that prayers be conducted without interruption or disturbance. The scrupulous are distressed when they notice noises coming from the outside into the prayer setting. They will typically experience multiple interruptions and suspend the prayer until the noise subsides. Others may start their prayers over because they feel the distractions "ruin" or "invalidate" them. The time it takes for the scrupulous to finish their prayers will be unpredictable and typically excessive.

Scrupulous patients arrive to treatment very confused about what is right and wrong according to their religious beliefs, and experience inordinate stress about how to functionally practice them to the point of dropping out of religious practice altogether, not because they want to, but because they feel they *should*.

Elements of Religious Rituals That Become OCD Symptoms: OCD rituals = Trying to Trick God

Here is how OCD complicates religious practice for Luke, Salima, Leah, Rani, Paul, and Lisa, among many others. Irrespective of religious faith, obsessions and compulsions manifest out of the same concerns: contamination, blasphemy, fear of offending God, and purity of soul. The most common rituals concern the needs for certainty, cleanliness, purification, contrition, reassurance seeking, perfectionism, and exactness.

Use of Water: Cleanliness Is Next to Godliness

Ritual Purification
Upon entering the church, Luke repeatedly dips his fingers in the holy water font to make sure he is purified enough before sitting down in the pew for Mass. Sometimes a small line of people stand waiting behind him to take their turns.

One of Salima's problems with praying is her obsessive concern about not adequately performed *wudu*. Paradoxically, her compulsive purifying washing causes her to feel guilty about having wasted water. She also worries that her prayer mat is not clean enough, so she always uses a damp towel to brush off any invisible matter she worries would profane her prayers to Allah. By the time she did prays, she is exhausted and has trouble focusing on the spirit of the prayer ritual. Because her midday prayer often makes her late in getting back to her desk at work, she stays later to make up the time.

Leah is the only scheduled appointment on the day of her mikveh, her monthly ritual purification bath, because of her obsessive slowness. In anticipation of how long the whole process takes, she begins the preparation process, normally completed within an hour or so, several days in advance. Leah spends time checking for hairs, loose skin, and for any other extraneous items on her flesh that would contaminate the pristine and sacred ritual bath (*mayim chayim*). Once there, the attendant (*balanit or tukerin*) inspects Leah's body after the last ritual is performed and tells her she is ready to enter the water. The attendant is familiar with Leah and braces herself for the many reassurance-seeking questions Leah has to ensure that she is, in fact, in a pure enough state for immersing herself in the water.

Excessive washing and purification rituals are common symptoms of Hindus who have OCD.[27] Rani is slow to move through her morning cleansing ritual because she wants to make sure she is presentable for prayer. Her obsessive fear of impurity also causes her to excessively clean anything brought into the house, including clothes, shoes, groceries, household items, books, money, and the like.

Cleanliness and Hand Washing before Meals

The first thing Leah does in the morning is use the bedside water to wash her hands. She obsesses that pouring out the "nail water" in the kitchen sink will contaminate the food she prepares for breakfast. Cleaning the sink has become as much a part of her daily ritual as the morning prayer itself.

Even though Jewish law may not require it, Leah washes her hands before every meal. While following the hand washing steps, she becomes anxious that the water touched her unclean hands. At times, she changes the water just in case this happened. She also obsesses that she lost count of how many times she has poured the water over her hands. She repeats the hand washing ritual until she feels sure that it was done according to the ritual law.

Food/Dietary

Salima takes great care ensuring her house is *halal*. She worries about bringing home forbidden items (*haram*). She experiences some anxiety when she puts the food away or prepares meals. She shops in stores that cater to Muslims and has to trust that the dietary laws have been sacredly kept. She keeps a supply of frozen dinners to have when she is tired and more vulnerable to her scrupulosity fears. When she is in a more distressing phase of OCD, she orders food online and has it delivered. Salima also plans dinners out with her family at *halal* restaurants that are somewhat out of the way. These latter options are more expensive, and she actually misses cooking for her family during these times.

Leah's OCD about germ contamination coupled with keeping the house kosher made grocery shopping and preparing meals difficult and complicated. While shopping, she obsesses about whether the items she put in the cart are germy or nonkosher for fear that she might cause an illness or spiritually exile herself and her family by eating nonkosher food. She compulsively checks food labels, not only for the common symbols provided earlier, but many universal others to make sure they suitable to buy.[28]

When she gets home, she also uses antibacterial wipes to clean the items before putting them away. To be extra sure about keeping food kosher, she puts the items in plastic bags as a way of creating a barrier between the items in case they touch.

Leah's kosher kitchen has two sinks, refrigerators, and freezers, normal in many observing Jewish households. If Leah loses track of what was where, she rewashes things, checks them for food particles before using them, or throws them away. If she isn't sure, she throws the egg out. During a certain period, she only used paper plates, napkins, and disposable utensils.

While cleaning, Leah worries she might stir up dust that would contaminate the house and transfer kosher/nonkosher particles to each other. For a time, she hired someone to clean the house and agreed not to watch how the person cleaned, but she still she didn't trust that it was being done properly; she fired the cleaner.

Rani maintains a strict vegetarian diet primarily to avoid any chance of profaning the Hindu gods she worships. She avoids buying any food she thinks might have been near or have traces of meat, even when there is no evidence that it has, and she cleans the surfaces in her kitchen just in case she bought something that had indirectly touched meat.

In keeping with the Mormon spirit of self-reliance, Lisa keeps an emergency supply of food in storage. For her, this has become a hoarding issue due to her fear of not having enough food for her family, as well as feeling responsible for other Mormons who might not have enough when events occur that threaten their ability to provide, including catastrophic natural disasters. Lisa's thriftiness compels her to accumulate coupons, which she uses to buy items that are on sale. She is preoccupied with collecting coupons and feels excessive guilt buying items without them.

Lisa was also obsessive about having only food designated on the list provided in *The Word of Wisdom*.[29] She adheres to recipes she finds through friends and on websites. Sometimes, though, her children, unwittingly, bring unauthorized snacks in the house. This triggers her OCD and causes her to vacuum and clean the areas where she saw the snack being eaten until she feels she has gotten all of it. Lisa is also uncomfortable attending non-Mormon events where alcohol is being served. She becomes moderately anxious that someone will spill their drink on or around her, leaving alcohol on her clothes.

Fasting

To be sure that he receives the Eucharist in a pure state, Luke begins his fast the night before and does not eat or drink anything until after going to church. Even if he has already done so, Luke rinses his teeth again right before walking out the door to eliminate the possibility that his fast might be broken by food stuck in his teeth. (According to the Roman Catholic Church, even if this happened, these remnants are considered digested and not of concern.)

Luke fasts and abstains from eating meat on Ash Wednesday, Good Friday, and all Fridays during Lent. Luke also practices the custom of giving up something pleasurable during the 40 days of Lent as a way to strengthen his spiritual will. Luke's sacrifice is forgoing dessert. He makes sure he keeps not only to the spirit, but also the letter, of the religious custom, even giving up tea because of his preference for sweetening it with sugar. He also avoids other sweetened food such as cereal, juice, and fruit just in case.

Salima begins her Ramadan fast before sunrise and eats only after the sun sets. For the entirety of the holy month, she abstains from eating, drinking, swallowing, smoking, using profane language, and having sexual intercourse. She wipes off saliva into a facial tissue if she thinks a speck of something got in her mouth that she might swallow. Preparing the meals is challenging—not from a temptation standpoint but because they are usually made big so that everyone has enough to eat. When the fast is broken, she eats less than her share of food to make sure there is plenty for others.

During Yom Kippur, Jews fast from sundown to sundown. Leah experiences similar anxieties to Salima's about serving the role of mother, wife, and religious observer. She feels guilty about not having the right mindset to honor the spirit and intention of the holiday. She worries about not being written into the Book of Life for the next year.

Rani adheres to the strict 24 hours of complete abstinence from food and drink. Rani, Salima, and Leah, all suffer more severe scrupulosity symptoms during their holidays because of the heightened importance of their personal and family roles in breaking the fast, cooking enough food, cleaning up, caring for the children, going to services, and praying the "right" way.

Religious Observance

Prayer

Luke's prayers were dutifully made, with humility, reverence, and trust. At least—that's how they started off. Because OCD scrupulosity abhors reverence, Luke suddenly thinks, "I pray to the devil," or "Mary is sexy." Luke always feels mortified and sinful when these kinds of obsessions are triggered. Luke considered giving up praying but felt that that might be worse. Luke continues to pray, repeating his prayers until the obsession is "undone" with a "good" thought. He experiences the same thoughts while saying the Rosary and often recites the prayer or the mystery until he achieves the "right" feeling.

For a time, Salima did avoid praying altogether. After countless dutiful and appropriate preparations and recitations, she never felt her body or her prayer mat clean enough. Her OCD also caused her to fear that she had lost her place during the prayer, doubting whether her prayers were said with enough sincerity. All these OCD symptoms led to her belief that she would offend Allah.

Leah obsesses about having the right mindset for prayer, not just going through the motions. She can't help notice the activity that goes on around her and worries that the distractions invalidate her prayers. She, too, repeats the prayers she doubts she has done thoroughly enough and is typically late in making breakfast and seeing her children off to school.

While chanting her mantras, Rani tries to forget herself and merge with the Divine. Achieving this perfection means that she is practicing Hinduism the "right" way. When her OCD gets in the way—and of course it does—she feels guilty about having failed to fully release her attention from herself. The more she tries, the stronger her OCD gets. Her prayers become ritualistic: She goes through the motions anyway, just in case doing so is good enough for the deities.

Paul has one particular obsession for which he has trouble forgiving himself. It takes God's name in vain: "Goddamn you G-d." Because he is afraid of committing the unpardonable sin, it became an obsession: "Therefore I say to you, every sin and blasphemy will be forgiven men, but the blasphemy against the Spirit will not be forgiven men. Anyone who speaks a word against the Son of Man, it will be forgiven him; but whoever speaks against the Holy Spirit, it will not be forgiven him, either in this age or in the age to come."[30] He has these obsessions because they are the worst thoughts his OCD could think to give him. Like the others, he prays until he feels he has compensated enough with good prayers to let it go for now. His goal is to pray without having any intrusions, but because of the nature of the disorder, this will never be achieved.

Paul also worries his prayers are empty because he feels he lacks the full intention and energy for them to count. Paul repeats his prayers until he "feels right," but then he worried these "vain repetitions" (Matthew 6:7) are self-centered attempts at seeking special attention from God.

Rites of Celebration

The enjoyment that is meant to be experienced in these events is sadly triggering for the scrupulous. Having pleasure means something bad will have to happen to maintain some mystical status quo. The scrupulous often make an effort to squash any good feelings or fun they are having. If they failed, they find ways of punishing themselves later.

Vergote and Aho both capture this dynamic in their writings. Vergote explained that

> another great religious theme that preoccupies the obsessive is the concept of debt. . . . Since everything man receives comes from God he remains infinitely indebted, but in order to enjoy the pleasures of his life one must be able to forget his debt. Thus pleasure naturally tends to forget its divine origin and makes man turn in upon himself, recalling what believers often admit: when they are happy, they do not spontaneously think of God.[31]

Aho traces the history of this moral indebtedness back to the medieval era as manifesting through materialism and a guilty conscience of abundance: Double-entry bookkeeping (DEB) arose from a sense of indebtedness on the part of late medieval merchants toward creator, Church, and commune. Burdened with this debt, they felt compelled to certify in writing that for everything they earned something of equal value had been returned and that for everything meted out something else was deserved. To rephrase the preceding proposition, then: DEB arose from a scrupulous preoccupation with sin on the part of the faithful medieval entrepreneur.[32]

We may all have a bit of superstition when something good happens. We may "wait for the other shoe to drop" or maintain a sense of humility by not bragging about it.

Confession, Forgiveness, and Atonement

Luke compulsively examines his conscience before he goes to confession. Having OCD, he checks, reviews, and repeats the process until he is sure he has thought of everything he needs to confess. In particular, he is troubled by his obsessive fear that he has mortally sinned by reading a novel with sexually provocative scenes. He enjoyed the book but feels guilty about having committed the sin of lust. He wasn't sure whether he really *was* guilty of sinful behavior, because reading is a deliberate action, or was he *not* guilty, because reading the scenes occurred in the context of the story? Either way, he confessed it just to be sure. Now he is nervous about what to read or not read going forward.

Luke told the priest in great detail what he had done wrong since his last confession to make sure he was given appropriate penance. "Our troubled and afflicted penitents . . . allege all sorts of pretexts for renewing confessions or making general confessions; something was forgotten; they did not express themselves clearly, or their contrition was insufficient."[33]

He starts repeating himself just in case the priest was distracted during his confession. The priest interrupted him and ended the confession. When Luke left the confessional, he worried his confession had not been heard properly, because he noticed the priest wore a hearing aid. He went back and loudly reconfessed to make sure that this time he was given the proper penance and was found worthy of receiving Communion. But new doubts set in about whether he had actually confessed *all* of his sins, and he left the church without receiving Communion, the divine sacrament for which he had so well prepared.

During Yom Kippur, reflection is made to identify mistakes that were made, especially in relation to others. Up to three apologies are said to seek forgiveness. If forgiveness was not given, the person can let it go. Leah seeks people out to apologize for (inconsequential) mistakes she thinks she made toward them over the past year. She annoys people, because they feel she has not accepted their forgiveness. They don't realize they have been brought into her OCD system of seeking reassurance. She has lost the spirit of atonement and forgiveness, because she treats her mistakes in an all-or-nothing manner.

We are all fallible. The scrupulous downfall about this is that

> the patient's complaint that he suffers from perfectionism. Such patients wear themselves out because they feel compelled to accomplish every task to perfection; then, because they never achieve that goal, they find themselves in a constant state of uneasiness and dissatisfaction. An obscure and internal sense of duty demands that they always do more and better. They feel the constant presence of some anonymous spectator watching over their shoulder, always ready to observe their slightest faults and errors.[34]

The tenet of having the "right" mindset for prayer is difficult for the scrupulous to achieve. Catholicism, Judaism (*kavanah*), Islam (*niyyah*), Hindu (*ucita mānasikatā*), and many other religions specifically address the importance of having sincere and focused attention during prayer. The other scrupulous prayer goal is perfect recitation. No intrusive thoughts, no mental mistakes, no sense of doubt about these things or about God are allowed, lest the prayers not count.

Scrupulous perfectionism is not limited to prayer, though. The same perceived excessive sincerity and thoroughness required in prayer is applied to almost all other aspects of life. Some scrupulous patients have said that being perfect was a survival strategy against being abused, being criticized, or calling negative attention from important others. They strive for it just to stay off the radar. Others fear committing the deadly sin of sloth, or laziness. We will see in the next chapter how moral perfectionism takes hold in a similar manner.

When Leah was a sophomore in high school, she began having scrupulosity symptoms. She was already very conscientious and respectful, but she became increasingly uncomfortable being around her gossiping classmates (*loshen hora*), gossiping being forbidden by Jewish law. Even though she wasn't in the conversations, she felt she was sinning just by being in the presence of it. So instead of going to band practice after school or hanging out with friends, she sought refuge at home, where she felt safe from sin. Instead of socializing, she poured herself into her homework and clarinet practice. Her diligence made her an excellent student and musician, and was praised by her parents and teachers for these accomplishments. The praise unwittingly reinforced her perfectionistic and avoidant behaviors. It wasn't until her senior year when her parents realized that Leah's lifestyle was limited and rigid. Because she was lonely, Leah agreed to see a therapist, who diagnosed her with OCD. Fortunately, she was able to get her symptoms under control, but her social development was somewhat delayed by her having missed out on age-appropriate enrichment activities such as clubs at school, attending parties, and dating.

This chapter has not exhausted all the scrupulous details that have affected people's lives. Some others involve giving up religious leadership roles because a person considers himself or herself unworthy; making pacts with God, then breaking them because they are unrealistic and unreasonable; avoiding dating; and mistaking scrupulosity symptoms as a calling from God to enter a religious order. One last problem to mention of the scrupulous is that they fail lie detector tests: They are too anxious when they take them!

Notes

1. O'Flaherty, *How to Cure Scruples*, 103.

2. Kilpack, *Scruples*, 5.

3. O'Flaherty, "Therapy for Scrupulosity," 222.

4. Vergote, *Guilt and Desire*, 83–84.

5. Vergote, *Guilt and Desire*, 84.

6. Harrelson, "Guilt and Rites of Purification": 218–221.

7. Ibid.

8. Lewis and Joseph, "Obsessive Actions and Religious Practices": 239.

9. All identifying information has been changed; the examples given are not case examples, but rather composites of various cases.

10. Gulevich, *Understanding Islam and Muslim Traditions*, 428.

11. Kassam, *Islam*, 116–117.

12. Bharath, http://bharathkidilse.blogspot.com/2009/10/bathing-snanam.html.

13. Ibid.

14. Besiroglu et al., "Scrupulosity and Obsessive–Compulsive Disorder": 3–12.

15. Bonchek, *Religious Compulsions and Fears*, 47.

16. *JPS Hebrew–English Tanakh*, 155.

17. From the Editors of Hinduism Today, "What Is Hinduism: Modern Adventures into a Profound Global Faith" (Kapaa, HI: Himalayan Academy Publications, 2009): 125.

18. Gulevich, *Understanding Islam and Muslim Traditions*, 141–153.

19. Ibid.

20. Steinberg, *Basic Judaism*, 122.

21. Hindu Resource Center, "Daily Prayers of Hindus," vedakalpataru.com.

22. Ibid.

23. The Church of Jesus Christ of Latter-Day Saints, "What is Prayer?".

24. Ibid.

25. Muhammed Ali, *The Holy Quran*, 36.

26. Vergote, *Guilt and Desire*, 77.

27. Khanna et al., "Sociodemographic Variables in Obsessive Compulsive Neurosis": 47–54.

28. To view more kosher symbols, visit www.eliyah.com/unclean/ingredients.html.

29. Widtsoe, *Joseph Smith's Concept of the Word of Wisdom*, chapters 9–16.

30. Matthew 12:31–32, The Holy Bible, *New King James Version* (Thomas Nelson, Inc., 1982).

31. Vergote, *Guilt and Desire*, 64.

32. Aho, *Confession and Bookkeeping*, xiv.

33. Raymond and Smith, *Spiritual Director and Physician*, 139.

34. Vergote, *Guilt and Desire*, 77.

Bibliography

Aho, James. *Confession and Bookkeeping: The Religious, Moral, and Rhetorical Roots of Modern Accounting*. Albany: State University of New York Press, 2005.

Ali, Maulana Muhammed. *The Holy Quran: Arabic Text, English Translation and Commentary*. 2nd ed. Lahore, Pakistan. Revised by the translator and republished in 1951.

Besiroglu, Lutfullah, Sitki Karaca, and Ibrahim Keskin. "Scrupulosity and Obsessive Compulsive Disorder: The Cognitive Perspective in Islamic Sources." *Journal of Religion and Health* 53, no. 1 (2014): 3–12.

Bharath, K. "Bathing (*Snanam*)." In *Hindu Rituals and Routines*. http://bharathkidilse.blogspot.com/2009/10/bathing-snanam.html.

Bleeker, C. J. "Guilt and Purification in Ancient Egypt." *Numen* 13, no. 2 (1966): 81–87.

Bonchek, Avigdor. *Religious Compulsions and Fears: A Guide to Treatment*. Jerusalem: Philipp Feldheim, 2009.

The Church of Jesus Christ of Latter-Day Saints. "What Is Prayer?" https://www.lds.org/topics/prayer?lang=eng.

Gulevich, Tanya. *Understanding Islam and Muslim Traditions*. Detroit: Omnigraphics, Inc., 2004.

Harrelson, Walter. "Guilt and Rites of Purification Related to the Fall of Jerusalem in 587 B.C." *Numen* 15, no. 3 (1968): 218–221.

Hindu Resource Center. "Daily Prayers of Hindus." Veda Kalpataru—A Resource Center for Hinduism. vedakalpataru.com.

Johnson, Linda. *The Complete Idiot's Guide to Hinduism*. Indianapolis: Alpha, 2002.

JPS Hebrew–English Tanakh: The Traditional Hebrew Text and the New JPS Translation, 2nd ed. Philadelphia: The Jewish Publication Society.

Kassam, Zayn R. *Islam*, vol. 5 in "Introduction to the World's Major Religions," ed. Lee W. Bailey. Westport, CT: Greenwood Press, 2006.

Khanna, S., P. N. Rajendra, and S. M. Channabasavanna. "Sociodemographic Variables in Obsessive Compulsive Neurosis in India." *International Journal of Social Psychiatry* 32, no. 3 (1986): 47–54.

Kilpack, Gilbert. *Scruples*. Wallingford, PA: Pendle Hill Publications, 1956.

Lewis, Christopher Alan, and Stephen Joseph. "Obsessive Actions and Religious Practices," *The Journal of Psychology* 128, no. 6 (1994): 699–700.

O'Flaherty, V. M., SJ. *How to Cure Scruples*. Milwaukee, WI: The Bruce Publishing Co., 1966.

O'Flaherty, V. M., SJ. "Therapy for Scrupulosity." In *Direct Psychotherapy*, ed. R. M. Jurjevich, p. 915. Miami: University of Miami Press, 1973.

Raymond, Viktor, and Aloysius Smith. *Spiritual Director and Physician: The Spiritual Treatment of Sufferers from Nerves and Scruples*. London: R. & T. Washbourne, Ltd., 1914.

Steinberg, Milton. *Basic Judaism*. New York: Harcourt Brace Company, 1947.

Vergote, Antoine. *Guilt and Desire: Religious Attitudes and Their Pathological Derivatives*. Translated by M. H. Wood. New Haven, CT: Yale University Press, 1978.

Widtsoe, John A. *Joseph Smith's Concept of the Word of Wisdom*. Whitefish, MT: Kessinger Publishing, 2010.

7

Moralosity: Nonreligious and Moral Perfectionistic OCD

[T]he extreme of perfect, abject, self-debasing, purposeful shaming of the self is . . . proscribed. It is not genuine humility.[1]

I call non-religious scrupulosity *moralosity*. Just as the scrupulous feel religiously contaminated, the moralous feel morally contaminated. In both instances, the compulsion is to purify the soul through perfectionistic rituals. The problem that makes it so difficult for people with OCD is that the disorder demands black-or-white certainty in these matters, and it creates false ultimatums: Either you either give in to the ritualistic urge, or the things you fear will happen. There is no gray area such as riding out the urge to see what actually happens.

Many people with this conscience-related OCD symptom are also concerned that there is a cosmic bookkeeper keeping track of every negative thought, feeling, and behavior for which, if uncorrected, they will receive some form of retribution. They feel compelled to maintain or restore a divine balance through deliberate and ritualistic positive thoughts, good feelings, and virtuous behaviors. Their obsessive conscience convinces them that mistakes are proof of inadequacy, negligence, laziness, or immorality. They worry that "karma" (what goes around, comes around) will come back to haunt them through bad luck, harm to loved ones, and unending punishment through failure.

Unconcerned about fashion, Dr. Lane typically shows up late to the office because he chooses what to wear until he feels they are the "good" items of clothing that will prevent "bad" things from happening, such as his wife being assaulted. Amir obsesses about whether he cheated on his income taxes ten years ago and lives in fear that the Internal Revenue Service and the police could come knocking on his door. This might seem like a rumination of a dishonest person, but OCD doesn't care that his repeated inquiries confirm the taxes were done accurately. Neither did repeatedly seeking reassurance from his patience-worn partner. Zoe was in a similar bind, obsessing about having been given a higher GPA in college than she earned, which means that she would have "lied" on her resume. Checking with the school and re-editing her resume didn't reassure her. She could only learn to live with the possibility that she got away with something she didn't want. And Sasha became distraught when she found out the mutual funds she invested in had holdings in tobacco and weapons companies.

One of the hallmarks of moralosity is a life of double standards. When I ask moral perfectionists whether other people should follow their same rigid moral rules, their answer is always adamant denial. They easily cut slack for other people when others make mistakes, but their OCD holds them to a doubly higher standard. Rick said, "It's okay that Maya laughed at that joke with racy undertones, but I should have known better." Rick left the party and went home, where he showered for two hours to cleanse himself from the emotional contamination he felt from laughing at the joke.

Kurt's existential moralosity could have been mistaken for scrupulosity. He wanted to believe in God, but he could not, because no scientific proof was extant, and such belief would thus be irrational. It was the same for his desire to believe in life after death. As shown in Table 7.1, Kurt's obsessions made his metaphysical belief system ambivalent about many things—the soul, the meaning of life, death.

Oren's moralosity came from being divorced. Being divorced meant he was an adulterer and that any future relationship would be tainted and sinful because of his having broken his wedding vows. He felt like a liar and a would-be cheater. Treatment was tricky: He worried that seeking treatment might mean that he was no longer sorry for his mistake, that symptom relief might be a way of cheating from the suffering he was supposed to endure, and that no matter what, he would always have a stain on his soul.

Priah's obsessions were about being right and about death. Being right was her attempt at perfection. To her, being wrong was a moral failure. She often argued and sought reassurance from people until she wore them down and they gave it to her. Sometimes she had trouble holding back and interrupted conversations to make "corrections." Sometimes she didn't speak at all because she was afraid of what it would take to end a conversation on the right note. People close to her loved her, but having conversations with her became less and less worth having.

Priah also reported, "I hold my breath whenever I see a hearse, drive by a cemetery, or a funeral home," fearing that someone she loved would die if she inhaled the "death air." She felt that death obsessions and death air contaminated her personality. To purify herself, she inhaled *good* thoughts and

TABLE 7.1   Kurt's Ambivalence about the Soul, the Meaning of Life, and Death

On One Hand	On the Other Hand
Maybe there is a soul, but belief in that is totally irrational.	Without a soul, life is meaningless.
Faith can only present a positive universe to me.	Faith is illogical.
My life has worth and will have meaning even thousands of years after my death.	My life has no worth except in the present and only to myself; compared to the entire infinite universe, I am nothing; in the long run, after thousands of years, my life was a useless gesture.
I am a spiritual being with power and knowledge beyond my comprehension.	The universe is beyond comprehension, and we are nothing in comparison.
I should not waste time. Every moment must be productive.	What's the difference between a meaningful and a lazy life? In the end, I'll be dead, but then enjoying life would make things fulfilling and simple.
I survive because of my fear of nothingness.	Survival is the purpose of life but has no meaning in the larger scheme of things.
Survival takes the least painful route; whether you are all "good" or "bad" is irrelevant.	I will do anything to survive as long as it does not hurt others.

exhaled *bad* thoughts. She repeated this behavior in series of fours, a number she felt was spiritually pure. She also texted family members under the guise of being friendly, but really as a way to hear that nothing was wrong. She felt a moral obligation to do whatever she could to prevent horrible things from happening.

Priah was afraid that her thoughts had special powers that could make or prevent things from happening. This is a similar godlike role that those with scrupulosity adopt when they feel the fate of others' is in their hands. Sadly, this OCD cycle is reinforced when nothing bad happens. The irony of it all is when, inevitably, something bad *does* happen, they respond rationally and do not blame themselves. Instead of the self-focus OCD creates, they appropriately attend to what needs doing under the circumstances.

Cognitive behavior therapy conceptualizes obsessive–compulsive, superstitious and magical thinking as thought–action fusion: Thoughts are actions. If thoughts are actions, I often challenge my patients to play the lottery, or pray for world peace, the point being that this system only seems to work one negative way. OCD causes a bias to the feared negative causal relationship and does not give equal thought to the possibility of neutral or positive thoughts and actions to work in the same way. Luckily for Priah, it didn't take that long for her to get control over these triggers by taking the risk to trust in normal behavior.

Some people with moralosity come from highly emotional, critical, or abusive households. In this way, moral perfectionism is a survival skill: "If I am perfect, I won't call negative attention to myself." They may have experienced or witnessed unexpected, unfair punishment, or other negative consequences that made making mistakes unsafe. Since the success of OCD treatment is based on the willingness to make mistakes, anxiety about being punished by parents makes adhering to the literal letter of rules and obligations the safest way to avoid negative consequences. If the person is unable to take such risks because of his or her history, he or she will likely benefit from a different treatment that is geared toward trauma, after which he or she will be ready to engage in ERP.

The Seven Deadly Sins

An easy way to think about moralosity is to consider the seven deadly sins (SDS). The idea of the deadly sins does not originate in the Bible, but is said to have been developed in the hermit communities of northern Egypt by Evagrius Ponticus (AD 346–399) as an aspect of monastic education.[2] Hill's investigation into the relationship between pastoral theology and psychiatric disorders found that Ponticus suffered from "demonic thoughts" common to what we now consider to be clinical obsessions. "If this is true, it offers a new perspective on the relation between pastoral theology and psychiatric disorders: the spiritual tradition which Evagrius helped found may, as a result, have tended to exacerbate such symptoms in others, but it also possessed the resources to address [the deadly sins] in a practical way."[3]

Taught in religious education classes in early childhood, the SDS set the stage upon which many OCD symptoms will, later, be played out. The SDS are said to characterize and organize human temptations and desires that are in need of being controlled. I have found that, developmentally, those predisposed to OCD often are stuck in the emotional and cognitive developmental stage in which the SDS are taught.

If a child is already suffering from OCD, he or she fears that deviating from the literal letter of the religious or moral law might result in punishment from God or the cosmic bookkeeper. Emotional maturity can become complicated when the need to please authoritative others, as well as being stuck at the cognitive level of literalness, overrides the natural process of individuating and separating. Lapsley describes this as a process of establishing a sense of self that is not psychologically or emotionally dependent on what caregivers expect or approve of, in order to develop one's own sense of identity.[4]

From a clinical perspective, the issue is not the committing of any of the deadly sins or virtuous acts. It's the false polarity that OCD creates.

Sufferers believe that things are absolutely one way or the other: either/ or, black/white, right/wrong, good/bad. People without OCD, for the most part, live by the rule of moderation in the gray area of personal judgment and responsibility.

Table 7.2 outlines the SDS and related virtues. Examples of how they are interpreted in the extremes by the moralous are provided.

TABLE 7.2   The Seven Deadly Sins and How They Are Interpreted in the Extremes by the Moralous

Cultural Deadly Sin/Vices	Cultural Virtues	OCD "Sin/Vices"	OCD "Virtues"	Life in Healthy Moderation
Pride	Humility	Feeling as if I have it better than most people	Seek forgiveness through mental chastising rituals and making pacts to donate more money, give to homeless	Trust Self-confidence
Avarice/ Greed	Generosity Charity	Wanting to buy new clothes	Returned clothes after buying them because felt too guilty	Self-care Spirit of abundance
Envy	Love	Wishing I could afford a nice house like theirs	Denial of pleasure; practice austerity	Spirit of gratitude
Wrath/ Anger	Kindness Patience	Angry/ resentful of boss because of negative comments	People-please, apologize even if it's not my fault	Self-respect Honor
Lust	Self-Control	Married person finding someone else attractive	Confessing to and seeking reassurance from spouse	Appreciation of beauty/ aesthetics
Gluttony	Temperance	Temptation to eat more than necessary; having seconds having dessert	Giving into temptation, now restricting to make up for being indulgent	Sense of enjoyment
Sloth/ Laziness	Motivation Diligence	Down time	Stay busy all the time so as not to waste it, even though exhausted	Courage Self-confidence

One additional virtue I would add to the list for people with OCD is *patience*. Anxiety makes it difficult to slow down. Waiting is like torture when your mind and body want things *now*. OCD sufferers are hard on themselves, or give up on things prematurely, because they feel as if they are failing if their efforts don't seem to be paying off (yet). Just like with so many things we've covered, all things happen in due time.

The Golden Rule

"Do to others as you would have them do to you."[5] The Golden Rule is yet another healthy social code that becomes an OCD guilt-inducing moral imperative to be fulfilled to the utmost degree. Here is a list of the beautiful sentiments that express the universal spirit of reciprocal respect:

- You shall love your neighbor as yourself. *Judaism and Christianity.*[6]
- Not one of you is a believer until he loves for his brother what he loves for himself. *Islam.*[7]
- Try your best to treat others as you would wish to be treated yourself, and you will find that this is the shortest way to benevolence.[8] *Confucianism.*
- One should not behave towards others in a way that is disagreeable to one-self. *Hinduism.*[9]
- Hurt not others in ways that you yourself would find hurtful. *Buddhism*[10]
- A man should wander about treating all creatures as he himself would be treated. *Jainism*[11]
- One going to take a pointed stick to pinch a baby bird should first try it on himself to feel how it hurts. *Nigerian Yoruba Proverb*[12]

Why the Opposite Golden Rule?

Like every best response to OCD, doing the opposite is what works. It has been helpful for people to turn the Golden Rule on its head: do unto yourself as you do to others. After all, the quality of what you give to others is reflected from the value you place on yourself.

From a values perspective, this may seem selfish. However, those with an obsessive conscience have gone too far in direction of not being selfish enough in the way that promotes self-care. These are considerations for understanding the range of effective interpersonal traits and styles:

- Being kind, empathic, compassionate, assertive, fair, honest, merciful, self-respectful, and altruistic
- Being nice, people-pleasing, overly guilty, overly altruistic, self-righteous, and passive

- Being selfish, self-important, pretentious, prideful, angry, and aggressive
- Being passive–aggressive, resentful, angry, expecting from others what you do for them

The Role of Humility and Pride

> True humility . . . never knows that it is humble, as I have said; for if it knew this, it would turn proud from contemplation of so fine a virtue.[13]

Although moralosity shows itself in all of the deadly sins, pride deserves special attention because of its insidious paradox. Pride is a personality trait addressed in both theology/religion and psychology. Pride was most commonly considered the foundation of sinfulness in the culture of the early Middle Ages.[14] In the age of psychology, being overly prideful is seen as a defense against and compensation for insecurity, with narcissism being the extreme form.[15] The corrective virtue for the sin of pride is humility, but as we will see, even humility can be prideful.

OCD sufferers are often surprised at their mistake when their practice of humility is actually prideful. "I feel so bad about myself. I'm the worst person. God has forgiven me, but I can't forgive myself," is a common refrain of the moralous. The double-standard form of pride here is "to err is human (for others, but not for me), forgiveness divine (for others, but not for me)." People think they can and should know things that are beyond their control, because they feel somehow responsible for bad things' happening. This failure to accept fallibility flies in the face of accepting one's humanity. Being hard on the self is not virtuous, but rather is a form of pride that rejects the grace of forgiveness from God, the universe, and, most important, from the self. This form of pride trumps any humility in that judgments are made from inhuman standards: This is not the intention, but it is the result. The antidote (letting go of things that are beyond control, accepting that mistakes are normal and not moral failures) seems to be the easiest way to go, and yet, for the moralous, it is the hardest.

Carl is a 54-year-old car mechanic, dressed in impeccably clean blue work clothes. He came to therapy because he took so much "pride" in his work. His perfectionism caused him to be overlooked for a promotion. He simply took too long to get routine tasks completed, because he needed to be sure everything was "just right." He feared causing a fatal accident if he left one bolt loose. He often broke bolts and wrenches because he turned things too tightly. Needless to say, the quality of his work was beyond reproach, but customers began complaining of very long waits when he was their mechanic.

Carl also admitted that his perfectionism manifests at home. He likes his environment to be neat and goes to great lengths to keep it that way. He gets anxious when there are guests in his house, because they (unwittingly) disrupt his order of things. When they leave, he puts everything back in place even after the rest of his family goes to bed. There were many other circumstances in which Carl tried to have needless control over simple tasks. Needless to say, he had trouble with spontaneity.

Carl is a very upstanding person in every way. There was no argument about that, but his OCD caused hardship on his customers and family. The pride he took in his work was largely based on the obsessive need to feel right, and until he made himself feel that way, he was unable or unwilling to move on. He knew he went beyond how other good mechanics ensure safety for the cars they repair. He was in a moralous bind, because he felt guilty if he was not perfectionistic in his work, *and* doing so affected his work productivity and caused customer complaints about the long waits. These symptoms were taking their toll on him, his job, and his family. Something was going to have to give.

Jorge has never been sexually active, but one of his obsessive fears revolves around semen. It contaminates him and could cause pregnancy. Using the bathroom, handling dirty laundry, sitting on chairs in public, and even being around females became too much. He avoided public situations and showered for long periods if it became absolutely necessary for him to run errands, such as to get his medication at the pharmacy. His insight was good, but the intensity of his fear was more powerful. We could joke about how many children he must have by now—but there was no humor when he was on his own.

Jorge's other obsession centered on safety. It was triggered when throwing sharp or toxic items in the garbage can: He repeatedly checked to make sure that what he threw away was in there. He worried someone in the house, including his dog, might swallow these things and be hurt. He stared into the trash until he felt sure items such as staples, household cleaners, and rotten food were out of harm's way. He also checked locks, the stove, and electrical appliances to make sure everything was secure before turning in for the night.

Jordan avoided shopping because he obsessed about unwittingly stealing things. He described the endless checking rituals he performed before he gave up going into stores. His checking behaviors made him look so suspicious that employees called security, who questioned him about what he was doing. He also felt anxiety going in and out of doors, causing people to wait. He felt guilty for being so much trouble, but not so guilty as his fear made him feel about having accidentally stolen something.

After a few initial meetings, Carl and I went grocery shopping. He spent excessive time inspecting items for imperfections. Five cereal boxes were rejected and put back on the shelf until he found one without any dents. I was surprised to see how many people made their selections in the time it took for him to be satisfied.

When Jordan was finally finished getting the items on his list, we approached the checkout line the same time as another man holding his 2-year-old daughter's hand. "After you," Jordan insisted. "No, you were here first," replied the father. "No, I insist," Jordan repeated. This dance went on a few more times until, finally, the man and his daughter took their place in line. The man thanked him after paying the cashier and all seemed well.

A good driver, Jordan follows the normal rules of the road, stopping and going, letting pedestrians pass, and the like. However, driving over a bump causes him uncertainty about whether he has run someone over. The real problem started not with the feared thought, but with driving back to check whether anyone was lying in the road. Because it is impossible to prove a negative, he could not confirm that he had *not* hit someone. Although he continued to feel uncertain and anxious, there was nothing more he could do but drive away. Then he obsessed being found guilty of leaving the scene of a crime, so he drove back to the area and checked again. Was Jordan's intention in going back over the route an action of care and concern for the well-being of someone hurt, or was it to cover his "assets" by making sure there was no crime scene at all?

Anxiety and guilt from not wanting to be found negligent, even homicidal, caused a bind in which he felt paralyzed. Leave? Stay? Leave? Stay? Check, check, check. He pushed himself to go by promising to check the 11:00 news on television and tomorrow's newspaper headlines for a report of a hit-and-run accident. He realized he could also call the police as a last resort to cover all the bases.

Meanwhile, his family was waiting for the groceries to fix dinner. They worried that something might have happened to him and felt stressed that he had not let them know he would be late. When he arrived home, the family was relieved, but then came endless "confessions" about possibly having hit someone with the car while putting the groceries away with utmost perfection. Jordan's anxiety was through the roof.

Asoka left the meeting at work but didn't "feel right" and worried (most likely because he was stressed about speaking in front of others, and about the status of the project) that he had not fully explained the challenges and progress he was making on his project. Unable to shrug it off after some time passed, he went to his manager's office to clarify the points he doubted he had made clear, but his manager was unavailable. Not knowing when he could speak to his manager, he went back to his office and spent the good part of an hour composing an email that covered what he thought was missing. Asoka never heard back from his manager about his lengthy email and was left feeling uncertain, anxious, and incomplete.

These are the common categories of moralosity obsessions that have been identified in treatment:

Mistakes of Omission

Feared Consequence: lying, cheating, stealing, causing damage, being wasteful

Compulsions: checking, seeking reassurance, repeating, cleaning, performing mental rituals to "undo" the "sin"

- If I don't stop someone from gossiping, it's the same as if I said it.
- Leaving out details while explaining something.
- Not moving an object out of harm's way, such as a shard of glass on the sidewalk or a stick in the road.
- I will get caught cheating on my income taxes if I don't check again thoroughly.
- I fear that my grade point average is wrong (overestimated) and that if I don't check/notify someone, I'll be accused of cheating.
- If I don't clean this, someone/pet may get sick.

Mistakes of Commission

Feared Consequence: lying, cheating, stealing, causing damage, being wasteful

Compulsions: checking, performing mental rituals to "undo" the mistake, seeking reassurance, repeating, inflicting self-punishment, checking, washing, seeking perfection

- I worry that I have these thoughts (obsessions) because I mean them. Ritualizing proves I don't mean them.
- Reusing these uncancelled postage stamps is stealing.
- Not recycling or reusing this is wasteful.
- Using online material, including shareware, is stealing.
- If I shop with this hangnail or dry skin, I will damage merchandise.
- If I park right next to this car, I may cause damage to it when I open my door.
- If I don't take home the food that's left on everyone's plates, I'm wasting it.
- I may have cheated that customer by giving him the wrong change.
- Just in case I caused harm by having the thought (obsession), I won't watch television tonight, eat dessert, or eat all my share of food to atone.
- If I do or think this perfectly, I won't make a mistake or cause harm.
- I'm afraid that my bad thoughts (obsessions) are causing harm in the universe.

Experiencing Pleasure

Feared Consequence: being guilty of indulgence, being guilty of a deadly sin

Compulsion: avoiding/denying self pleasure, confessing, punishing self if experienced or perceived self as experiencing pleasure, going to related 12-step program for particular "indulgence," seeking reassurance

- I am guilty if I enjoy sex, eating, playing cards, music, dancing, reading the horoscope, drinking alcohol, etc.
- I must make myself suffer just in case my enjoyment was "sinful."
- If I watch television, I risk "sinning" if I don't ritualize, because I might see or hear sexual content, swearing, off-color humor, etc.
- Avoidance of pleasure will keep me pure and good.
- I will avoid eating "treats" or food that tastes good.
- I am taking too much risk if I don't suffer.

Miscellaneous

Feared Consequence: causing harm, committing a deadly sin

Compulsions: confessing, performing mental undoing rituals, inflicting self-punishment, making decisions out of obsessive guilt and not choice, avoiding responsibility

- Telling someone of potential harm no longer makes me responsible.
- What if I really meant that bad thought (obsession) and I don't do something (ritualize) about it?
- I am afraid my bad thoughts (obsessions) are causing harm in the universe; ritualizing will cancel them out.
- Concern about wasting food.
- Vegetarianism out of fear of violating the commandment "Thou shall not kill."
- Denial of food as punishment or as penance for having an obsession or for having skipped performing a ritual for an obsession, which would be indulgence for slothfulness.

This chapter closes with the thoughts: Was OCD causing these sufferers to be "selfish" by giving into the demand of settling the obsessive doubts for as long as it took to assure moral goodness, while at the same time creating real negative consequence to their coworkers and families? Or were they being unselfish by ensuring that all was good and right? Did the obsessive need to be sure take precedent over their concern for the toll OCD takes on their loved ones? These are not real questions for which there are real answers. What is important is realizing that abiding the obsessive fear, doubt, and guilt *never* works, and that OCD can be overcome with courage, strength, support, and a healthy sense of humor!

Notes

1. Knapp, "Narcissism, Pride, and Humility": 13.
2. Hill, "Did Evagrius Ponticus Have Obsessive–Compulsive Disorder?": 49–56.
3. Ibid., abstract.
4. Lapsley and Stey, "Separation–Individuation," 188–210.
5. Luke 6:31, Holy Bible, New International Version®, NIV® Copyright © 1973, 1978, 1984, 2011 by Biblica, Inc.® Used by permission. All rights reserved worldwide.
6. Leviticus 19:18, *JPS Hebrew–English Tanakh*.
7. An-Nawawi, *An-Nawawi's Forty Hadiths*, 70.
8. Douglas, *Confucianism and Taoism*, 108.
9. Shoemaker, *The Theology of the Four Gospels*, 264.
10. Sharp, *Book of Life*.
11. Ibid.
12. Stoneham, *Why Religions Work*, 23.
13. Luther, "Sermon on the Mount and the Magnificat," 375.
14. Newhauser, "Introduction: Cultural Construction and the Vices." [Two Summer Seminars funded by the NEH at Darwin College, Cambridge University, on "The Seven Deadly Sins as Cultural Constructions in the Middle Ages."]
15. Campbell et al., "Running from Shame or Reveling in Pride?"

Bibliography

An-Nawawi. *An-Nawawi's Forty Hadiths*. Translated by Ezzeddin Ibrahim. Kazi Publications, 1982.

Campbell, W. Keith, Joshua D. Foster, and Amy B. Brunell. "Running from Shame or Reveling in Pride? Narcissism and the Regulation of Self-Conscious Emotions." *Psychological Inquiry* 15, no. 2 (2004): 150–153.

Douglas, Robert K. *Confucianism and Taoism: Non Religious Christian Systems*, 5th ed. London: Kessinger Publishing, LLC, 1900/2004. Facsimile reprint.

Hill, Jonathan. "Did Evagrius Ponticus (AD 346–99) Have Obsessive–Compulsive Disorder?" *Journal of Medical Biography* 18, no. 1 (2010): 49–56.

JPS Hebrew–English Tanakh: The Traditional Hebrew Text and the New JPS Translation, 2nd ed. Philadelphia: The Jewish Publication Society.

Knapp, Richard D. "Narcissism, Pride, and Humility." *Journal of Psychology and Judaism* 24, no. 2 (2000): 205–222.

Kuchler, Bonnie Louise, ed. *One Heart: Universal Wisdom from the World's Scriptures*. New York: Marlowe and Company, 2003.

Lapsley, Daniel K., and Paul Stey. "Separation–Individuation." In *Corsini's Encyclopedia of Psychology*, eds. I. Weiner and E. Craighead. New York: Wiley, 2010.

Luther, Martin. "Sermon on the Mount and the Magnificat." In *Luther's Works*, eds. Jeroslav Pelikan and Helmut T. Lehmann, p. 383. St. Louis: Concordia, 1956.

Newhauser, Richard Gordon. "Introduction: Cultural Construction and the Vices." In *The Seven Deadly Sins: From Communities to Individuals*, ed. Richard Newhauser. Leiden, Netherlands: Brill, 2007.

Sharp, Michael. *Book of Life: Ascension and the Divine World Order*. Rantoul, IL: Avatar Publications, 2004.

Shoemaker, Mel. *The Theology of the Four Gospels*. Bloomington, IN: WestBow Press, 2011.

Stoneham, Eleanor. *Why Religions Work: God's Place in the World Today*. Alresford, Hants, SO24 9JH, UK: John Hunt Publishing Ltd., 2012.

8

Obsessive Guilt

One reason for the frequent urge of human beings to accept guilt and responsibility where they have none is a deep-seated need to feel power over their lives, whether by influencing fate or by authoring events. It suggests, in other words, that accepting guilt may, on occasion, be the only way of attributing efficacy to oneself—and, as a corollary, that the pain of guilt may, in such circumstances, be less than the pain of irrelevance.[1]

Obsessive Guilt: The Emotional Aspect of OCD

"I deserve OCD. I must have done something wrong and OCD is my punishment!" Like most people, Leila wanted a reason for why things happen to her. It was easier for her to live with her explanation of OCD being a form of punishment from an unknown source from unknown mistakes, rather than having OCD for no reason at all. Assuming responsibility in this way gave her the illusion of having control when she really didn't. Leila's treatment was complicated because of the obsessive bind she found herself in: Keeping her life limited by OCD would fulfill her obligation to suffer, but at the cost of knowing that this suffering was a product of her OCD and unnecessary. Engaging in treatment meant betraying her duty to suffer, but not engaging in treatment meant she would be denied her right to a normal life. Either way, she felt selfish and greedy.

Obsessive guilt also complicated Naomi's OCD. She was an excellent surgical nurse and struggled with OCD contamination and thoroughness. She blamed herself for not being with her father when he died, because she believed that if she had been there, she could have saved him. Her excessive guilt and doubt began to interfere with her focus and concentration during surgery, and she became afraid of making fatal errors. Getting into treatment helped her grieve the loss of her father, unburden her sense of responsibility for her father's death, and resume her career to save other countless lives.

The patients I've treated have taught me that although observable OCD symptoms (washing, checking, repeating, apologizing) readily respond to exposure and response prevention (ERP) therapy, which requires people to face their obsessive fears while resisting urges to ritualize, is not always sufficient in maintaining treatment gains over the long run. When faced with stressful conditions (such as illness, loss, and other unforeseeable negative life events), one vulnerability factor for relapse is unaddressed and underlying obsessive guilt. No matter what the OCD trigger, people become conflicted about not ritualizing because the need to be "good" overrides the ability to withstand the anxiety and guilt to resist them. The motivation becomes avoiding the negative feeling of guilt more than the anxiety of challenging the feared situation. Most, if not all, OCD subtypes appear to have elements of obsessive guilt that compel sufferers to either ritualize or avoid experiencing it.

Guilt across OCD Subtypes

The Yale–Brown Obsessive Compulsive Checklist identifies the following categories of obsessions.[2] Next to those are some examples of guilt-related feared consequences people have expressed for those obsessions (see Table 8.1).

Aggressive/Harming Obsessions

Brian's obsession consisted of a vague but strong fear that his mere presence might taint every place he went. Before moving from one task to the next, he looked for evidence, or lack thereof, that he did not cause any harm in his wake. At store entrances, people used a different door, or just walked around him because he was in the way. On some occasions, store clerks called security to see what he was up to, because he looked suspicious. He was unaware of how he looked while lurking over a product for a long time, trying to decide whether it was the *right* one to buy.

When anxious about being a few minutes late to our meeting (from finishing his car checking rituals), Brian began apologizing, not so much because he was sorry but more to feel *right* before starting the session. Being a frequent target of compulsive apologizers, I sometimes risk using humor in a nice way. To point out to Brian that he *was* actually having a negative effect on what was *really* going on in the room, I said, "You're not really sorry, because that's what you said the last time!" He looked at me, blinked, then smiled and sat down. It's all but certain that his behavior has the same effect on polite others, who are not as inclined to call it out.

We have said that it doesn't matter what type of OCD you have to feel guilty. Ironically, the content of obsessions change according to shifts in the culture, and guilt follows suit. We can't help but notice and be affected by the cautionary

TABLE 8.1 Examples of Guilty Obsessions across OCD Subtypes

Obsession	Guilty/Feared Consequence
Safety	
"I have a thought that someone I love might be in a car crash."	"That thought may cause it if I don't do a ritual to counterbalance it."
"When preparing food, I have an image of stabbing whoever walks into the kitchen."	"That thought/image might mean I want to hurt them. I worry I will lose control of my impulses and will actually stab someone."
"Whenever I'm driving, I think I hit someone."	"I drive back and check to make sure nothing happened."
Contamination	
"I feel gross if I or my kids touch things in public."[a]	"If I don't wash my hands *and* my kids' hands, it will be my fault if they get sick."
"I might get someone pregnant if I sit on this chair."	"I shower before I go out. Sometimes I wear an extra pair of underwear, or a pair of shorts under my pants."
Sexual	
"I worry that when I have my period, my pheromones will cause someone to commit rape."	"If I don't shower enough, it won't be safe." "I'll just stay home so nothing will happen."
"Whenever my sister changes her baby's diaper I think, 'What if I accidentally— *wait!* maybe on purpose—touch her in a sexual way?'"	"Maybe I am a child molester. Lately, I've been avoiding my sister and my niece."
"I feel so ashamed. . . . I get these images of having sex with my best friend."	"I worry the thoughts mean I want to act on them unless I convince myself otherwise."
Hoarding/Saving	
"If I throw this away . . ."	"I am betraying the person that gave it to me." "This could be important information for me to have later." "I am losing a part of myself and my memories."
Religious	
"What if my prayer went to the devil instead of God?"	"I might go to hell if I let this go. I will keep praying until I'm sure."

(Continued)

TABLE 8.1 (*Continued*)

Obsession	Guilty/Feared Consequence
"I have inappropriate, blasphemous images of the Pope."	"I committed a sin but if I don't perform a ritual, I will have 'sinned' by omission."
"Some of the music I like might offend God."	"I say a prayer when a song comes on and change the radio station."

Superstitious

"If I don't touch the sink five times perfectly (without having an obsession), I must touch it another five times to make sure nothing bad happens to my family."	"I will be responsible for something bad happening to myself and those who depend on me."
"I get really anxious on the thirteenth of every month because that's the date my dad died, and I don't like the number thirteen anyway. I make the station of the cross on those days and whenever I see that number."	"I'm afraid something bad will happen again if I'm not careful enough."

Miscellaneous

"I have to know and remember details or I might miss something important."	"I'm not sure I heard the last thing my teacher said. I might get a bad grade and disappoint my parents."
"I have a fear of saying certain things because they might make someone mad."	"I will feel guilty if I insult or offend someone. I might misrepresent myself."
"I am afraid of not saying just the right thing."	"I might be lying, or not telling the exact truth."
"I have a fear of losing things. It doesn't matter how valuable (or not) the things is."	"Losing things is wasteful. It would be careless."
"I am bothered by certain nonsense sounds, noises, words, or music."	"Maybe someone's in danger and they need my help."
"These numbers are unlucky: 13 and 666 and their multiples. I get anxious on a certain date at a specific time because it's the anniversary of when something bad happend. I don't like uneven numbers."	"I'm playing with the devil if I don't substitute a good number. Something bad will happen and I'm asking for bad luck if I leave anything off on those numbers."
"These are lucky numbers: my family's birthdays, even numbers, but also the number three."	"These numbers are auspicious. Something good is going to happen. Three is good because of the Father, the Son, and the Holy Ghost."
"I believe these colors have special significance."	Red = devil or blood; black = death; green = envy; blue = sadness; gold = goodness.

Obsession	Guilty/Feared Consequence
"I get anxious when I get twinges or sensations or notice things on my body."	"Uh-oh, that bump on my back could be cancer. If I die, my kids won't have a father. I must see a doctor immediately."

[a] Several mothers I have worked with have stripped off their clothing and their children's clothing to keep "outside" dirt/germs from coming inside. When these children went to their friends' houses to play, they instinctively started to take off their clothes upon arrival, to the horror of the hosting parents!

news in the media. In the World War II era, the message was "Clean your plate. Children are starving in Europe." After that, people with contamination symptoms were obsessed about contracting the sexually transmitted diseases syphilis and gonorrhea. These fears became obsolete when the mandate to prevent contracting AIDS was to have "safe sex." Deadly substances such as anthrax and asbestos became obsessive fears, as well as computer viruses and identity theft. What is important to keep in mind with *all* obsessions is that there is always a kernel of reality to them, and that there is always a level of probability and possibility that these things could happen. Although we may be anxious about what is happening in the world right now and feel less in control of our circumstances, most of us will get on with our normal daily routine in spite of it. As OCD sufferers know, though, OCD will always be looking for new uncertainties to latch onto. So although there have been real and fatal cases of AIDS, anthrax, and asbestos exposure, as well as violations in our electronic world, we can help those with OCD and ourselves by keeping things in perspective.

The current cultural theme is green guilt, defined as "the uncomfortable feeling that some people experience when they believe that they could and should be doing more to preserve the environment than they are, in fact, doing."[3] People with OCD obsessively think, "Am I being 'green' enough? Do I abide by the standards set to reduce, reuse, and recycle?"

This obsession often results in *green* hoarding. Stacy, a successful physician, stops along the highway to pick up redeemable cans and bottles to put, as she claims, toward her children's college funds. She considered this a doubly worthy duty: helping the environment *and* saving money. Why is it a problem? The can and bottles, along with other reusable items overtook space in her basement and backyard. The cans and bottles have yet to be redeemed. As for the reusables, they never are put to use—even if they were, there is not enough time left in her life to use them up. Also, if you are getting a ride from Stacy, you will be late because of the multiple recyclable rescue stops she makes along the way. Her obsessive guilt about leaving them to waste is beyond reasonable, but she remains undeterred.

Seeing food left on plates was another trigger for Stacy about being wasteful. When she went out to dinner, she asked to take the food home that was left on others' plates. When she didn't end up eating the food at home, she had to throw it out.

Healthy and Unhealthy/Obsessive Guilt

Healthy guilt is a survival instinct that promotes empathy and helps us coexist. Most of us do not intend to cause harm or hurt others, but when we do, inevitably, we try to make some form of restitution directly to the person when we can (apologize, recompense financially, offer to do a favor, etc.), find an indirect way when we can't (make a donation, do volunteer work, etc.), and, when there may not be *anything* we can do about it, resolve to do better the next time. At some point, letting go of the guilt is the healthy end to the process.

Healthy guilt occurs when we have violated our own personal rules, morals, or ethics. We know when we made a mistake, because it *really* happened. We saw the look on someone's face when we said something hurtful. We went against our own code of conduct and felt appropriately bad about it. Someone gave us feedback about a negative experience. Taking responsibility for these events and seeking forgiveness are good steps toward resolving the guilt.

Some examples of how healthy guilt may play out in our lives are

- Even when you are in a rush, you stop and help someone who needs it, because you've been in those situations (such as helping someone fix a flat tire, or giving directions to someone is lost).
- We keep our plans with someone even when another friend calls with a better offer. We choose to be reliable, because we value and respect this friendship, rather than canceling for a more immediately gratifying experience.
- We feel guilty when we didn't keep a secret and the person who confided in us became aware of it.
- Guilt inhibits impulsivity and destructive urges. Our judgment stops us from acting on negative/addictive/self-destructive urges and prevents our getting into situations that are likely to have a bad outcome and that could cause us regret.
- We take care of ourselves while respecting others' rights to do the same.

Unhealthy guilt, on the other hand, is misguided and is an excessive assumption of responsibility and blame for things that are out of our control. We all have a degree of unhealthy guilt, but it is a luxury that those who have conscience-related OCD cannot afford. If you have it, you may become emotionally burnt out, as your guilt compels you to fix things that aren't broken. Obsessive guilt sentences sufferers to life in OCD prison for failing to make everything good and right. In her book *Guilt is the Teacher, Love is the Lesson*, Joan Borysenko nicely sorts out the different roles guilt plays in our lives: "Unhealthy guilt entails fear and doubt created by guilt-driven behaviors such as perfectionism, overachievement, lack of assertiveness, and self-sacrificing as a means of avoiding 'self-responsibility.'"[4] Borysenko also adds that "unhealthy guilt can be a product of anxiety and depression out of which life is lived to function around the need to avoid fear rather than the desire to share love. When we persist in prolonged and disproportionate self-criticism, we maintain unhealthy guilt."[5]

Aly reported, "If I see a stick in the road, I have to move it or else it will be my fault if someone gets hurt. Also, if I drive over a bump, I have to go back and check to make sure I didn't run someone over by mistake." Afraid of offending, Chris allowed his basketball coach to call him the wrong name for all his high school years (under normal circumstances, even the shyest of kids probably would have corrected the coach). At night, Sandra reviews her "wrongdoing" list of the day and mentally apologizes to each person or situation before she feels worthy of sleep. Guilt-related topics that seem to stoke obsessive fears into wildfires of anxiety and emotions follow:

- *Doubt* about having done something wrong (not an actual event)
- How suffering is maintained by the obsessive need to please others and avoid conflict (survival); social anxiety
- Bad thoughts' being assumed to be the same as bad actions
- Problems with decision-making

Some treatment goals for these issues are accepting doubt/uncertainty as a fact of life, accepting never knowing how others perceive you, being willing to let go of the need to know how others perceive you, realizing that how you judge yourself is the dynamic you carry into how you relate to the world, and realizing that trusting your *own* judgment and intuition for making decisions is the best way of making the right decisions for yourself. Everything flows from that self-trust. I'm often asked, "But how do you do that?" The portion on assertiveness in chapter 10 provides some help for this.

Anne suffered from OCD symptoms of incompletion. She had trouble moving from one task to another until she "felt right." This is a difficult type of OCD to treat, because it is more of a vague sense of something's being wrong accompanied by physical discomfort. Anne's guilt was feeling negligent and irresponsible that something bad would happen if she didn't check to completion. She constantly checked for fear of losing something material, but, more important, she feared losing part of herself physically—or losing part of her soul. She performed her checking rituals four times each. If she felt "incomplete," she would repeat the checking in series of fours until she felt okay.

Another manifestation of her OCD was the transferring a part of her identity to a material object. She stated, "If I lose something, a part of myself (which becomes attached to a material possession) it is somewhere unsafe in the world. I will be left feeling incomplete and mourning for that 'missing piece' of myself from the puzzle of my being. As hard as I sometimes try, I can't stop imagining that possession 'beckoning' to me to be found. My keeping track of every insignificant item is confirming that none of those things are mine, therefore forbidding anything outside of my environment from entering through."

Anne had made lists and catalogued every item she came in contact with. She brought these with her to treatment, as well as every item she picked up along the way. She saved receipts and pieces of paper that had her name on them. She felt extremely guilty about her sense of connectedness and spirituality to the world being through material objects.

On two occasions in Anne's life, she found herself in a convent, mistaking her sense of perfection, guilt, and excessive responsibility for a vocational calling to God. She was in a bind: She was afraid that letting go of the way she did things would cause her to be unsafe, but staying stuck in this pattern prevented her from living the kind of life she imagined for herself. She recognized her behaviors as senseless but had great difficulty taking the risk to give them up.

Anne's treatment challenged her fear and guilt by categorizing what she had saved into levels of difficulty. She started by throwing things away from the easy pile and then graduated to the medium and then difficult levels. She ended up saving some things that were especially sentimental to her, but she discarded most of the items. She also agreed to resist urges to take and save things.

To target her fear of losing a physical part of herself, we developed a systematic way for her to resist the urges to check behind her when leaving places. She began by leaving home and work without checking. Eventually, she was able to go to places in public she had been avoiding because of the intensity of her symptoms, and she worked hard at not checking. Her anxiety, fear, and guilt subsided to the point that she could go anywhere without anticipating her obsession's being triggered.

Ellen explained in our first meeting that the only acceptable standard set by her OCD for cleaning her house was "beyond reproach." She was the daughter of a career army officer and his lesson was *good enough means settling for less.* Her friends often commented on her perfect physical appearance and home decor. She did not consider these compliments, but rather a sign of having gotten away with the flaws she knew were there. About six months ago, though, her body and her will "gave up." She was simply too tired to keep up the routine.

She came to see me because the all-perfect house became a nothing-mess. She felt guilty about how consumed she had been over valuing *appearances* over function, and now feeling guilty about being *too lazy* about bothering with the house at all. Embarrassed by the condition of the house, her kids no longer invited their friends over.

One of the initial problems we addressed was perfectionism:

Is perfection really achievable?

What is the value of it?

What does it provide?

How long does it last?

Does striving for it cause guilt and dysfunction if you can't get it "right"?

Do you blame yourself for having faults?

Are things only good or bad, right, or wrong?

Does the desire to make "just right" choices end up in procrastination or complete avoidance?

To address her contamination symptoms, she would touch triggering items, then cross-contaminate the house to make one world out of a clean and dirty one. Even though Ellen's house had been a mess, it did not take long before it became neater. Normalizing her behavior helped her feel as if she could finish the tasks without the exceedingly high expectations for the outcome.

Then we addressed people-pleasing, another indicator of excessive guilt. Ellen worried about what other people though about her. She was concerned about disappointing them. She put others' needs ahead of her own because she wanted to be liked (not unreasonable), to keep the peace and avoid conflict (e.g., not be hated and retaliated against). Focusing on others' needs was a form of distraction, a convenient way to avoid her negative emotions. She said what she thought other people wanted to hear without ever knowing what was, rather than sharing her true thoughts and feelings. She dodged being responsible and the fear of being negatively judged for decisions by going along with other peoples' preferences. She could have had more confidence from the experiences she had when what others opted for was what she would have suggested in the first place. She also used self-blame as a control strategy. "It was my fault," became her default way of settling uncertainties about social interaction, possible mistakes she made, and even for things that she had nothing to do with.

Big Bad Emotions That Trigger OCD

[E]motional guilt involves a kind of self-punishment where the agent has some control over whether he experiences that unpleasant feeling. But it is important that, if anger is thought of as originally grounded in an animal urge to attack, guilt comes out not as a self-directed version of the urges—an urge to attack oneself—but rather as a less aggressive counterpart of it, requiring in the first instance reparation, or some way of making amends. Guilt may thus involve self-punishment as a form of reparation along with the readiness to submit to attack or to other punishment from others; but in developed form it is not simply inwardly directed anger.[6]

OCD, by nature, causes discomfort and not right feelings, now clinically considered not-just-right-experiences (NJREs). Almost all OCD *is* NJREs. OCD sufferers who have NJREs may not have obsessions at all but ritualize as a way of getting it right. In other cases, obsessive thoughts seem to overlay the physiological not-just-right-experience and appear as explanations for why something feels wrong without anything's actually being wrong. Then at least something, like ritualizing, can be done about it. The closest I have ever come to knowing what this feels like is when I forget something. I don't feel right, and I want to remember whatever it was to feel right again, even if it wasn't important. Sometimes the harder I try, the more frustrated I get. Obviously, OCD NJREs occur with a much stronger sense of urgency than just forgetting something, and the most natural response to this feeling is: *Get rid of it!* Rituals are performed and obsessions are strengthened, and the cycle lives on.

The experience of having negative emotions also triggers OCD, because having them feels wrong. Negative emotions are normal but are often experienced by people with OCD to be "bad," a kind of moral failure to be avoided. The OCD brain causes any action, mental or physical, not to feel right, as if something dreadful is wrong.

To varying degrees, as children, we were sensitive to the anger and criticism of our parents and other authority figures as they tried to teach us how to become good people. If, as we matured, we felt too guilty to come into our own codes of conduct because it meant betraying those critical authority figures, we may still be living by those lessons in the same way they were taught.

In service to developing a personal sense of identity, most adolescents test the validity of the rules taught by authority figures by challenging them as a way to internalize those lessons. Mistakes are made, appropriate guilt is experienced, and lessons are learned to help forge a personal sense of morality. Those with an obsessive conscience may find this so overwhelming that instead of taking risks, they avoid moral mistakes by living to the literal letter of laws taught in childhood.

Other common negative emotions that are problematic are fear, anger, shame, blame, regret, resentment, hostility, frustration, impatience, irritation, loneliness, rejection, and worthlessness. These emotions provoke or reinforce obsessive anxiety and guilt, and rituals are used as coping strategies to "make them go away" (even though they don't).

Paul was angry with his father for criticizing his homework and began having violent obsessions about his father's falling down the stairs and breaking his neck. Paul felt guilty and anxious because of the obsessions and spent twenty minutes stuck in place repeating to any receptive mind reader, "Please keep my dad safe; please keep my dad safe" until he felt "right enough" to move on. He then walked by the den, where his father was using the computer, to check whether he was safe. Full of guilt, he made another appeal to the nameless mindreading force out there not to make him have these thoughts again. "Please don't make me think about my dad falling down the stairs," which *is* having the thoughts again. As people with OCD know, this strategy always backfires when used as a way of getting rid of anxiety and guilt.

Misguided altruism is another way in which the rigidity of OCD can be problematic for others. Oakley, O'Connor, and their colleagues have studied and reported on pathological guilt and pathological altruism: "Pathological altruism might be thought of as an extreme form of any behavior or personal tendency in which either the stated aim or the implied motivation is to promote the welfare of another or others. But, instead of overall beneficial outcomes, the 'altruism' instead has irrational substantial negative consequences to the other or even to the self."[7]

Although adaptive guilt serves to inform individuals when they have truly wronged another or violated a personal standard for which rectification is appropriate, pathological guilt (PG) drives an intense need for certainty over a "normal" incident for which rectification is neither necessary nor appropriate. Within the religious setting, religious rituals have emerged to address and absolve guilt, whereas the therapeutic approach aims to identify dysfunctional guilt, religious or otherwise, and to provide the means to normalize it. Both religious and clinical spheres have their benefits and limitations.[8]

Notes

1. May, *Nietzsche's Ethics and His War On "Morality,"* 76.
2. Goodman et al., "The Yale–Brown Obsessive Compulsive Scale": 1012–1016.
3. Sudindranath et al., "'Green Guilt' and 'Green Behavior.'"
4. Borysenko, *Guilt Is the Teacher, Love Is the Lesson*, 20.
5. Ibid.
6. Greenspan, *Practical Guilt*, 153.
7. Oakley et al., eds., *Pathological Altruism*, 4.
8. Shapiro and Stewart, "Pathological Guilt": 63–70.

Bibliography

Borysenko, Joan. *Guilt Is the Teacher, Love Is the Lesson*. New York: Warner Books, 1990.

Goodman, W. K., L. H. Price, S. A. Rasmussen, C. Mazure, R. L. Fleishman, C. L. Hill, G. R. Heninger, and D. S. Charney. "The Yale–Brown Obsessive Compulsive Scale." *Archives of General Psychiatry* 46 (1989): 1012–1016.

Greenspan, P. S. *Practical Guilt: Moral Dilemmas, Emotions, and Social Norms.* New York: Oxford University Press, 1995.

May, Simon. *Nietzsche's Ethics and His War on "Morality."* Oxford: Oxford University Press, 2004/1999.

Oakley, Barbara, Ariel Knafo, Guruprasad Madhavan, and David Sloan Wilson, eds. *Pathological Altruism.* New York: Oxford University Press, 2011.

Shapiro, L. J., and E. S. Stewart. "Pathological Guilt: A Persistent yet Overlooked Treatment Factor in Obsessive–Compulsive Disorder." *Annals of Clinical Psychiatry* 23, no. 1 (February 2011): 63–70.

Sudindranath, Manisha Masher, Lynn E. O'Connor, Jack W. Berry, David J. Stiver, and Reeta L. Banerjee. "'Green Guilt' and 'Green Behavior' Associated with Better Mental Health." In *Association for Psychological Science.* Poster presented at the Association for Psychological Science Annual Convention, San Francisco, CA, May 22–25, 2009.

Part III

"You Want Me to Do *What?*"

9

Taking Control Where You Can and Must

Do the thing you fear the most and the death of fear is certain.[1]

Exposure and response (ERP) therapy is doing the thing you think you cannot do—but must. Exposure consists of facing your feared situation. Response prevention is not performing any rituals to reduce your anxiety during exposure. ERP is simple, but it is not easy. In OCD terms, patients have to be willing to take a leap of faith and jump off a mountain of *exaggerated* risk to prove that the threat of the obsession is nothing. This is easier said than done, but having a therapist at both the top to cheer you on *and* the bottom as a safety net can help boost your confidence and morale. Being that cheerleading safety net for people when they take their leaps of faith and land with more confidence and less obsessive fear is a privilege I continue to cherish in my work!

Neuroimaging research has shown that ERP causes therapeutic changes in the left orbitofrontal cortex.[2] Essentially, the rule of exposure therapy is to do the opposite of what your obsession is telling you to. When your obsession says, "You like looking at fashion magazines because those models are attractive—you know it's lustful and disloyal to your girlfriend," your exposure task is to look at high-end fashion magazines and let yourself naturally have whatever thoughts or feelings occur, without pushing them away. Eventually, your nervous system will get used to seeing attractive people without your getting anxious. After this happens, you can accept that the thoughts and feelings can't really, or should be, helped. You will also be able to let go of the obsessive guilt that having the obsessions meant that you were being unfaithful to your partner. Thoughts and feelings are not the same as actions. Later this chapter, we will review the concept of thought–action fusion.

Medications can work well, minimally, or not at all in taming OCD. Although ERP is the gold-standard treatment in getting symptoms under control, it is not always sufficient in maximizing treatment gains or in maintaining the gains over the long run, because patients' unaddressed nagging *obsessive conscience* still compels them to "*feel right*" and do the "*right thing.*" Typically, the combination of medication and ERP treatment maximizes potential gains in how much control you achieve with symptom control and to what extent you maintain the gains in recovery.

Treatment outcome from ERP, though, can vary thanks to other complex factors such as how willing and motivated you are to experience the anxiety you may be trying to avoid, how much insight or belief you have that your obsessions are exaggerated thoughts, how much tolerance for risk you are willing to have, and how ready you are for changing your life, among other issues. As happens with many disorders, relapses occur for a variety of reasons, such as sudden noncompliance with medication or behavior therapy, unexpected life stressors, illness, and so forth.

History of ERP

Exposure and response prevention was started using a method of behavioral treatment called *apotreptic therapy* (designed to dissuade) introduced by the psychologist Victor Meyer on an inpatient unit at Middlesex Hospital in London.[3] With staff assistance, Meyer gradually exposed two patients with severe contamination and scrupulosity symptoms to triggering items while blocking ritualistic behaviors.[4] In the 1970s, researchers such as Rachman, Marks, and Foa began to improve on Meyer's apotrepic therapy, and eventually they turned it into the exposure and response prevention therapy that most therapists are familiar with today.[5, 6, 7]

Clinical research yielded improved treatment strategies to this form of treatment. Therapists used modeling techniques that demonstrated normalized behavior, such as touching contaminated items and then having the patient engage in the same behavior.[8] After the patients were comfortable with that situation, they moved on to more challenging OCD triggers, and eventually the need for the therapist was eliminated.[9]

How to Conduct ERP

ERP is the same process as when we work to change our conditioned fears. Like many people, I have the most common phobia: fear of public speaking. Sharing my clinical work and research is a strong value of mine, but I was terrified at the idea of standing in the front of a sterile function room and speaking coherently to strangers who might not know what I was talking about—or, even worse, colleagues who knew *more* than I did. I knew that my fear was irrational and that I would regret not taking advantage of these speaking opportunities, so I promised myself that I would not turn down any invitations. Most important, however, I did not want to be a hypocrite to my patients by not challenging my own fears. I have presented my work dozens of times over the years in conjunction with dozens of panic attacks. But I must admit that I do feel less anxious when the next talk is on the horizon. I'm glad I challenged myself—even though, truthfully, it's still not the thing I do best.

When a patient makes the decision to undergo treatment, it is highly recommended that upon initial contact with a therapist to ask whether he or she has experience treating OCD with exposure and response prevention. If the therapist says anything but yes, say thank you very much and look for someone whose answer is a definitive yes. You may find, however, that ERP treaters are not always available in every community. Consult the International Obsessive Compulsive Disorder Foundation (IOCDF) for help finding behavior therapists with ERP experience.[10]

You and your behavior therapist will meet a few times to get to know each other and identify your symptoms. Typically, a fear hierarchy is created that consists of rating your OCD triggers on a scale between 0–100. The scale measures your subjective units of distress (SUDS). A zero rating would probably mean you were asleep. Anxiety between below 60 would indicate that you feel noticeably anxious but that you can resist ritualizing. Rating your anxiety in the range between 60 and 100 means that you have more intense physiological symptoms of anxiety and that rituals become harder to resist. Some of these symptoms are increased heart rate, shallow breathing, sweatiness, muscle tension, and desire to flee the situation. You might also feel very guilty, irritable, full of dread, and ashamed. The hierarchy provides a road map of how your symptoms will be treated. Patients prefer to start at a level of challenge that will provide a noticeable difference but will not be overwhelming.

In vivo exposures are conducted "in real life." Being in the environment in which the obsessions are triggered is the ideal setting for facing down the fear. Doing so is usually logistically problematic for outpatient treatment owing to time, geographical, and financial constraints. A 50-minute session does not lend itself to traveling to a patient's home, a shopping mall, a restaurant, a workplace, or other community-based triggering situations. Video chatting and use of electronic apps have been helpful in facilitating exposure, and some patients conduct daily ERPs, as outlined in the therapy sessions, that connect the patient and therapist during the actual exposure task.

For ERPs to take effect, they must be repeated daily. Problems carrying out the exposures every day may be because the patient is overwhelmed. If this is the case, the plan can be modified by breaking the exposure task down into more specific and focused steps. If the exposure turned out to cause more anxiety than anticipated, the plan can be changed to an item lower on the hierarchy.

Here are some principles of ERP my colleagues at the OCD Institute and I have developed to keep in mind for successful treatment:

- Reading psychoeducational material that describes OCD and behavioral treatment can help you have a better understanding of what will be involved and expected in treatment.
- Understand that previous trials of exposure therapy may not have been effective because the chosen task may have been too intense and thus was attempted prematurely. Maybe there was not enough support available to help you stay motivated to endure the anxiety and maintain good response prevention.
- Remember that ERP involves putting the cart before the horse. Changing behavior *first* sets the stage for a reduction in physiological, cognitive, and emotional symptoms to the obsessive fear.
- In vivo exposure (exposure that is conducted in real life) is the gold standard approach to getting symptoms under control. Brain chemistry changes when the feared situation is faced in the natural setting in which it is triggered.
- Exposures should always be set up to include and exactly match all the elements of the obsession. Two people with the same fear of lying will have their own versions of the obsession. Sean's exposure is to deliberately tell "white lies" and not confess or take them back later, whereas Drew's exposure is to have a fluid and spontaneous conversation without choosing his words carefully before speaking.
- The goal of ERP is habituation. Habituation occurs naturally when the feared situation is confronted until the anxiety peaks and drops off naturally, without any purposeful attempts at reducing it with mental or physical rituals. Habituation will occur only by staying in the exposure and experiencing the decrease in anxiety. This happens because the nervous system does not sustain high anxiety indefinitely. The subsequent exposures will be entered into with less anticipation because of the physiological memory of the previous exposure ending at a lowered anxiety level.
- When obsessive fears cannot be replicated in vivo—because they would be dangerous or they cannot be replicated in reality—imagined exposures are often helpful. A "script" is written with as much detail as if the obsessive fear were happening *right now*. For detailed instructions, refer to *When Once Is Not Enough*.[11]
- Paying attention to distractions interferes with the ERP process. Stimuli in the environment or the mind wandering, to name a few things, are natural distractions that disrupt the focus on the exposure. Refocusing attention back to the exposure task will facilitate habituation.
- Exposure without response prevention is an exercise of torture. Being in the feared situation without experiencing any benefit due to ritualizing is cruel.
- Track your distress or anxiety level and urges to ritualize during exposure, using the Subjective Units of Distress Scale (SUDS) for measurement (0 [lowest] to 100 [highest]).

- Exposures must be conducted *daily* if they are to work. Your nervous system won't habituate without consistency. This is a common reason why people say that ERPs don't work. Finding a way to be accountable for doing them is usually what makes the difference between just complying with the plan and feeling its rewards.

- Remember that experiencing less anxiety and habituating is a *good* thing. Some people feel guilty about this because they worry it means that they are becoming insensitive or that they don't care about the feared situation and consequences any more. What it really means is that the playing field of uncertainty is put back to the same level as it is for everyone else.

- Don't be perfectionistic about treatment. Finding the "perfect" exposure is obsessive and is more of what got you into the situation in the first place.

- Although complete response prevention is the goal, don't expect it go perfectly. ERP is incredibly hard. Ritualizing is not a crime, and feeling guilty about ritualizing only sets you back. The best thing is to chalk it up to being human and move on.

- Analyzing obsessions are mental rituals. You will never figure it out. If you could, you would have already.

- Maintain the exposure task even after the exposure session. If your exposure for perfectionism is to disorganize your office or home, leave it that way until fixing it is an easy choice and not for providing anxiety relief.

- It's okay to cry. In fact, it's good to cry. Crying means you are *in* the exposure and not cognitively or emotionally avoiding it. It won't be long before the situation does not elicit a tearful response—even if you feel guilty about what the exposure entails.

- People are not expected to do things that others wouldn't do. It may seem like it, or feel like it, but this will not be the case. If someone with OCD raised you, treatment will allow you to learn what the norm is. Sometimes people without OCD may cringe if you tell them what you are doing in treatment, but they would agree that they could do those things if they had to.

- No one will ever be able to know how you truly experience your OCD. Some people are unable to move forward unless they feel that someone (family member, partner, friend) completely "gets it." Along with being an unreasonable condition for treatment, it is another form of avoidance—it can never happen.

Treatment

Making Fear Hierarchies

These are the fear hierarchies of some of the people we have gotten to know in this book. Luke's hierarchy is the longest because, to avoid repetition, it incorporates some of the symptoms that overlap with the other patients, highlighted in bold print. His story also represents the 32 percent of 959 patients at the OCDI who identified Catholicism as their religion (32%).[12] Although everyone had several other OCD symptoms, the hierarchies focus on the ones that are most conscience-related. OCD and its treatment are paradoxical and counterintuitive. Luke and all other sufferers who have an obsessive conscience wince at the idea of purposely embracing their obsessions by doing the opposite of what the obsessions demand, without apology and without excuses. At the same time, though, no one is asked to sin: Jews will not be asked to eat a cheeseburger; Muslims will not have to drink alcohol, Hindus won't be eating meat, and so forth. They may practice these exposures in imagination, but not in reality. The point is to get people back to practicing their faith in the most meaningful way.

In the next chapter, I will present other types of helpful strategies to augment ERP therapy, one of those being clergy involvement. I mention this now to assure sufferers that clergy with whom patients and I have consulted have sanctioned exposures even when they appear to contradict religious teachings. They know that obsessions are a product of the disorder and are do not represent intended sacrilege. Martin Luther, for example, took control over his OCD in the spirit of: *agere contra* (do the opposite).[13]

Scrupulosity

Luke

Luke was in college on a football scholarship when he suddenly starting having fears that God disapproving of his drinking and partying at school. He had worked hard to get where he was, because he had already gone through a serious OCD episode that jeopardized his high school and college career. He had been an honor student, popular, and athletic. He began praying throughout the day because of having sexual obsessions he hated. The more he had them, the more he prayed. The more he prayed, the more obsessions he had. Because Luke was confessing the same things over and over, Father Joseph suspected that Luke had OCD/scrupulosity and referred him to a therapist who specialized in treating it. Luke began taking medications that helped take the edge off the obsessions, and he was able to trust his therapist and did a good job with ERP treatment. He still had some residual symptoms, but he maintained a good level of functionality. But now the stress of living away from home, his academic workload, and football practice had caused his OCD to flare up (see Table 9.1).

Although it seemed impossible to maintain all his obligations, Luke agreed that the OCD was not going to get better or just go away. Since my office was close to where he was in college, Luke came in to get going on facing his fears and get back to focusing on school. Luke's initial ERP plan targeted the triggering words associated with the Devil, evil, and the like. First he said them aloud until he could say them without hesitation. Then, he wrote them down over

TABLE 9.1 Luke

SUDS	Triggering Situation	Obsessive Fear	Ritual	Exposure	Response Prevention
100	Receiving Communion	Committing sacrilege; disrespecting God and religion; getting away with something	Avoidance; self-reassurance; skipping breakfast	Receive Communion without hesitation;	Resist mental checking; eat no sooner than one hour before going to church
100	Confessing in church	Forgetting to confess sins of omission or commission; lying to God; God will think I am trying to get away with something; going to hell	Repeat the confession, even at different churches if necessary (church-hopping); mental reviewing; seeking reassurance from the priest	Confess only what you remember since the last confession; write a script about lying to God and the feared consequences	No mental preparation or checking of past sins; resist reconfessing
90	Examining the conscience	Not being thorough enough; lying; going to hell	Mental reviewing; re-examining past actions	Skip this step and go to confession; rely on faith and that mental rituals have already recognized faults/ sins	Resist urges caused by obsessive doubt to review for unconfessed sins
90	Having morbid thoughts	Having a stain on soul before dying or being administered Last Rites	Praying	Have morbid thoughts on purpose, such as "I might die today without a pure soul and go to hell"	Repeat exposure thoughts if I reassure myself
85	Having intrusive thoughts while praying and saying the Rosary	Prayers are contaminated; prayer was incomplete; God will be offended; praying to the Devil; going to hell;	Pray equally pray to the Father, Son, and Holy Ghost; 40–50 morning and evening ritualistic prayers; pray and recite the rosary until perfect/"just right"	Pray in mentally fluid manner and keep going; limit rosary; limit saying the Rosary to 15 then to 10 minutes; set a timer; skip a step on purpose; repeat the intrusive thoughts on purpose	Reduce prayers to 1–2 times/ day; keep praying fluidly; don't stop, repeat, reassure self, or fix intentional "mistakes"
85	Movies: *Rosemary's Baby, The Omen, The Exorcist;* anything with time travel and the paranormal/ supernatural	Becoming possessed; losing my soul; going over to the dark side; forsaking all that is good; becoming evil	Avoid all situations that might be triggering; leave places when topics come up	Watch the movies repeatedly until habituated; read books by Edward Cayce and Nostradamus, play Ouija board with someone	Resist neutralizing anxiety by thinking "good" words, images

(Continued)

TABLE 9.1 (*Continued*)

SUDS	Triggering Situation	Obsessive Fear	Ritual	Exposure	Response Prevention
85	Feeling angry	Going to hell	Turn anger inward; turn the other cheek	Write out uncensored angry thoughts including curse words, swears, etc.	Resist being *nice, rational*
80	Dipping finger in font; making the sign of the cross	Contaminating the water; not feeling pious enough	Wash hands before entering; repeat crossing self until sure it was done "right"	Leave home without washing hands and directly into church; dip hands in font and cross self once	Resist urges to redo, go back and fix it
80	Committing unpardonable sin by mistake or on purpose	Going to hell	Wash hands before leaving for church; repeat it until feels right	Thinking, saying the unpardonable sin until habituated	No reassurance seeking from priest or family; no thinking "I didn't mean it"
75	Fasting for Communion, Ash Wednesday, Good Friday	Offending Jesus/God; cheating; going to hell	Restricting eating; checking teeth	Eat no earlier than one hour before going to church	No rinsing mouth in church bathroom
75	Praying/reciting the Rosary	Praying to the Devil; having blasphemous sexual thoughts while praying	Repeating prayers/rosary until the bad thoughts are *undone* with good thoughts	Search the Internet for triggering pictures of attractive men; let the obsessions run their course; have them on purpose	Rethink obsession if ritualized; block neutralizing mental images
75	Sexual/homosexual/blasphemous obsessions (Jesus is sexy)	Really worshipping the Devil; "the Devil is telling me to do this"; going to hell	Push away/undo thoughts/images with good ones; reassure self didn't mean them; punish self for having them	Use treadmill at gym, keep eyes up and notice the women; let the obsessions run their course; have them on purpose	Keep walking on treadmill with eyes up; casually focus on the women with the most exposed skin (but not in a creepy manner)
70–75	Being around immodesty	Lusting	Averting eyes; avoiding the beach and the gym	Use treadmill at gym, keep eyes up and notice the women	Keep walking on treadmill with eyes up; casually focus on women with the most exposed skin (but not in a creepy manner)

SUDS	Triggering Situation	Obsessive Fear	Ritual	Exposure	Response Prevention
70	Words: Adorable Evil Demonic Possession Lucifer Scary Ugly	Think opposite thoughts/words: "I only adore God," good; innocent; heaven	Being contaminated with evilness; committing evil acts toward those I love, or anyone	Write, read, say the words; use them in conversations; write a story about being possessed	Being contaminated with evilness; committing evil acts toward those I love, or anyone
70	Colors: Red Black Green	Someone will die, get sick; greediness	Think/imagine white to purify self	Wear the avoided colors; type, print out, and post the words in their colors around the house	Keep the clothes on for the entire day; look at the triggering words instead of avoiding them

and over until his anxiety level decreased. He agreed to do this exposure every day for an hour, as well as to refrain from ritualizing about these triggers when the obsessions occurred naturally over the course of the day.

Luke's next exposure consisted of going to places on campus and noticing how women were dressed. He went into stores at the mall, browsed Vogue and other magazines, and watched racy movies. One man's pleasure is another's pain. Luke was initially embarrassed and mortified by these exposures, but with practice he was able to tolerate being places he had previously been avoiding. The goal was not for Luke to *like* being around immodesty, but rather to not have it limit his ability to go wherever he wanted and or watch media that might be incidentally suggestive.

Working up the hierarchy, Luke's ERP for Luke worked on his sexual obsessions by allowing them happen as well as having them on purpose. He wrote triggering words and phrases without taking them back or asking others for reassurance about whether he was gay or whether he had blasphemed. Although it sounds easy, Luke was quite distressed and was not always able to maintain the ERP. Clergy were consulted about this and other symptoms for him to be able to move forward.

Putting his faith forward even more, Luke worked on reducing the rituals he performed while saying the rosary. He broke the process down into three steps and used a timer that prompted him every five minutes to move on to the next step if hadn't already. When 15 minutes were up, Luke dropped what he was doing, put the rosary down, and went on about his day. The tricky part about this plan was making sure he didn't just perform his rituals faster. The other goal was not to have the time limit become obsessive by checking the timer too often, thus overtaking the actual exposure task of reducing the time spent on reciting the rosary.

By the time he was to face his fear of having committed the unpardonable sin, he was more ready. In similar fashion, Luke then worked his way up the hierarchy and conducted the ERPs facing his fears of going to hell, offending God/Jesus, and being controlled by the Devil.

The final challenges were as difficult as he predicted, though. When it came time for Luke to examine his conscience before going to confession, he checked, reviewed, and repeated the process until he was sure he had thought of everything he needed to confess. In one instance, he was troubled by the fear that he had mortally sinned by reading a novel in which there were sexually provocative scenes between characters. He enjoyed the book but felt guilty of lust. He thought, "Was I really guilty of sinful behavior because I read the book on purpose, or was I not guilty because reading the scenes occurred in the context of the story?" He ending up confessing this transgression and became nervous about what he might decide to read or not read in the future. He agreed to reread the book and resist confessing similar "gray area" concerns in the future.

While in confession, he told the priest in great detail what he had done wrong in order to make sure he was given the appropriate penance. Luke started repeating himself, just in case the priest had been distracted while he was confessing. The priest interrupted him and ended the confession.[14] Luke was upset and doubted whether he was in a worthy state to receive Communion. He was tempted to leave, but decided to act in faith and completed the sacrament.

Luke's OCD disrupted the rhythm of college life. He did manage to keep playing football and maintain grades to keep the scholarship. The support of family, friends, teammates, clergy, and therapy helped Luke not feel "weird" about having OCD, which helped him also maintain a social life, even if he didn't go to blowout parties.

Salima

Salima worked in the office of a software company. Her prayers began taking longer and cut into her work time. She started getting to work late because her morning prayers were taking too long. When she got home, the OCD started affecting how she cooked dinner, and she kept her hungry family waiting until she felt it was properly prepared. Shopping, household chores, and even socializing were more work than pleasure, and she looked for ways of getting around doing them.

Salima's treatment began with grocery shopping. Salima avoided shopping and preparing meals because of her obsessive fear of breaking religious law. She understood the need to trust that the stores she shopped in were compliant with the Islamic dietary laws. She made a list and selected items to put in her cart without checking them. She agreed to limit how many frozen meals to buy as a way to keep to the treatment plan of preparing her own meals, which was her goal. When she got home, she put away food and nonperishables without cleaning them.

Like almost all people with scrupulosity, feeling good was difficult to tolerate. Feeling good caught her off guard and caused her to feel bad. She knew this was irrational, but to her, letting that guard down meant she was being negligent. Instead of compensating for this "lapse" in mental rituals, she decided to stay focused on and involved in the source of the enjoyment. She knew the obsessive fear might start in on her again later, so she prepared herself to stay strong (see Table 9.2).

Moving up to preparing meals, Salima decided to set a weekly menu and stuck to cooking the meal planned for the day. This helped her stay on track, because obsessive doubt would tempt her to change her mind about the meal's being *halal*. She stopped ordering food online for delivery. She and her family agreed not to eat out until she and I agreed that enough progress had been made that doing so would be out of enjoyment, and not as an OCD avoidance behavior. Within a month, Salima was rewarded with being able to make a reservation at her favorite restaurant. She and her family celebrated her success at eliminating the food and meal rituals and resumed enjoying the times shared around meals.

Her imam helped get the OCD out of her praying behaviors. On Fridays, the special prayer day of the week, and as often as she could manage, her imam recommended that she pray at the mosque as a way to keep pace with the other women in prayer. Praying with the community would help her feel more connected to her faith and less obsessive when practicing praying by herself. He reviewed the rules about *wudu* and set limits about performing the washing rituals and how long it should take, and she agreed to use a timer to keep track of the time. Praying five times a day gave her a lot of practice, and there were many times she had trouble sticking to the plan. Her imam agreed to meet with her weekly to help support the behavioral plan and get her back to being a spiritually functional Muslim.

The OCD involved in Ramadan was harder to treat, because it is occurred only once a year. Special preparation would be necessary to set guidelines that complied with both her religious and treatment interests. Firstly, Salima's OCD convinced her that swallowing was breaking her fast, even though this is religiously allowed. She agreed not to carry tissues on her and not to put extra tissue boxes around the house. Her imam instructed her to do no more or less than what was expected of other Muslim women, as well as maintaining therapy sessions during Ramadan as much as possible. She agreed to let family members help out to ease the heavy sense of responsibility she felt for keeping the sanctity of everyone's religious standing.

TABLE 9.2 Salima

SUDS	Triggering Situation	Obsessive Fear	Ritual	Exposure	Response Prevention
100	Performing *wudu*	Not being clean enough; offending Allah; not following the proper order	Excessive rinsing; repeating rinsing when unsure; following perfect order and going back if was distracted/had an obsession	Perform *wudu* as taught; keep moving through steps	Resist rewashing/ going back over doubted areas; expect to not feel right
100	Fasting for Ramadan	Performing sacrilege by swallowing anything; dishonoring Allah	Excessive spitting and wiping mouth off with tissues	Swallow saliva normally	No purchasing extra supply of tissue boxes; don't keep tissues in purse, pockets, up sleeve, etc.
95	Preparing meals during Ramadan for breaking fast	Food isn't *halal*; not enough food for everyone	Overbuying food quantities; excessive checking, cleaning	Shop for food casually (okay to shop in *halal* store); put food and items away fluidly	Resist label checking; resist checking food and items before putting them away
90	Praying	Forgetting/ skipping something/losing place; prayer mat soiled; being disrespectful; not having the right mindset for prayer; not being sincere in prayer	Repeating prayers; excessive amount of time cleaning mat; waiting for that *just right* feeling to begin prayers	Reduce prayer time to 10–15 minutes; pray at mosque and keep time with the others; pray even if have not achieved "right" mindset	Focus on fluid motions; keep moving through steps prayer even when you don't feel you have "finished" each of them completely
75	Having fun	Getting away with something; something bad will happen to self or family	Saying punitive mental rituals for being careless	Interact socially; go to movies; spend time doing favorite leisure activities; put these in a schedule	Engage in these activities even when you don't feel like it; keep commitments to people with whom you have plans
75	Grocery shopping and preparing daily meals	Food is *haram*; countertops are religiously unclean; will cause family and herself to be religiously unclean	Visually checking items before buying them/using them; buying frozen dinners; eating at *halal* restaurants; ordering groceries online/having it delivered; washing/wiping/ cleaning food; overcooking	Shop for food casually (okay to shop in *halal* store); put food and items away fluidly; make weekly menu and stick to it	Resist label checking; resist checking food and items before putting them away; don't change menu or throw food away because of obsessive doubt

Leah

We know that Leah's scrupulosity started in high school. Now a wife and mother, Leah came for treatment in the summer because Yom Kippur was in September, six weeks away. She felt guilty that the holiday was causing her so much distress: Having had OCD for some years now, she anticipated it with dread. Although there was some time pressure to get to the top of her hierarchy, we were able to start at the moderately difficult level of her contamination and kosher obsessive fears (see Table 9.3).

I could tell Leah was a compulsive hand washer because she bore the telltale sign of looking as if she had scrubbed for surgery. She looked as if she waere wearing gloves because of how the red chappedness ended at her wrists, after which her normal skin color began. To get a sense of how often she washed her hands, Leah agreed to keep a log of how many compulsive hand washes she performed during the next week. At our next session, she logged an average of about 20 per day and stated that this was less than usual: Keeping track made her more aware of her urges, allowing her to resist some of them.

Because handwashing rituals ran through many daily tasks, her exposure was designed to target this behavior rather than moving through the specific situations. We reviewed when and how hand washes were done legitimately for religious and functional purposes. Leah wanted to negotiate the hand washing plan—how long, how many times, what it my hands are greasy . . . *oy veh*. Compromising with OCD leads to one negotiation after another and is a form of control and avoidance. After having this explained, she agreed to follow the guidelines we set up together for addressing her contamination, fear of breaking kosher laws, and prayer obsessions. This meant having to tolerate feeling impure, unclean, and imperfect.

Because compulsive apologizing and reassurance seeking is a regular behavior, Leah agreed that working on this aspect of her OCD would help her be better prepared for *Yom Kippur*. She kept track of the number of times she of times she acted on the urges *and* the number of times she resisted. Her family was instructed to not respond to her compulsive apologies and not to answer her obsessive questions. They were allowed to validate her anxiety and support her effort to stick with her ERP plan by suggesting that she "let it go" as code for "You're ritualizing now, aren't you? Hang in there!" This was frustrating for her, but effective. After getting control over these symptoms, her apologies became more sincere, and people took them more to heart. By the time Yom Kippur came, even though she still felt anxious about her responsibilities, she was much less bothered by doubting thoughts about not having addressed interpersonal mistakes she thought she had made.

Treatment for the contamination obsessions preceded the *traif* (unkosher) obsessions. Germs were easier to combat than sins. We set up the course for exposure work, starting with touching surfaces inside and outside of home,

TABLE 9.3 Leah

SUDS	Triggering Situation	Obsessive Fear	Ritual	Exposure	Response Prevention
100	Mikvah	Will contaminate the pure water	Excessive checking for extraneous body remnants; excessive washing/rinsing; reassurance seeking from the attendant	Make preparations under the supervision of the attendant; move fluidly through the steps, being mindful of the time[1]	Don't argue about the rules; trust her direction without seeking reassurance before and after; resist body checking after each step; adhere to the time limit
90	Fasting and seeking forgiveness on Yom Kippur	Breaking the fast and being unholy; not being forgiven	General vigilance; excessive apologizing/reassurance seeking	Be around food during fast; help cook the breaking fast meal; refrain from apologizing because already did it in the past when it happened	Don't avoid being around food; don't check food for evidence that bites were taken; don't ask reassuring questions from the women you are helping; don't seek reassurance from people to whom you have already apologized; no new "doubtful" apologies
75	Preparing food	Will contaminate the food with germs; will contaminate food by mistakenly mixing meat and dairy cookware	Repeated hand washing; checking to make sure using the right cookware and utensils; rewash everything again separately	Wash hands only before cooking; trust how items have already been separated and use them in spite of doubt	No extra hand washes; no checking cookware; use cookware even with obsessive doubt; no asking others for reassurance
75	Grocery shopping	Buying nonkosher items; touching *traif* items	Excessive label checking; hand washing	Put items regularly bought into cart without label checking; okay to look for kosher symbol once; assume touched something *traif*	Put items in cart with label down; out them away at home without checking and with labels facing toward the back; no hand washing
75	Praying	Not having right mindset/ *kavanah*; imperfect prayers	Stay stuck in place until achieve right feeling	Approach prayer spontaneously; move forward in prayer in spite of doubt about *kavanah*	No repeating portion of prayer if triggered; no mental reviewing of prayer after finished

SUDS	Triggering Situation	Obsessive Fear	Ritual	Exposure	Response Prevention
70	Coming back home	Germ contamination; house isn't kosher	Remove shoes; wash hands; wash hands; wipe down purse and keep if in special/ safe spot; wipe down anything new	While out, touch germy and unkosher things; keep shoes on and walk through the house; place purse on surfaces around the house	Don't clean/wash contaminated areas in the house; don't vacuum where walked with shoes on; don't wipe purse off
70	Cleaning the house	Germ contamination; spread nonkosher dust	Avoid cleaning; excessively clean until surfaces are perfect; check to make sure done properly; wash hands when triggered	Wipe dust off living room table, then use towel and wipe it on surfaces around the house	Leave areas dusty; no reassurance seeking or asking someone else to dust or clean
65	Cleaning up after meals	Mixing meat and dairy kitchenware	Rerun the dishwashers; hide items in the basement; throw items away; wash hands between steps	Put items in dishwasher and put them away once	No looking at items until certain what category they are; no asking others to look for you or asking them to put them away

[1] Total time needed to prepare1 hour and 10 minutes to 1 hour and 42 minutes—see more at http://mikvah.org/article/ocd_mikvah_preparation_checklist#sthash.P4kisBqP.dpuf. This checklist has also been approved for women who have OCD by Dr. Baruch Trappler, a psychiatrist and a renowned expert in trauma research.

not washing her hands and cross-contaminating the germs thoroughly around the house. She understood the concept of having *one world* instead of keeping track and separating "clean" and "dirty."

Like many others who have followed this exposure plan, she felt relief from not having to be controlled by the OCD contamination system. Family members also felt relief from the OCD rules, and the atmosphere in the household became more relaxed.

When we moved on to her obsessive fear of buying nonkosher food, Leah shopped at a different supermarket, but one that carried the same items Leah was used to buying. When she found the items on her list, she took the first one off the shelf and put it in her cart without looking for the kosher symbol. In keeping with the contamination plan, she unpacked the items in the kitchen without checking or cleaning them off.

Leah did not need much of a plan for cooking, because the gains she had already made from treatment generalized to this task. She did have obsessive thoughts about meat and dairy items' being mixed up, but she was willing to take the chance.

Perfectionistic praying is difficult to change, because it feels sacrilegious. Leah was afraid she would just be going through the motions if she did not have the right mindset. The other problem, of course, was feeling guilty for having obsessions while praying. We reviewed the guidelines for normal prayers. She identified what prayers she would say, when they should occur, how they are to be said, and for how long. When we consulted her rabbi, he posed this question about doubt and certainty: How wet is wet? What he meant was to sum up the unending nature of questions that have no answer. He advised her to adhere to the behavioral principles of ERP by letting the obsessions happen but keeping going. He reminded her that everyone has other thoughts while praying and that the intention of the spirit was what was essential.

Leah had already had several menstrual cycles by the time she was ready to tackle the challenge of getting the OCD out of this sacred religious ritual. Over the months, as she anticipated going to the mikvah, we had discussed several modifications she could make in reducing the time she spent on certain preparations. Instead of cutting her nails at home, she would cut and scrub them at the mikvah house. If something caught her eye that needed more attention, she would do so. She would trust the attendant's overall approval for being ready. Other steps were carried out in the same manner, transferring aspects of the preparation from home to the mikvah house, allowing the attendant to lead her to the water without pointing out "imperfect" details. Because the mikvah is not a daily practice, it took many months for the behavioral changes to become easier. Her perfectionistic urges continued to drive her wish to fix "just one more thing," but with the help of the attendant and treatment, she was able to resist acting on them. Her thoughts and feelings began to shift from dread and fear to the purpose of the mikvah, which was to be spiritually renewed.

Rani

Rani's spiritual contamination fears about bringing impurity into the household from outside were similar to Leah's and were treated accordingly. What was different for Rani was her fear of bad karma. As with most fears about death and the unknown, there is no proof about, if any, afterlife and what the outcome might be. Karma refers to intentional moral actions that affect one's station in this and next lives. The law of karma says that all of life is governed by a system of cause and effect, action and reaction, in which one's deeds have corresponding effects on the future. Western culture's version of this is "what goes around comes around." Needless to say, OCD exploited Rani's obsessive conscience as she questioned the morality of every move she made. Her religious life became secondary to her obsessive fears, and her concern for spiritual perfection overrode her ability to recognize all the other healthy and life-affirming aspects of her faith (see Table 9.4).

TABLE 9.4 Rani

SUDS	Triggering Situation	Obsessive Fear	Ritual	Exposure	Response Prevention
100	Morning cleansing ritual	Not pure enough to pray; creating bad karma; being regressed and punished in the next life	Slow/thorough wash until feels *right*	Use appropriate allotted amount of water and time; expect to not feel right	Stick with the time limit no matter the anxiety level or obsessive fear that not pure enough for prayer
90	Praying/ meditating	Spiritual contamination; imperfect praying; prayers won't count; having obsessions while meditating is failing at the practice; creating bad karma; being regressed and punished in the next life	Wait for right feeling; mental prayer rituals for almost every action taken; stuck in or avoid meditation due to obsessions	Recite prayer according to regular practice; use prayers only for appropriate purposes according to the list; practice meditating and allow obsessions to run their course	Don't repeat or go back when triggered; stop the prayer when the timer goes off; skip urge to pray if situation is not on the list; resist urges to dwell on obsession and let it pass
75	Fasting	Spiritual contamination; creating bad karma; being regressed and punished in the next life	Start fasting earlier than necessary	Begin fast along with others; drink water and take medication	Spiritual contamination
70	Grocery shopping	Buying food contaminated by meat; offending gods; creating bad karma; being regressed and punished in the next life	Avoids buying it; clean the kitchen before cooking in case trace of meat was there from before; checks items for red spots or streaks before buying	Put food away in normalized manner; make food even though unsure if contaminated	Don't wash food or surfaces when cooking; don't check for spots or streaks; don't "warn" family or seek reassurance
70	Coming inside the house	Spiritual contamination and creating bad karma; being regressed and punished in the next life	Family leaves shoes outside; changes clothes in mudroom and puts clothes in laundry before going into rest of the house; cleans, washes items brought into house	Everyone to keep shoes on and walk through the house; keep same clothes on; immediately cross-contaminate entire house; let impurity settle in	Don't clean/wash contaminated areas in the house; don't vacuum where walked with shoes on; no hand washing after getting home

Because the principle of karma extends to the very minutiae of life, Rani's insight during this episode was only fair. In rational discussions, she admitted that her fears were excessive, but she could also argue about their validity. To help improve her flexibility and not selectively focus on only one aspect of her religion, Rani was willing to take a step back by teaching me about the four broader values of living a good Hindu life. *Dharma* is the fulfillment of one's life purpose; a*rtha* is the goal of prosperity; *kama* is the pursuit of pleasure and desire through sexuality and enjoyment; and *moksha* enlightenment through transcendence. It is interesting that as a religion, Hinduism explicitly states that pleasure and desire are important factors that add to the meaning and quality of life. It was going to be a challenge for Rani to accept that pleasure, anathema to scrupulosity, was going to have to become a routine part of her lifestyle!

First, the OCD rules set for her and the family were no longer valid. Everyone was to return to normal functioning. Rani did not like this, but the option of trying to control others was no longer available. After people came and went as they usually did, Rani had to give up trying to keep track of what was and wasn't clean. Rani's prayers, meditations, and fasts and were next. Because of the frequency of prayers, Rani wanted to reclaim the time she needlessly spent on them. It was easy for her to agree in theory but harder when she was actually doing them. We broke them down into singular steps and made a hierarchy for the order in which she would conduct them as ERPs.

Fasting is considered a form of self-discipline to purify the body and soul and is an act of sacrifice. Unlike people she knows, Rani fasts according to the 24-hour traditional fast practice and abstains from all food and drink. The rules of fasting have changed over time, and people can now occasionally drink milk or water. She said that she would be open to following what her family and friends did, but they were not consistent. Her decision to fast the same way she had been doing all along, because she still felt it was the right way for her, was respected.

Lisa

Attending events outside of the Mormon community was rare, but Lisa wanted to feel more comfortable during them. Her husband has a leadership position in the church, so she felt some pressure to make sure her behavior was impeccable. Her husband teasingly assured her that if she wasn't already a good person, then he wouldn't have married her, but she still worried about making mistakes that would reflect badly on herself and her family (see Table 9.5).

In order for Lisa to be able to work on being more at ease around alcohol, she and her husband had a date night and went out to eat at a pub. It was loud and servers glided through the dining room with drinks on their trays. Lisa

TABLE 9.5   Lisa

SUDS	Triggering Situation	Obsessive Fear	Ritual	Exposure	Response Prevention
90	Having the *right* food in the house	House will not comply with food recommended in *The Word of Wisdom*; forgetting what foods are safe to have in house	Label checking; checking *The Word of Wisdom* for certainty	Shop somewhere new; choose items fluidly	No label checking or looking in The Word of Wisdom for reassurance; no asking others whether food purchased is okay
85	Having enough food in the house	Won't have enough food when it is needed	Hoarding	Make list of what is needed for the week and stick to buying *only* what is on the list	Refrain from adding to the list at the store because *forgot* to write it down
75	Being thrifty enough	Being wasteful	Hoarding; excessive coupon clipping	Shop without coupons	Reduce time spent and amount of coupon clipping; buy one when two-for-one sale
70	Fasting	Breaking the fast; cheating	Abstains from food/drink the entire day	Eat when food is served to family	Don't avoid by "not feeling hungry"
60	Being at a party where alcohol is served	Violating the Mormon code of conduct; being contaminated with vice	Avoid/keep distance from people with drinks; create distance between self and others dining at the same table	Attend invited events; go out to eat where alcohol served; order something to drink directly at the bar	No checking/ smelling clothes, hands; no asking anybody whether they smell alcohol on you; put clothes in laundry with other clothes and wash them all together

kept breathing instead of waiting for them to pass out of her safety zone. Her anxiety level reached a 90 during those moments, and she gave her husband panicked looks. His response was to take in a huge breath of air into his belly so that he would also be contaminated. They laughed, talked, ate, tipped the server, and went home. Lisa kept the clothes she wore on her dresser and in the morning cross-contaminated them to her other clothes. She also made visits to liquor stores and casually picked up bottles and read the labels.

Food issues were next on the list to tackle. On fast days, Lisa ate with her family. This exposure was straightforward enough. Food shopping and storage were more challenging symptoms, because these were behaviors passed down from her mother. In hindsight, Lisa realized that her mother may have had OCD but that it hadn't seemed to take over her mother's life. Lisa had trouble reconciling the idea that changing her behavior meant "rejecting" her mother's ways. This was an emotional hurdle, and she had trouble complying with the exposure plan.

She did agree to cut down on clipping coupons by putting ads in the recycling bin and to stop the ritual of going online to find bargains for the items on her list. She was allowed to use the ones she already had and then get rid of the little accordion coupon organizer she had kept them in. The buy-one-get-one-free offers were difficult to resist, and on several occasions, she gave in. The reduction in the quantity of food made for a noticeably positive difference in the family budget. Although she felt guilty about the lack of input into her storage supply, she realized that she still held the value of being thrifty, just in a different way.

The exposure for fear of not having the *right* food in the house was similar to Leah's. Lisa agreed to rely on her own judgment about what the appropriate food was to have in the house and not check the Word of Wisdom website beforehand. She shopped in a different store and did not necessarily buy the same brand of items there. After a few months, Lisa enjoyed going back to shopping at her favorite store and not having her OCD rituals make her time there so agonizing. She stopped tracking things that came into the house and stuck to a normal cleaning schedule.

Moralosity

Obsessive fear of offending someone or "lying" in conversations by not saying thoughts with the right/perfect words, intent, or sentiment is one of the most common symptoms people with OCD have. Many people also have a general feeling of anxiety in social situations that constrict their spontaneity and comfort in being themselves out of fear of negative judgment by others. Most of the people included in this book have had these fears and, to avoid repetition, are described by Kurt's situation.

Kurt

After assessing Kurt's OCD, I explained to him the aspects of moralosity and perfectionism. He understood that his obsessions drove him to "analysis paralysis" and that committing to any decision was going to feel wrong. Kurt was a natural and deep thinker. OCD turned his wisdom against him and caused him to doubt things he already knew in his core being. His judgment was skewed and too literal. He took everything, including himself, too seriously (see Table 9.6). He gave me feedback about being insensitive and uninterested in his take on things. It was true that I did not want to get into specifics about existential matters, even though it was tempting, and that is what I told him. I also told him spending more precious time going over these timeless issues would keep him stuck. He gave me the "evil eye," then conceded.

To free up his thoughts, emotions, and body, I recommended that he start hanging out with friends again. Yes, they were superficial and boring, but they

TABLE 9.6   Kurt

SUDS	Triggering Situation	Obsessive Fear	Ritual	Exposure	Response Prevention
100	Thinking about the meaning of life; is there a God; is there an afterlife; having conflicting information; being uncertain	Believing in "nothingness"; believing everything matters; not figuring things out before death; possibility of going to hell	Reading/looking up existential philosophy; analyzing conflicting beliefs; grilling others about their beliefs; discounting own beliefs	Write out obsessive scenarios; spend a week assuming there is a God; same for no God; same for an afterlife; no afterlife; live with uncertainty	Stop collecting/ reading/ checking/ asking for more information; don't think reassuring thoughts
95	Deciding what to do	Making the wrong decision; wasting time	Mentally review all the options; avoid deciding; go back to bed	Make decision based on what you *want* to do and stick with it; accept uncertainty about it being the *right* decision; follow through on it	Resist analyzing the decision; put decision into motion step by step; don't second-guess while taking each step; be spontaneous
90	Wanting to buy a video game	Wasting money; giving into gratifying urges	Avoidance	Decide on the video game you want to have and where you will buy it	No second-guessing whether made the right choice; no procrastinating by price comparing
85	Wanting to play a video game	Being selfish, indulgent, childish	Avoidance	Play video game that same day and everyday	Stick to commitment and not put it off; okay to enjoy it; no punishing self
75	Having or hearing a conversation	Inaccuracy; say something wrong; say something hurtful	Think the perfect words before speaking; make verbal corrections if it didn't feel right, or if think someone didn't get the idea; hearing someone say something inaccurate; avoid conversations or talking	Be spontaneous in conversation; say something innocently untrue about yourself; make mistakes; be a good listener by focusing on the topic	Don't correct what you said to people or in your head; don't seek reassurance or confess about the "lie"; don't correct others' mistakes

were also spontaneous and funny. He would sit with family and get involved in conversations. Let inaccuracies go—both of grammar and of "facts." Give opinion without censoring. Tell little white lies.

Decide on a video game to buy, including where and when to purchase it. It was okay to go with someone if he needed support. He should install the game and play it by the next day for at least 10 to 15 minutes (or longer), but not on end. He should play the game daily for 15 to 30 minutes, letting himself enjoy it. He should let worries about wasting time be there and keep going, as well as thinking about what other "timewasting" and enjoyable things he might be willing to do. He should then plan to do one of those things within a few days, resisting self-punishing rituals for wasting time and having fun.

The last phase of Kurt's exposures would be writing out his obsessive scenarios: Everything matters, nothing matters, wasting time matters and I waste enough, wasting time doesn't matter and I could have enjoyed myself; there is a God, there is no God; there is an afterlife, there is no afterlife. He would exhaust all possible feared consequences. After doing so, he was still bothered by existential uncertainties and not having a clue what the meaning of life was, at least for now. He did set a goal for accepting the uncertainty and to become more flexible in his thinking.

Priah

Priah's exposure work started with not pushing the spontaneous death obsessions away. She could have the thoughts and tell herself that having them meant she was a bad person. Naturally, this is an upsetting experience; anyone might feel guilty about doing this. The good news is that just as with other OCD symptoms, Priah began to feel some distance between herself and the thoughts. She even said to herself, "I am the master of death and my thoughts will get rid of anyone I don't like." Priah lost her grandmother when she was eight years old. She remembered the sadness of losing her, but especially the open grieving of her family. This experience sensitized her to death and, of course, is what the OCD gave her as symptoms. Her sense of guilt about her thoughts, and especially about "wishing" death on purpose, required many discussions about how obsessive guilt was another trick OCD used to stay in control (see Table 9.7).

We worked out a plan that went according to a pace that Priah considered manageable. As described in her hierarchy, she exposed herself in graduated steps to watch, write, and think about death and about the things that reminded her of it that she had avoided. In stepwise fashion, she drove by local cemeteries, parked and stayed in the cemetery until the anxiety came down, walked around in them, read headstones, touched headstones, and walked on grave sites. She told herself while breathing in, "whenever I see a hearse, drive by a cemetery, or a funeral home, someone will die."

Many tears were shed for these exposures, and they were emotionally exhausting. There was no need to rush through the steps, and she took the time necessary to habituate to one before moving on to the next. Priah's treatment took about a year to complete, with monthly maintenance sessions thereafter.

TABLE 9.7   Priah

SUDS	Triggering Situation	Obsessive Fear	Ritual	Exposure	Response Prevention
95	Driving by a cemetery or funeral home; seeing a hearse while driving	Loved one will die, get sick, have an accident; being negligent/ uncaring	Hold breath; think good thought; call/ text family; avoid looking	Drive to local cemeteries, funeral homes; let death obsessions happen; write imaginary scripts about causing loved ones to die	Breathe in death; don't avert eyes; no mental ritualizing by having good thoughts; stay focused on obsession during script writing; don't use distraction to avoid anxiety or emotions
90	Watching television or movie and seeing death-related triggers	Loved one will die, get sick, have an accident; being negligent/ uncaring	Hold breath; think good thought; call/ text family	Watch/read triggering shows/movies/ books/articles, etc.; write down death-related words; make recording of "my family will die and it will be my fault"	Don't fix thoughts/images
85	Spontaneous death thoughts	Having the thoughts means wishing it happens	Push thoughts away; think good thoughts; call family to check they are okay	Repeat death thoughts; keep death thoughts in mind; wish for death; tell self only bad people have these thoughts	Resist calling family for reassurance; no thinking self-reassuring thoughts

Carl

Carl considered disorder a character flaw. He determined that if things weren't perfect, he was slacking. When things weren't arranged perfectly at home, he took it as a personal insult that nobody cared enough to make the effort to keep things in order. He admitted to being controlling, but he could not stand being around what he considered chaos. Even when people did make the effort to make things neat, he fixed what they had done so that they were perfect. He got upset when someone took out a magazine or needed a paper and messed up the stacks that he had so carefully arranged. Rationally, he knew that his behavior was extreme, and that it wasn't fair to his family to expect them to abide by such perfectionistic standards (see Table 9.8). When he agreed to start leaving things the way they were, he explained to his family about the plan and told them that they no longer had to modify their behavior according to the OCD rules. He explained that he might have some bad days when he would

TABLE 9.8   Carl

SUDS	Triggering Situation	Obsessive Fear	Ritual	Exposure	Response Prevention
90	Working on cars	Making a fatal mistake; wasn't careful enough because of laziness	Checking work; tightening bolts; asking others to check work; explaining to customers what was done	Get job done in normal timely manner; trust your skills	Don't check or second guess what was already completed; don't ask others to look at your work; no contact with customers except to say hello; keep going in spite of doubt
90	Having guests over	Order is disrupted in the house	Avoid having people over; put things back perfectly after people visiting family leave	Invite people over; engage in conversation	Don't track what they touch or handle; leave things the way they were when they left
90	Clutter; mail/ papers/ newspapers left around; messiness	No fear but annoyance at imperfection; visually offensive; people don't have good values; things being messy are mistakes	Demand that family arrange things the way you like them; align/square off stack of papers	Put things out of order around the house and leave them that way; tell family about exposure so they can live normally	Resist urges to straighten, or tell others to straighten things
80	Taking care of personal business: bills, mail, financial reports, leaving voice mails, sending emails	Making mistakes; not being perfect; being negatively judged	Check for mistakes until feel "sure"	Pay bills and cover what you filled out on the check as you go along; make mistakes on emails/voice mails	No checking that information is correct; no resending email to explain/clarify, same with voice mails

give into temptation to fix things, be irritable, and ask them to ritualize for him. His family praised his effort at changing his rigid behavior, but especially for wanting the atmosphere in the house to be more friendly and relaxed, and possibly having better interactions with him. No one changes over night, they were warned, but they all agreed to do what they could to help.

Carl's wife took responsibility for paying the bills and taking care of family finances, because Carl took so long to finish the tasks that they ended up paying finance charges because they were sent in late. Carl brought bills to the session, and we set out to get them done. We used a piece of paper to block each item after he filled it out on the checks. He was not allowed to look at them when they were finished. I flipped the checks over while he took out the envelopes to put them in directly without checking them. We did the same blocking technique for addressing the envelopes, then found a mailbox that he put the envelopes in, again, without checking. The whole process took fifteen minutes. He was initially upset, and I knew he was angry at me while we went through the process, but then he felt relief that the bills were paid on time, that they were now out of his hands.

Work was more challenging, because the problem there was not one of aesthetics, but of his obsessions—life and death. One mistake could cause a fatal accident. Because I don't know anything about the technical aspects of car repair, Carl agreed to use the standards his fellow mechanics follow to set the behavioral norm. He described in general what he was working on and what his typical jobs involved. He identified what his rituals were for his safety obsessions and worked out the steps he would take to decrease, then eliminate them. He would not ask his co-workers to check his work or seek reassurance by asking them how they would perform the task as a way of checking that he had done it right. He would no longer greet the customers and tell them everything he did as a way of "confessing" and as a ritualistic way of transferring responsibility to them now that they knew what was done.

Carl's work performance improved, and he was more productive than ever. His sense of humor returned on the job and at home. He took pride in what he did but was not prideful. He still pressed his work uniforms to look nice, but that was by choice, not perfectionistic obligation.

Misha

Misha was very proper. His hair was cut short and slicked back, his shirt was tucked in, his pants were perfectly pleated, and he was very polite. He was raised in a strict conservative household and had little patience for pity. It was painful meeting with him, because in his culture, psychiatry and mental illness were considered indulgent—and only weak people took advantage of treatment. He made it very clear that he was *not* going to take medication and that he was going to get his OCD symptoms under control by sheer force of will (see Table 9.9).

I asked him and his wife to sit down. He said he only came in because his wife insisted that he talk to someone about the stress his behavior was causing in the household. I could tell he didn't want to be there or talk about his symptoms. After a half hour, we agreed for his wife to have a seat in the hall and to wait until Misha and I had a chance to talk in private. He reiterated his position that, yes, there were something going on but he was already doing better. He said that he tried not to think about the things that bothered him and that he was managing. He did not want to make another appointment, as because he felt he knew what to do, but that it had been nice meeting me—I was a nice lady. When he opened the door, his wife stood up and asked how it went. We

TABLE 9.9   Misha

SUDS	Triggering Situation	Obsessive Fear	Ritual	Exposure	Response Prevention
100	Being around women	Getting them pregnant	Avoid going out in public; handwash 15–20 times/day; extra showers	Go to public places and sit as many places possible	No wearing extra layers of clothing; no checking or wiping where sat
95	Bathroom—fear of semen/feces/urine on self/clothes	Contamination; being lustful	Wash/change clothes if unsure	Use bathroom/masturbate; cross-contaminate around house	No washing cleaning beyond normal behavior
90	Laundry—fear of touching dirty clothes	Contamination	Hand wash, rewash clothes wearing gloves	Wash contaminated clothing in with the other laundry; put all clothes away together	Don't separate "clean/dirty" clothes; wear all contaminated clothes every day before wearing clean clothes; don't change clothes during the day
90	Harming thoughts while around children, people in general	Caused harm without knowing it	Fix "bad" thoughts with "good" ones; avoid children; go back and check area where triggered	Go to children's stores/departments at the mall; have obsessive thoughts	Leave without visually or mentally checking
80	Throwing something away while having sharp or harmful item in pocket	Causing harm because threw something sharp or harmful away; being bad person because too lazy to ensure safety by checking until sure	Hand wash; check pockets four times to be sure object is still in there and didn't fall out (staple, pill); count to four while staring at the shape/color of the item, repeat counting to four until feel right stare at it, stare at the shape of it	Throw away "dangerous" items—staples, tacks; leave trash where it is	No counting, checking or removing item from trash; no putting trash out prematurely; no warning/confessing to people
75	Running track when women there	Contaminate them with semen/bodily fluids; being lustful	Avoid them; check mentally/visually that they appear safe	Run where women are; purposely run near women; say hello if appropriate; assume they will become pregnant	No checking or asking reassuring questions

SUDS	Triggering Situation	Obsessive Fear	Ritual	Exposure	Response Prevention
70	Leaving for somewhere or moving from one task to the next	Causing harm	Visual checking to make sure no harm done	Leave/move on while having the obsession that might harm someone; think "so be it"	No checking; no reassuring self or asking someone whether you are a good person; no asking someone to get something from where you left as a subtle reassurance ritual
75	Closing house up for the night	Being responsible for family being harmed	Counting and order of checking: stove, door locks, appliances/plugs; asking someone else to do it	Go to bed without checking and allow obsessive thoughts; write scripts about how you neglected to secure the house and it caught fire/robber came in/family was murdered	No asking someone else to close up the house; no getting up to check; no rationalizing during catastrophic script writing

were speaking to a disappointed face when I said we would hold off for now but that Misha could call me if he changed his mind. Misha had my card and knew how to contact me.

A few months later, Misha called and said he wanted to come in because things didn't really change; in fact they had become worse. We went systematically through his hierarchy and he performed appropriate ERPs for his symptoms.

When it came time to address his fear of impregnating women, Misha stopped wearing layers of extra underwear or shorts under his pants. He casually navigated through women's clothing stores, the gym, running track, and other public places without wiping the seat after getting up or performing other checking behaviors. We joked about how many children he must have by now. Through DNA testing, women would be knocking on his door for child care support, and that it would be only a matter of time before they grew up and tracked down their father. He would have a multitude of grandchildren and his genes would live prolifically on!

Jordan

Stuck standing there, Jordan was breathing rapidly as he repeatedly checked his pockets up and down. He was obsessing about maybe having stolen something from the store without realizing it. He even asked me whether I saw him take anything that he hadn't put in his shopping cart (this is a ritual called reassurance-seeking). Jordan is the last person in the world who would ever act on this obsession, but he was not willing to run the risk of cashing out until he felt sure (see Table 9.10). He "nicely" let a few more people go ahead of him. With much encouragement about moving along in spite of the uncertainty, Jordan put his items on the checkout belt while monitoring his items to make sure the cashier scanned them properly. He worried that if he did not pay attention, the cashier might skip an item that ended up in his cart as a stolen good. He paid and was then coached to not check his pockets or grocery bags despite the strong urges. After a simple but prolonged shopping trip, we finally made it out of the store.

TABLE 9.10   Jordan

SUDS	Triggering Situation	Obsessive Fear	Ritual	Exposure	Response Prevention
100	Driving downtown; around schools	Killing/maiming someone; causing harm	Drive back to triggering spot—repeat until achieve certainty no one hurt; reassurance seeking; checking car for damage, blood; checking whether hit-and-run accident reported by local news		
95	Driving by people running, walking, bike-riding on small roads; neighborhoods	Killing/maiming someone; causing harm	Drive back to triggering spot—repeat until achieve certainty no one hurt; reassurance seeking; checking car for damage, blood; checking whether hit-and-run accident reported by local news		
90	Driving on surface streets	Killing/maiming someone; causing harm	Drive back to triggering spot—repeat until achieve certainty no one hurt; reassurance seeking; checking car for damage, blood; checking whether hit-and-run accident reported by local news		
85	Shopping	Stealing; getting caught; going to jail	Visual checking in store; mental reviewing after leaving; reassurance seeking		
80	Experiencing pleasure; need to suffer because others have so little	Will be punished because didn't fix moral mistakes; will be punished by being deprived of a good life	Avoiding dancing, reading, movies, music, family, friends, shopping, gym, using Facebook		

How is this prideful? Although Jordan truly is a nice man, the center of focus was on himself. He was stuck in place obsessing that he might have mistakenly taken store merchandise and put it in one of his pockets. His real intention in giving way to the other customer was to stall for time to compulsively check his pants and jacket pockets. Jordan was still distressed over the idea that it might be just a matter of time before the police find and arrest him.

While driving home, Jordan told me at our next session, his OCD told him to make sure that he did not hit someone with his car. He had turned around after being on the road and went back to where he was triggered. Nothing was there, but he kept looking. He was late getting home, even though we had ended our session at 2:00 p.m. We drove together under the conditions that spiked his anxiety, with me riding in the back seat so that he couldn't rely on my reactions while he drove by pedestrians and cyclists as reassurance. There were many—pardon the expression—bumps in the road, but with persistence, he was able to get where he had to be, for the most part on time.

Obsessive Guilt

Naomi

Naomi was "a mess," as she described herself when she came to treatment. She wrung her hands and demolished the tissue she had been using to wipe away her tears. She sobbed as she described what happened in the hospital when her father died. She and her coworkers said that she had not been the same since his death. She had always followed hospital and surgery protocols to a T, but now her work was hindered by her being too careful, too detailed, and too thorough, taking too long to get things done. Timing was everything in surgery, and she had kept people waiting (see Table 9.11).

Naomi was referred to a therapist by her hospital employee assistance program for grief work. After making progress, her therapist diagnosed her with OCD and recommended that she see a psychiatrist for medication therapy. Along with medication, her psychiatrist recommended that she seek a behavior therapist who treated OCD with ERP.

A few sessions were spent going over the events of her father's death, the guilt she had for allowing it to happen, and her blaming herself for not stopping it. She said she had come to better terms with all of this in her work with her grief therapist, but she was still afraid of causing harm to other people through negligence. It was taking a toll on her, her work, and her social life. She was isolating from friends and felt that if she allowed herself to have fun, it would mean that she no longer felt sorry for her mistake. She felt that suffering for what happened was at least one way of expressing her sorrow and paying respect to her dad.

TABLE 9.11   Naomi

SUDS	Trigger	Obsessive Fear	Ritual	Exposure	Response Prevention
100	Assisting in surgery	Killing the person; mistakes will be result in death that will be blamed on others; making careless mistakes	Excessive washing; having "right" thought to be able to focus/concentrate; feel emotionally "clean"	Follow normal protocols; think obsessive thought on purpose	Resist checking and seeking reassurance
95	Dressing and scrubbing for surgery	Not being sterile; not washing properly	Change scrubs when not sure they are sterile; being too careful; taking too long; keeping others waiting	Only one set of scrubs allowed—no changing; follow normal protocols; think obsessive thought on purpose	No extra or longer washing/scrubbing
95	Getting tools organized and ready for surgery	Making mistakes and not having appropriate tools ready; not putting them in the right order	Prepare tools ahead of time to make sure they are perfect	Arrive at regular time to make preparations, not early; arrange tools once	No visual checking of tools; no asking others to check
75	Having fun	Being selfish	Restrict favorite food for a week; stay home alone	Make at least one social plan per weekend; spend some time doing relaxing activities	Don't procrastinate or cancel plans; don't avoid leisure—even 10 minutes in the evenings is okay

She reported having some OCD in the past, especially in nursing school. She was perfectionistic about her studies and had very high standards. This is why it was so hard for her to accept having made a mistake.

Over some weeks, we reviewed her OCD symptoms, how they were interfering with her functioning, and what her goals were for getting them under control. We talked about the role of guilt and the extent to which it was obsessive. It took some time for her to understand the difference between healthy and unhealthy guilt, that imposing suffering was contributing to her distress, and that the OCD rules she was setting for how to live would not be normal for others in the same circumstances. Her avoidance of pleasure and fun were not serving any purpose other than keeping her miserable and alone. After this process was achieved, she agreed that hanging on to her symptoms was an inappropriate way of grieving, and that her father would not approve of her doing this on his behalf.

Reconnecting with friends and going out was the first challenge. They had been reaching out to her anyway, so it wasn't hard to make plans. Sticking with the plans she made with friends did not always happen. She just didn't feel like making the effort. Because she was starting a pattern of avoiding and canceling plans, she started inviting people over. Things started to loosen up for her. She had some good laughs and some good cries with the people she trusted.

Getting back to normal working habits took the normal ERP course of identifying, in stepwise fashion, the obsessive fears and behaviors she was willing to work on. Like the treatment of others we have covered, she identified the normal procedures of how to perform her duties and agreed to stick to those. She could follow the behavior of her coworkers as they prepared for surgery. She performed imaginary exposures involving messing up during surgery and causing the deaths of patients. She knew from her years of experience that inevitably some patients would die in surgery. She knew that surgeries were conducted with a team of people, some of whom could mess up, and that assigning blame was a reaction to fear. There could be cases of malpractice, but the probability was extremely low.

She still missed her father, but she was once again the effective and reliable nurse she had always been. She cried because she missed him, but she accepted that his death was natural and that it was his time to go. Her friendships were alive, and she began to enjoy even the smallest everyday things in life.

Stacy

Stacy was a medical doctor which meant that she was smart and successful. This made it hard to challenge her authority, so to speak. She was used to being right and making clinical recommendations to remedy illness. Her symptoms were a little more in line with her values than other types of OCD. She did agree that her fears about being wasteful were taking over the household. Her family complained of finding rotting food in the fridge, tripping over cans and bottles, and there being clutter in places that used to be neat and clean. People also complained that she would get distracted when she saw recyclable or reusable items while being out socially. The worst was going out to eat, when after the meal she would ask to take home the leftovers—anyone's leftovers, no matter how little was left (see Table 9.12).

Although she performed many collecting/saving rituals, Stacy would target the most problematic areas in her treatment. Like many hoarders, she would always think of how things could be reused. The problem was that it would take many lifetimes to use up the amount of things she already had.

Stacy drove to areas she knew would tempt her to stop and pick up bottles. The highway was always littered with five-cent returnable bottles and cans. Stacy told herself that there were probably others who could use the money from collecting them and left them alone. She still felt pangs of guilt that they might just sit there indefinitely, and that she had a responsibility to be a good steward of Earth. She knew there were many other responsible ways she was

TABLE 9.12   Stacy

SUDS	Trigger	Obsessive Fear	Ritual	Exposure	Response Prevention
95	Having green guilt on seeing cans, bottles, or other items in public that could be reused/recycled	Being wasteful; being too lazy to pick them up; ruining the environment	Pick them up, bring them home	Drive through neighborhoods and keep going; bring hoarded items to redemption center or throw them away	Resist stopping and picking up bottles, reusables
85	Food left on plates	Being wasteful	Ask to take food left on others' plates at a restaurant	Leave food on plate	No doggy bags

accomplishing this goal and came to terms with those ways' being enough. She couldn't completely shake her guilt about being wasteful but kept at letting it run its course, which it did—and stopped running her life.

Anne

Like Stacy, the range of Anne's anxiety was narrow and high. Everything she did felt wrong, not right, as well as bad. Her obsessive fear was, she admitted, farfetched. The problem was the inability to prove a negative. Like fear of hitting someone while driving, there is no way to prove something did *not* happen (see Table 9.13).

Anne was going to have to get used to not feeling *right*. The nature of her symptoms made it difficult to conduct exposures that were based in practicality or could be faced directly. She would put herself out in public and let the chips fall regarding where parts of herself might be left to exist without her. She rode the subway, took buses, and went in and out of stores while resisting checking to see whether anything of herself was there. She pictured her lonely soul being somewhere strange and unsafe.

To help her leave things where they were, she adopted the phrase "it doesn't belong to me." It worked as a way to help her not personalize everything in which she came into contact. She still felt mostly unsure and incomplete. The moral contamination feeling told her that someone might take on her personality if they came across a part of her left behind. Although there were aspects of herself that she liked, the traits someone might pick up of hers weren't the nice ones.

Dave

A busy executive, Dave did not have time for his OCD or for treatment. His jobs, relationship, and kids kept his schedule busy and stressful. His partner also worked full-time, but they managed to work out a fair division of

TABLE 9.13 Anne

SUDS	Trigger	Obsessive Fear	Ritual	Exposure	Response Prevention
100	Leaving places	Her soul or part of self will be lost; some cosmic order will be disrupted and will cause harm; feeling guilty from abandoning that part of self	Make list of things she felt part of herself was left on; visual checking before leaving places	Go to public places and leave part of yourself behind on purpose; remind self not complete, that something is missing	Keep going forward and take the risk that something was left behind; let yourself feel "incomplete"
95	Moving from one task to the next	Unsure whether all of self was complete	Repeat behavior four times/series of fours	Leave off/ finish things on uneven numbers	Retrigger obsession when unintentionally used four as mental ritual
90	Seeing things on the ground	Left herself/ anything behind	Made lists; catalogued every item she came in contact with; item she picked up along the way; saved receipts and pieces of paper that had her name on them	Be willing to lose a part of yourself; live with the uncertainty and not knowing whether this happened; write name on pieces of paper and leave them around	
85	Feeling incomplete	Left herself/ anything behind	Checking that didn't lose something material; collecting things considered having an emotional attachment to	Rearrange items in house to create disorder; rearrange things again to create new disorder; go in and out of stores fluidly; put something down and leave it for a few minutes; graduated process of discarding items that had an emotional attachment but are now considered useless	Leave things out of order; pick things up without visually/mentally checking to make sure of what it is

responsibilities. Dave felt guilty about having harming obsessions and how annoying his checking and reassurance-seeking questions were to his partner and kids. He kept promising himself that he would stop doing these rituals and just ignore the thoughts, but that didn't work (see Table 9.14).

TABLE 9.14   Dave

SUDS	Trigger	Obsessive Fear	Ritual	Exposure	Response Prevention
100	Intrusive harming thought	Family hurt/dead	Excessive checking; reassurance-seeking	Think harming thoughts on purpose; wish harm/death on family	No reassuring mental rituals; no seeking reassurance or checking
100	Intrusive harming thought	Might mean them; want them to happen	Reassuring thoughts that are to convince self they aren't true; avoidance of being around people/family because of how strong they are around them		
90	Intrusive harming thought	Being a bad person	Mentally chastises self; overcompensates by people-pleasing		

Dave's exposure consisted of writing out his obsessions in great descriptive detail as if they were really happening. Dave wrote in great length, and in great distress, about his daughter being kidnapped. This type of exposure is very emotional, but it did not consist of anything he hadn't already thought about in his imagination but tried to push away. He also wrote out the phrase "I might be a bad person" over and over while resisting the urge to perform mental rituals. Instead of analyzing whether this was true, he was to focus on the uncertainty. He was instructed to stop every 20 minutes and read the phrase out loud to himself. He also read them aloud in sessions and cried for how badly he felt about having these thoughts.

Dave's conducted this exposure until he had faced all the awful and possible scenarios given to him by his OCD. He wrote them, typed them, and read them out loud. In time, he no longer was afraid of having his obsessions, and was able to cope when he had them. Because he had done the exposures so effectively, the obsessions were much less frequent and intense. When he had them, he let them their course. They no longer interfered with whatever he was doing

Ellen

Many people with contamination, perfectionism, and NJREs end up in a paradoxical situation with their OCD fears. The level of ritualizing becomes so detailed and labor intensive that they simply burn out and avoid dealing with the triggering situations altogether. Their houses are in shambles because they are exhausted. This was the case with Ellen (see Table 9.15).

After a few meetings and some friendly cajoling, she put her fear on the line and agreed to have me visit her house. Just as she described, laundry strewn about, toys and papers lay around, dust settled on the glass end tables in the living room and den, dust bunnies lived in the corners of her floors, and dishes overflowed in the sink. She took me through the three bedrooms, two bathrooms, and the basement. Overall, it was a disorganized mess. Ellen needed help believing that relaxing her standards would get a good—not a perfect or failed—job done, and that this change didn't mean she was betraying her father, or that she was a slob. She agreed good was better than nothing but had lost her sense of knowing what that was.

Even though Ellen's SUDS about doing the laundry was rated as a 90 on the anxiety scale, she wanted to start with this because of the stress is caused in the household. People with OCD find doing laundry especially tedious, because making a mistake in any of the steps that can cause the contamination each

TABLE 9.15   Ellen

SUDS	Trigger	Obsessive Fear	Ritual	Exposure	Response Prevention
100	Anything having had contact with the floor	Being imperfect/ inadequate; being negatively judged by others; being seen as lazy; contamination will spread to self and family	Avoids cleaning because too excessive	Sit on the floor, then sit on all chairs in the house; touch the floor, and cross-contaminate to the rest of the house; touch the floor, then cross-contaminate to skin and hair	Keep wearing the same clothes; don't check for lint or hair on clothes from the floor; leave it wherever you happen to see it; resist washing hands, face, hair
90	Doing laundry	Clothes won't be clean enough	Avoid doing them		
90	Household chores	Won't do them perfectly; will be considered a slob			
90	Having clutter	Imperfection; messiness; making mistakes	Avoid sorting through and discarding things		
80	Making a decision	Making mistakes; not being perfect; being negatively judged by others; making trouble for others	Check for mistakes until feel "sure"		

step of the number of steps involved, all of which can cause the person to start the process all over again, or just avoid it altogether. Because we were conducting the exposure at home together, we would see how she managed doing the laundry and design her daily exposure plan accordingly.

Ellen gathered up the dirty clothes, putting them in the laundry basket, and then into the washer. Ellen poured the normal amount of soap into the cup and then turned the washer on. She resisted checking the setting dials or opening the lid to check that the washer was running and did not perform any pre or post hand washes. After walking away from the washer, we went back to her living room and sat to assess her anxiety. When the washer shut off, she followed the same procedure for putting the clothes in the dryer: no checking or hand washing. Getting the clothes out of the dryer was done without checking for anything she thought she might have left in there. She folded the clothes in a fluid manner, leaving wrinkles alone, and put them away without perfect symmetry/exactness.

Ellen's anxiety ranged from 90 to 60 in an up and down manner. She admitted the exposure was not as bad as she expected and felt confident that she could practice doing it the non-OCD way for homework. Although she still felt somewhat guilty for not having it done perfectly, she was willing to accept that having it done was the better option. It would take some time until the all the clothes around the house were laundered and put away, so Ellen was instructed to do no more *and* no less than what the plan specified (for people without obsessive guilt, doing less is easy, but it is very hard for people with it, who to adjust their morals to accept that getting things done does not have to mean doing them the nth degree or suffering—you can still adhere to the norm *and* be moral).

The relief she felt in opting for *good* then helped her with other tasks such as paying bills, returning emails, and grocery shopping without doing time-consuming and mind-numbing rituals. Her guilt was allayed when she met her goals for herself and her family, albeit imperfectly. Working through the steps even became entertaining as she spoke aloud the feared consequence that previously haunted her conscience: "On no! When my son wears this wrinkled shirt to school, he will be ruthlessly teased about it, all because his mother didn't care enough to iron it!"

OCD is like a mental gambling game that the dealer always wins because it has a tricky deck of cards consisting of anxiety, doubt, fear, and guilt. The best trick you have is to fold your hand and walk away.

Notes

1. Mark Twain, http://www.goodreads.com/quotes/60285-do-the-thing-you-fear-and-the-death-of-fear.

2. Moll et al., "The Neural Basis of Human Moral Cognition": 799–809.

3. Schwartz and Begley, *The Mind and the Brain*, 59.

4. Meyer, "Modification of Expectations in Cases with Obsessional Rituals": 273–280.

5. Rachman, Hodgson, and Marks, "The Treatment of Chronic Obsessive-Compulsive Neurosis": 237–247.

6. Marks, Hodgson, and Rachman, "Treatment of Chronic Obsessive–Compulsive Neurosis": 349–364.

7. Foa and Goldstein, "Continuous Exposure and Complete Response Prevention": 821–829.

8. Wilson, ed., *Principles and Practice of Relapse Prevention*, 32.

9. Ibid.

10. www.ocfoundation.org/treatment_providers.aspx.

11. Steketee and White, *When Once Is Not Enough*, 133–146.

12. Unpublished data.

13. St. Ignatius gives us his famous principle of *agere contra*:

> If the scruple presumes that the incident was a sin, the counselee should presume that it was not a sin.
>
> If the scruple howls for attention, the counselee should give it the utmost contempt.
>
> If the scruple puts out bait for an argument, the patient should adamantly refuse to become involved.
>
> If the scruple makes the patient feel desperate, the patient should remain imperturbable.
>
> If an emotion tricks the patient to an extreme, the patient should trick the emotion back to the mean. If an emotion does anything at all, the patient should do just the opposite.
>
> O'Flaherty, "Therapy for Scrupulosity," 122.

14. On occasion, penitents who have OCD will receive dispensation from their priests to receive Communion without confessing. Performing the sacraments are sacred acts, but the spirit of their meaning becomes lost when they become ritualized acts driven by fear, instead of a heart open to love and grace.

Bibliography

Foa, E. B., and A. Goldstein. "Continuous Exposure and Complete Response Prevention in the Treatment of Obsessive–Compulsive Neurosis." *Behavior Therapy* 9 (1978): 821–829.

Marks, I. M., R. Hodgson, and S. Rachman. "Treatment of Chronic Obsessive–Compulsive Neurosis 2 Years after In Vivo Exposure." *British Journal of Psychiatry* 127 (1975): 349–364.

Meyer, V. "Modification of Expectations in Cases with Obsessional Rituals." *Behaviour Research and Therapy* 4, no. 4 (1966): 273–280.

Moll, Jorge, Roland Zahn, Ricardo de Oliveira-Souza, Frank Krueger, and Jordan Grafman. "The Neural Basis of Human Moral Cognition." *Natures Reviews Neuroscience* 6, no. 10 (2005): 799–809.

O'Flaherty, V. M., SJ. "Therapy for Scrupulosity." In *Direct Psychotherapy: Twenty-Eight American Originals*, ed. R. M. Jurievich, pp. 221–243. Miami, FL: Miami University Press, 1973.

Rachman, S., R. Hodgson, and I. M. Marks. "The Treatment of Chronic Obsessive–Compulsive Neurosis." *Behaviour Research and Therapy* 9 (1971): 237–247.

Schwartz, Jeffery. M., and Sharon Begley. *The Mind and the Brain: Neuroplasticity and the Power of Mental Force*. New York: Harper Collins, 2002.

Shapiro, Leslie J., Christina Gironda, Jason Elias, and S. Evelyn Stewart. "Treatment Outcome of Scrupulosity in Residential Patients Attending a Weekly Psychoeducational/Support Group at the OCD Institute." In *McLean Hospital Research Day*. Belmont, MA: McLean Hospital, 2011.

Steketee, Gail, and Kerrin White. *When Once Is Not Enough: Help for Obsessive–Compulsives*. Oakland, CA: New Harbinger Publications, 1990.

Wilson, Peter H., ed. *Principles and Practice of Relapse Prevention*. New York: Guilford Publications, Inc., 1992.

10

Helpful Treatment Augmentations

Motivation, ambivalence, fear of life without symptoms, and improved quality of life are issues that affect treatment and recovery. In working with patients who never had, or who have lost, functional, social, and vocational skills, these are the prominent themes that must be addressed in treatment. There are several techniques that complement ERP while transitioning from being functionally impaired by symptoms to improving quality of life and preventing relapses. Please note that none of these techniques will produce the effects that are accomplished with ERP.

Continued behavior therapy and exposure and response prevention maintenance is, of course, recommended until you and your therapist agree that the symptoms are under good control. Keep challenging your obsessions by doing the opposite, even if they are just background noise. One patient threw his bread on the kitchen floor every morning before toasting it to stay on top of his contamination symptoms. Some people phase out of treatment by reducing how often the sessions are held. Other people phase out completely over time. And some people prefer monthly or periodic check-in appointments because symptoms can wax and wane according to life events and stress.

The following strategies can help people who have had trouble engaging in ERPs, help expand self-awareness about other thinking, beliefs, and behavior styles beyond OCD. They can help round people out and improve the quality of life and relationships.

Cognitive Therapy

The role of cognitive therapy for OCD is to help people recognize distorted/faulty beliefs that underlie and maintain dysfunctional behavior patterns. In doing so, finding strategies that help patients challenge these underlying thinking styles can help motivate them to do ERP work if it has been avoided.

It also helps to recognize faulty beliefs that developed over time from negative experiences.

Cognitive Domains Specific to OCD

In 1997, several of the world's CBT experts sorted through the types of thoughts and beliefs people with OCD had and identified six specific cognitive domains:[1] perfectionism, inflated responsibility, overestimation of threat, intolerance for uncertainty, overimportance of thoughts, and importance of controlling thoughts. Clinical data showed improvement in overall insight into symptoms, as well as that the obsessive belief in the importance of thoughts and the need to control thoughts became more rational.[2] Understanding which domains apply to your symptoms or thinking style can help you identify ways to change how they are distorted.

We know that perfectionism is a strong trait in people with OCD. Thinking becomes polarized and demands absolute results. When perfect results are expected, but not achieved, people can blame themselves for doing things wrong, or believe that they are just fundamentally bad or lazy. Perfectionism is problematic for people who may not even have a particular obsessive fear but who feel the need to get things "right."

Inflated responsibility is another tricky domain for the obsessive conscience. People feel overly responsible for the outcome of events that have nothing to do with them. They feel guilty if they don't make every effort to prevent any negative consequences, even though there is no actual or imminent presence of danger. Their self-imposed expectations differ from those they have of others.

Obsessive fear also causes sufferers to overestimate levels of threat because of the anxiety they experience in triggering situations. Because certainty cannot be achieved, the default belief becomes: If there's something I *can* do to prevent it, I *should*.

People with OCD have a low threshold for uncertainty. OCD is considered the doubting disease, and the normal doubts we all have seem unbearable for OCD sufferers. The obsessive need for certainty, need to know, need to remember, and need to be sure are not casually dismissed. People have a sense of urgency about their doubts and have trouble waiting to manage them better with more time. Lost is the sense of priority and proportion to the actual doubting situation and whether it needs any attention at all.

The domain of the importance of thoughts and importance of controlling one's thoughts is of special interest for people with an obsessive conscience. People believe that their obsessive thoughts are important because their physiology is telling them so, and because they think the thoughts are abnormal and bad. People also believe that thoughts and actions are the same. People with exaggerated intrusive "bad" thoughts believe that they have sinned if, for example, they have an inappropriate sexual thought. Performing a "good" ritual gives them a sense of having done *something* to make up for it.

Within the importance of thoughts domain there are two subtypes: likelihood and moral thought–action fusion. If people believe that having their obsessions increases the likelihood that their feared consequences will happen, then wanting to prevent them makes sense. People also judge themselves as morally inept because of the nature of their obsessions and feel the need to prove their good moral worth. Rituals seem to be a recourse taken to make things safe and good.

The other last and pertinent domain is the belief that if there is a way to have control over thoughts, every effort should be exerted not to have them. Importance of controlling one's thoughts means that it is possible and obligatory to have complete control over intrusive thoughts, images, and impulses. When this fails, the person tries to make up for having had them by trying even harder, which only makes them stronger.

Evaluating Automatic Thoughts

Evaluating automatic thoughts was established as a fundamental assessment tool in understanding a patient's thinking style. We all distort reality in some way to make sense of it, so there is some truth to some of the conclusions we automatically make about how and why things happen. Getting good at realizing when we are exaggerating or making false assumptions about how someone treated us or why things happen frees us up to consider alternative reasonable explanations.[3, 4]

1. *All-or-nothing thinking* (also called black-and-white, polarized, or dichotomous thinking): You view a situation in only two categories instead of on a continuum; black-or-white, all-or-nothing.
2. *Catastrophizing* (also called fortune-telling): You predict the future negatively without considering other, more likely outcomes. You expect disaster. You notice or hear about a problem and start "what ifs": What if tragedy strikes? What if it happens to you?
3. *Disqualifying or discounting the positive:* You don't take positive experiences, deeds, or qualities into consideration.
4. *Mental filter* (also called selective abstraction): You laser focus attention on one negative detail instead of seeing the whole picture of the situation.
5. *Magnification/minimization:* When you evaluate yourself, another person, or a situation, you unreasonably magnify the negative or minimize the positive. You exaggerate the importance of your problems and shortcomings, or you minimize the importance of your desirable qualities.

6. *Tunnel vision/binocular trick*: You filter out and only see the negative aspects of a situation.

7. *Negative predictions*: Your pessimism based on earlier experiences of failure prematurely or inappropriately predicts failure in a new situation.

8. *Overgeneralization*: You see a single negative event, such as a romantic rejection or a career reversal, as a never-ending pattern of defeat by using words such as "always" or "never." You make a sweeping negative and exaggerated conclusion about the current situation. Or you come to a general conclusion based on a single incident or piece of evidence. If something bad happened once, you expect it to happen that way over and over again.

9. *Mental filter*: You pick out a single negative detail and dwell on it exclusively. You neglect other factors that provide a more realistic context. You assume a constructive comment to be criticism and rule out all the other positive feedback you received. You obsess about this for days and ignore all the positive feedback.

10. *Discounting the positive*: You reject positive experiences by insisting that they "don't count." If you do a good job, you may tell yourself that it wasn't good enough or that anyone could have done it as well as you did.

11. *Jumping to conclusions/ Mind reading/ Fortune-telling*: You interpret things negatively when there are no facts to support your conclusion. Without checking it out, you assume that someone is reacting negatively to you. You predict that things will turn out badly. You believe you know what others are thinking, failing to consider other, more likely possibilities.

12. *Emotional reasoning*: You think something must be true because you automatically "feel" and then believe it strongly, ignoring or discounting evidence to the contrary. If you feel stupid and boring, then you must be stupid and boring. You assume that your negative emotions explain that that's how things really are.

13. *Labeling*: You put a judgmental and subjective label on yourself or others. Labeling does not allow for openmindedness. You may label your self as a "loser" if something didn't go the way you wanted it to. If someone rubs you the wrong way, you tell yourself that he or she is "stupid" and assume that that person is like that all the time. You see him or her as totally bad and rule out the possibility of getting to know the person or understanding that he or she may have been having a bad day.

14. *Personalization*: You believe others are behaving negatively toward you, and you take it personally. You think that everything people do or say has something to do with you instead of having a more general understanding of what is going on. You also compare yourself to others and try to find faults as a way to feel better about yourself.

15. *Mind reading*: You make assumptions about what people are feeling and why they act the way they do based on how you feel about yourself. Your assumptions are taken as truth.

16. *Fallacy of change:* You expect that other people will change to suit you if you just pressure then enough to see your point of view. You need to change people so that they will understand how right you are about things and to consult you about problems.

17. *"Should," "Must," "Ought," and "Have-to" statements (also called imperatives):* You tell yourself that things should be the way you hoped or expected them to be. When you make a mistake you berate yourself because you should have known better or done better. Should statements toward yourself lead to guilt and frustration. Should statements toward others lead to anger and resentment because you think things should be done your way. When you say, "I should, must, ought, or have to," you leave yourself little choice and flexibility. Unnecessary rules and standards get set either by experiences you had growing up or because you think they will motivate you. You feel as if you have failed when you don't live up to them.

18. *Personalization and blame:* Personalization occurs when you hold yourself personally responsible for an event that isn't entirely under your control. You blame yourself as a way to take control of a situation to fix it. Personalization leads to guilt, shame, and feelings of inadequacy. Sometime people might use you as a scapegoat by blaming you for something over which you had no control. You assume that they must be right and feel guilty not to have known. If you blame other people, you don't take responsibility for problems, and you give away your power.

19. *Control fallacies:* You feel externally controlled, see yourself as helpless, and as a victim of fate. You surrender control because you feel at the mercy of the universe. The fallacy of internal control is the belief that you are responsible for whatever happens to everyone around you.

20. *Fallacy of fairness:* You feel resentful because you think things are unfair. You get angry at others when you feel or see an injustice and expect someone to do something about it.

21. *Global labeling:* You generalize one or two qualities into a negative global judgment.

22. *Being right:* You are continually on trial to prove that your opinions and actions are correct. Being wrong is unthinkable and you will go to any length to demonstrate your rightness.

23. *Heaven's reward fallacy:* You expect that all your sacrifices and self-denial will pay off, as if someone were keeping score. You feel righteous and resentful because the reward never comes.

Cognitive Restructuring

Once people get better at identifying their automatic thoughts, cognitive restructuring is a way that helps normalize the assumed negative assumptions that have been made.[5] When a person notices having an automatic thought, he or she looks for evidence that the negative assumption was true. Jane was in a conversation and saw that the other person looked at her watch and noticed that she was personalizing the situation from having the thought: *I must be really boring and she wants to leave.* Jane then generated some alternative and more objective explanations for her friend's action instead of assuming that checking the time meant something about her. Jane considered that her friend may have to be somewhere at a certain time, that her friend just wanted to see what time it was, or that her friend wanted to make the best of the time they had together. Jane also realized that she could ask her whether she was pressed for time or had to be somewhere to check whether there was a reason to have to manage the time. Jane's restructuring her thoughts helped reduce the negative judgments about herself, feel more relaxed while spending time with her friend, and reinforced the ability to reality check her assumptions instead of believing they were true. With OCD, it may be useful for helping people challenge the underlying thinking and beliefs that drive and maintain their obsessions and compulsions, especially what sufferers think about themselves based on their intrusive thoughts.

Constructive Self-talk versus Self-reassurance

People always wonder whether how they talk to themselves while being triggered is a coping strategy or a form of ritualistic self-reassurance. The way to tell the difference is by examining the intention: Are you trying to stay with the anxiety caused by the obsessive fear until you habituate, or are you trying to avoid it? People also ask about the use of "affirmations," thinking good and positive statements repetitively until people are convinced they believe them. They tend not to work because of the idea that they will magically become true, in a way similar to though-action fusion. People with OCD might try to use affirmations by thinking "I am a good person," "Nothing bad can happen," "If I try harder I will be perfect." We know that one of the most reliable methods for change is through action and behavior. Thinking alone is a difficult way of getting motivated.

Constructive self-talk has to ring true and be realistic. Using words such as *always* and *never* keep the false obsessive dichotomy alive. Thinking and being in the gray area of life levels the playing field from trying to force existence at the lonely polar ends of certainty.

But there are many statements that promote flexible thinking:

- I have to live with uncertainty.
- Analyzing my thoughts will only make things worse.
- Unless there is unequivocal evidence of something wrong, I must keep going.

- I know I'm obsessing when my thoughts start with "What if . . ."
- If I'm catastrophizing about something, I can remind myself I will cross that bridge when I get there.
- Having the obsessive need to know is not the same as needing to find something out for realistic reasons. My body and brain may make it seem urgent to know something *now*, but I can delay acting on the urge and decide later whether it is important.
- Whenever I want to avoid something out of obsessive fear, I can prove to myself that the fear is irrational by doing it anyway.
- If it is reasonable for someone else to take the "risk," then I can take it, too.
- My rituals don't keep things safe or serve the purpose I want them to. I can change the way I approach my fears a little at a time until that situation is normal again.
- My family and friends can't really assure me of anything, and when they do, I don't believe them, anyway.
- My obsessions pass when I don't act on the fear. This one will pass, too.

Here are some coping statements I developed for helping manage conscience-related OCD symptoms:

Yourself to Yourself

- My very being and soul is unique. The world loses what I have to offer when I am not being myself. I *have* OCD, but I am *not* my OCD.
- Assume innocence until there is actual evidence of wrongdoing
- I have learned that adhering to social norms protects me and others from acting on destructive urges. They provide safety for me and others. Beyond that, I am free to take creative and curious risks, and originality can lead me to my own brand of creativity.
- Anxiety indicates a challenge, not a danger.
- Maturity requires that I deconstruct negative lessons from authority figures (parents, teachers, coaches, clergy, etc.) that are no longer helpful. I can trust to know the truth when I challenge myself to listen to my instincts about what is right and wrong for me.
- "Mistakes" are lessons from which I learn about how to take the next step toward my goal. They cannot and should not be avoided. They teach me what I need to know about my own process. Every successful person has made mistakes or outright failed. These were the lessons they were given in how to get to the next step.
- If I don't have confidence in myself, no one else will. When I function and interact with people from a place of fear, my fear is what they are getting.

- Validation from others might be nice, but I can't count on it for evidence of my worth. It's like reassurance: It may seem nice, but it never works.
- I may envy what someone else appears to have or how they seem to be— they are probably doing the same thing about me.

Yourself to Other(s)

- Guilt is a negative motivator. Who are you helping when you make decisions from it? You will know when you have truly hurt someone and can then make restitution. If there is any doubt about the triggering situation, it's OCD and should be resisted against acting on.
- Inverse empathy: Put yourself in the other person's place: was the degree of *possible harm* worthy of involving the other person in your OCD? Would you be upset if the same *harm* was done to you? Would you expect the same degree of excessive attention to it from the other person? Would repeatedly being asked the same question—until the person felt *right*— get on your nerves? Try to rate the degree of the *offense* on a scale of 0–10 using inverse empathy as a guide. If you wouldn't be bothered about it, neither would the other person. Challenge yourself to let it go and see what happens.
- Try to delay an apology to get more clarity and distance from the situation, then decide how to address it. Is it really all that urgent or important?
- Do you think the person was actually affected or noticed what you are obsessing about? If you are not sure, let it go. Doubt means that it *is* OCD.
- Do not perform subtle checking or reassurance-seeking rituals (interpreting body language, initiating small talk, etc.). This is considered cheating.
- Focus on other aspects of yourself and your life instead of allowing the obsessions to divert you away from your goals.
- Trusting oneself is exciting and scary at the same time. Guilt and distress create a bind between fear and creativity. You sense or know your potential and are frustrated because there is no guarantee of success up front. That is the level playing field of life.
- How can you presume to know that your contribution won't be of value to others? What's the worst that can happen if you take the chance? Is the worst realistic? Is the worst really *that* bad? Would finding out help inform you for subsequent attempts? What's the worst that can happen if you don't take the chance? What is the best that could happen?

Yourself in Relation to God or Spiritual Connection

- Does the obsessive concern *clearly* match what you were taught about right and wrong?

- Are you being too literal and perfectionistic out of obsessive fear and doubt so that you cover the bases "just in case"? Does that count as a meaningful expression of faith?
- Do you have trust/faith enough to accept that the intensity/severity of the triggering event is an obsession, not worthy of any response?
- Are you asking too much from God to provide reassurance for an obsessive thought?
- Do you really know what God wants? Wouldn't you have to have special power or knowledge?
- Might God expect you to do your part and take responsibility for handling the obsessive doubt for what it is (e.g., God helps those who help themselves)? God cannot forgive you if no mistake has been made. It will be better to ask God for help when a real-life event has occurred (such as asking God to help you have the courage and faith when facing your fears that will result in a better relationship with God and loved ones)!
- An obsessive "bad" thought does not a sin make. If it weren't for the OCD, would it be more of a passing thought? Everyone experiences the same types of thoughts that become obsessions for people with OCD (see appendix).
- Obsessions are made from whatever "taboo" thoughts you find objectionable. They are not a reflection of who you are as a person. Thus analyzing obsessions serves no productive purpose. You have OCD, but it does not define who you are.
- Rituals never serve their intended purpose. They actually express a lack of faith. No rituals performed or ever to be performed will cause or prevent the feared outcome. They provide the illusion of control but do not give real control, which is what you get when you resist them. There is never proof that performing a ritual prevented a car crash. When real-life situations happen, people with OCD manage them normally and effectively. The hypothetical possibilities are a product of an active mind, not premonition or prediction.
- Wanting to control things that are beyond you is a normal human wish, but accepting the limits of control shows humility. You will have healthy results when you take responsibility for what is yours and get unhealthy results for efforts made at controlling what isn't.

Emotion Regulation and Distress Tolerance

As is the case for many people, with or without OCD, emotions can run high in stressful situations. Along with anxiety, people who have OCD can react to negative experiences with emotions that are seemingly out of proportion to the event that triggered them. Obsessive guilt becomes complicated when it is experienced as an internal form of self-punishment for feelings of anger, which is deadly sinful.

Emotional avoidance and emotional dysregulation are maladaptive responses to strong emotions. Negative emotions are often experienced by people with OCD as "bad," a kind of failure to be avoided. To varying degrees, as children, we were sensitive to the anger and criticism of our parents and others as they tried to teach us how to become good people. As adults, we may still be conditioned to live by these lessons if we are afraid that maturing out of them will mean betraying our parents. Some of us rebelled as teenagers to test the validity of the rules taught by the authority figures in our lives, but many who have an obsessive conscience continue to live by them. Guilt over the idea of challenging authority can be so overwhelming that many live to avoid making mistakes by living stuck in the literal letter of the rules.

Other common negative emotions that are problematic are fear, anger, shame, blame, regret, resentment, hostility, frustration, impatience, irritation, loneliness, sorrow, rejection, and worthlessness. These emotions provoke or reinforce obsessive anxiety and guilt, and rituals are used as coping strategies to "make them go away" (even though they don't).

Concepts found in acceptance and commitment therapy (ACT) and dialectical behavior therapy are designed to help people better manage how they experience and express strong negative emotions. The skills taught in ACT and DBT can help OCD sufferers who also have these strong emotional experiences.

ACT stands for

- Accept your reactions and be present: Notice them, accept them, and experience them instead of avoiding them.
- Choose a valued direction: Clarify your values and ask yourself whether your behavior is compatible with your values,
- Take action according to your values.

Like other CBT skills, ACT teaches people to notice, accept, and embrace them the cognitive, emotional, and physiological experiences they are trying to avoid.[6] A particular function of ACT is to help people identify their values, make compatible decisions, and commit to putting them into practice. ACT views the core of many problems to be due to the concepts represented in the acronym FEAR: Fusion with your thoughts; Evaluation of experience; Avoidance of your experience; and Reason-giving for your behavior.

The six core principles to help clients develop psychological flexibility:

1. **Cognitive defusion**: Learning methods to reduce the tendency to reify thoughts, images, emotions, and memories
2. **Acceptance**: Allowing thoughts to come and go without struggling with them

3. **Contact with the present moment**: Awareness of the here and now, experienced with openness, interest, and receptiveness
4. **Observing the self**: Accessing a transcendent sense of self, a continuity of consciousness which is unchanging
5. **Values**: Discovering what is most important to one's true self
6. **Committed action**: Setting goals according to values and carrying them out responsibly

Act employs mindfulness as a skill that enhances the capacity to notice the present moment without judging how you are experiencing it. Similar to thought–action fusion, people are encouraged to take a step back to observe them rather than get entangled in them. As previously stated, this won't work for obsessions but will for other negative experiences.[7]

Dialectical behavior therapy emphasizes learning to bear inevitable pain skillfully. Much like with ACT, people who use DBT are taught to accept without judging self and the current situation. Becoming objective reduces the need for external validation and approval from others. The goal is to become capable of calmly recognizing negative situations and their effects, rather than becoming overwhelmed or hiding from them. This allows individuals to make wise decisions about whether and how to take action rather than falling into the intense, desperate, and often destructive emotional reactions that make any problem situation worse. Interpersonal effectiveness, emotion regulation, distress tolerance, and behavioral scheduling are skills that help to improve communication and express emotions in ways that allow for mutual validation of feelings.[8]

Assertiveness Training, Compulsive Apologizing and People-Pleasing

A hallmark of obsessive guilt is compulsive apologizing (see Table 10.1). How can one person be responsible for so much wrongdoing that he or she express sorrow for every move he or she makes? There are many ironies to OCD. In this case, humility is the flip side of the deadly sin of pride. Apologies become meaningless when they are given compulsively. If people express them for all situations, they appear not to be able to discriminate between imagined and serious wrongdoing. The receivers of these apologies dismiss them and may not take a meaningful apology seriously. It is not a gesture made from strength or healthiness.

People-pleasing is another indicator of excessive guilt. Putting others' needs ahead of our own is not an act of selflessness, but self-preservation. Instead of acting on altruism, the ulterior motive is avoiding conflict, wanting to be liked (e.g., not hated and retaliated against), avoiding one's own negative emotions (focusing on others as a distraction), avoiding negative judgment by others

TABLE 10.1   Healthy versus Obsessive Apologizing

Healthy	Obsessive
Performed once	Performed compulsively for reassurance
Honest expression	Overapologetic to "feel right"
Direct and to the point	Performed until obsessive need for certainty achieved
Clear and specific to the problem	Intention and effectiveness of the apology is lost because the motivation becomes the obsessive need for certainty, completion, and reassurance

(saying what I think people want to hear, not what I think, to keep me safe), problems with decision making (if I commit to a decision, then I have to take responsibility for it), avoiding mistakes (if I act perfect, I won't call negative attention to myself), and so on.

New to treatment, Petra said, "Oh, we don't do that in our family." She read some material on assertiveness that I had given her and shrugged her shoulders when I asked her whether she had gotten anything out of it. "Read it again," I instructed her. After dutifully rereading the material, she asked where to start working on this communication skill. After taking risks and practicing standing up for herself, people asked, "Who *are* you?" Staying strong, she was now in control of her decisions, able to set limits, and was overall less stressed. People could no longer take advantage of her, and she commanded respect even from her mother, who had always intimidated her.

Assertiveness is the antidote to guilt and low self-esteem. Having self-respect means that you decide what is worthwhile for you and your life. You trust your natural sense of (positive self-regard naturally lends itself to others. There is a mutuality of self- and other-respect, because when you are comfortable with yourself, people are more naturally comfortable with you. They do not threaten your self-worth, and they naturally respect you, because you are in charge of where you leave off and another begins. It helps people let go of feeling responsible for other people's problems. They also stop blaming others for their own problems. The need to please others or to be liked becomes secondary. They acknowledge that they can't always please other, but that they can decide and live by what is right for them.

Following is a list of assertive rights (not privileges, rights!):

Basic Assertive Rights[9]

1. The right to act in ways that promote your dignity and self-respect as long as doing so does not violate others' rights.
2. The right to be treated with respect
3. The right to say no and not feel guilty

4. The right to experience and express your feelings
5. The right to take time to slow down and think
6. The right to change your mind
7. The right to ask for what you want
8. The right to do less than you are humanly capable of doing
9. The right to ask for information
10. The right to make mistakes
11. The right to feel good about yourself
12. The right to offer and accept a workable compromise
13. The right to offer no reasons or excuses justifying your behavior
14. The right to judge whether you are responsible for finding solutions to other people's problems
15. The right to say "I don't know"
16. The right to say "I don't understand"
17. The right to respectfully disagree

Interpersonal Communication Styles

Understand that being kind and being a "people pleaser" are not the same thing. To disagree with someone does not necessarily mean you are being unkind (see Table 10.2). It is possible to be kind and state your own needs at the same time. Passivity is the typical end of the spectrum for the guilty. They don't feel they have rights or power. Aggression is the other end. People fear they will "lose it" and be out of control. Do not label standing up for yourself as selfish or wrong. It is not.

TABLE 10.2   Interpersonal Styles of Relating

Nice/passive	Kind/assertive	Mean/aggressive
Passive	Empathic	Aggressive
People-pleasing	Compassionate	Blame others
Avoid conflict	Assertive	Selfish
Taken advantage of	Fair	Exploiting
Fear of negative judgment	Honest	Self-important
Learned helplessness	Merciful	Pretentious
Self-effacing	Self-respectful	Grandiose/arrogant
Dependent	Self-responsible	Demanding
Need to be liked	Genuine	False front
Timid	Spontaneous	Impulsive
Living in fear/avoidant	Living in the present	Living in the past/resentments
Isolation	Healthy relationships	Controlling

Many people who have OCD also suffer from social anxiety and panic disorder lack assertiveness. Many other people were never taught assertiveness skills, because their role models may have never learned them, either. Assertiveness is practicing one's personal rights, responsibilities, and self-care. It is not a burden to others. On the contrary, assertiveness commands respect and trust from others, because they know where you stand and how you feel. Assertiveness manages stress by addressing a problem situation in the moment. Stress is alleviated by honestly and effectively communicating about yourself. It enables letting go of anger and resentment so that these feelings do not boil up and become expressed inappropriately to the immediate situation at hand.

Good Skills to Have

Setting goals is a way of organizing getting what you want and how to get there in achievable steps. Having realistic goals that are measurable and that have an end point can help reduce procrastination or feelings of being overwhelmed. If the goals that were set were too big, break them down into phases that have smaller steps. Wanting to be fluent in Russian is a good goal, but it takes learning a new alphabet, language semantics, vocabulary, and so forth. It will not be achieved overnight, perhaps not even within a year. But practice and keeping your eye on the goal will eventually get the goal achieved.

Decision making, as we know for people with OCD, can be paralyzing. Accepting that while there is no perfect solution, a cost–benefit analysis can be a helpful way of weighing the options. One of the most important strategies for OCD sufferers is to make a decision, and stick with it, no matter what the doubt or second-guessing. The grass could always be greener on the other side, but maybe the side you are on is really *is* the greener side.

Support

Family and friends mean well by trying to help the OCD sufferer cope with his or her symptoms. They see their loved ones suffering and want to help the person, in whatever ways they can, to find some relief. Sometimes the symptoms are so severe that they affect all aspects of how the every other person in the household, even the household itself, functions. Reassurance is provided and loved ones become involved in the rituals, either because they want to help ease the burden or because the circumstances have become insufferable. After family and friends learn about their responses to the symptoms and, often, their role in maintaining the disorder, they realize there are better and effective ways of managing how it affects daily life.

OCD symptoms can negatively affect family relationships, leisure activities, and interactions, possibly resulting in financial and emotional stress for the entire family. Family interactions around OCD depend on where the person with OCD is in the course of his or her illness, what his or her family role is (child, parent, spouse, sibling), the stress tolerance level of family members, and the personalities of all involved.

Additionally, loved ones need to understand the treatment process and their role in the treatment of their loved one. After family members feel equipped to support and help a loved one, family interactions, communication styles, and the quality of relationships can be improved and the severity and frequency of OCD episodes diminished. Most important, family members can be taught to identify and minimize those behaviors that accommodate the OCD symptoms. When families function around the OCD symptoms (e.g., waiting at the request of the sufferer until he or she ritualizes or washes his or her hands), they are accommodating the OCD, which may unwittingly lead to the OCD's becoming the head of the household. After families learn how to provide support to their loved ones without being controlled by the OCD, they can feel confident that they are truly helping. Families can assess their accommodation using the family accommodation scale.[10] When symptoms are accommodated, it keeps the OCD in charge of the household, it maintains the life of the episodes, it gives a message to the sufferer that he or she is unable to manage his or her anxiety, and it fosters anger and resentment in accommodating people that they are involved in the OCD system. After support people learn what to do instead, whether the OCD sufferer is on board or not, a better semblance of order and routine is established in the house, people feel less controlled by the demands of the disorder, and the sufferer may start making improvements after people stop doing things for him or her. Learning how to provide support that is not reassurance is a healthy skill to have.

Groups

Groups help people to learn they are not alone with the conscience-related aspects of their OCD. Groups for OCD can be either conducted by a mental health professional, or in a self-help manner. There are pros and cons of each. Professionally led groups usually cost money but are well facilitated to help people set goals and have accountability for how they were or were not met. There is a sense of commitment and accountability to the group, and members offer mutual support. Self-help groups are free but can devolve into obsessive discussions about medications and complaints about symptoms, not producing constructive outcomes.

In the scrupulosity group I run at the OCDI, we often find moral gray areas in discussing issues related to the Ten Commandments, the seven deadly sins, and obsessive guilt. One example of how scrupulous people think differently is talking about people's responses to finding money on the ground. For some, it's easy. They say they would or would not take it. Others take the conditions under which the money was found into consideration. We can get a bit obsessive about what those conditions are (where was the money was found, how much was it, and so forth). Even though people in the group may be polarized in their strict beliefs about what is right and wrong, they provide helpful feedback to others.

Clergy

Clergy are helpful adjuncts in working through these issues of the problem is well understood by them. The Catholic and Jewish clergy I have consulted in my practice are unanimous in holding that scrupulosity is not a form of religiosity consistent with the spirit of their faith. They agree that the way the scrupulous use religion is beyond the expectations and standards of a healthy religious life, and they invariably support the strategies used in cognitive-behavioral therapy.

Martin Luther took control over his OCD in the spirit of *agere contra* (doing the opposite):[11]

1. If the scruple presumes that the incident was a sin, the counselee should presume that it was not a sin.
2. If the scruple howls for attention, the counselee should give it the utmost contempt.
3. If the scruple puts out bait for an argument, the counselee should adamantly refuse to become involved.
4. If the scruple makes the counselee feel desperate, he or she should remain imperturbable.
5. If an emotion tricks the counselee to an extreme, he or she should trick the emotion back to the mean.
6. If an emotion does anything at all, the counselee should do just the opposite.

To identify a balance between the two extremes of scrupulosity and autonomy, the scrupulous should consult a *trusted* clergy member, preferably with the cognitive–behavioral therapist, to discuss the parameters of the problematic areas in question. Acceptance of this counsel is essential and needs to be contracted for before such a meeting is held, given the propensity to "doubt the dissonance." Although this treatment strategy appears to encourage the acceptance of another externalized system of religiosity, it provides a context for internalizing the same tenets that were previously taught but that were incorporated into the OCD. At best, this process will support the scrupulous in letting go of their rigidity, their need for certainty, and their need to be perfect.

The scrupulous who are committed to orthodox forms of religion must be encouraged to do so out of choice, not fear. As adults, it may not be realistic or reasonable for the scrupulous to "hedonistically" rebel due to life circumstances and responsibilities. However, along with appropriate religious counsel, a compromise between scrupulosity and hedonism can be reached and realized through a cognitive–behavioral treatment plan.

Another question is whether autonomy and self-determination are humanistic values that are biases of the mental health profession. Are they specific to certain cultural values? Do these values pose a conflict to those committed to traditional religious faiths? Can the scrupulous consider autonomy and self-determination to be morally acceptable, or should another standard be set? The dual nature of the problem obligates theologians and mental health professionals to reconcile these questions. When clinically treating scrupulosity, the professional must be aware of his or her own biases or prejudices that may emerge in the clinical relationship, because cognitive–behavioral therapy directly addresses and challenges the scrupulous' belief systems. Likewise, clergy must be educated about the psychological nature of scrupulosity and not mistake frequent requests for reassurance or confession of guilt for sin.

Finding Humor

If I were a doctor, I would prescription a healthy dose of humor to go along with obsessions. It is unfortunate that finding humor in obsessions only seems to come when people are transitioning into recovery (indeed, it is a real sign of recovery). Humor works because it puts some distance between what we take seriously and what it looks like as an observer. Like mindfulness and meditation, it takes the self out of the center and into the sidelines, where things become more objective. Humor also sets off the pleasure neurotransmission of endorphins.[12]

In closing, successful treatment requires humility in accepting that to err is human, trusting that commitment to the treatment process leads to mental and emotional clarity, and that leveling the moral playing field to the same standards as others leads to deeper compassion and social participation. Taking the proverbial "leap of faith" will lead to a freer life that get people back to taking healthy and life-fulfilling risks.

Notes

1. Obsessive Compulsive Cognitions Working Group, "Cognitive Assessment of Obsessive–Compulsive Disorder": 671–674.

2. Adams et al., "Obsessive Beliefs Predict Cognitive Behavior Therapy Outcome": 203–211.

3. Beck, *Cognitive Therapies and Emotional Disorders*, 203–211.

4. Burns, *Feeling Good*, 33–43.

5. Hyman and Pedrick, *The OCD Workbook*, 98.

6. Hayes et al., *Acceptance and Commitment Therapy*, 49–80.

7. Öst, "The Efficacy of Acceptance and Commitment Therapy": 105–121.

8. Linehan, *Cognitive-Behavioral Treatment*, 120–165.

9. Jakubowski and Lange, *The Assertive Option*, 80–81.

10. To assess your family's accommodating behaviors, visit www.dmertlich.com/assets/FAS.pdf.

11. O'Flaherty, "Therapy for Scrupulosity," 234.

12. Abrami, "The Healing Power of Humor in Logotherapy": 7.

Bibliography

Abrami, Leo Michel. "The Healing Power of Humor in Logotherapy." *International Forum for Logotherapy* 32, no. 1 (2009).

Adams, Thomas G., Bradley C. Riemann, Chad T. Wetterneck, and Josh M. Cisler. "Obsessive Beliefs Predict Cognitive Behavior Therapy Outcome for Obsessive Compulsive Disorder." *Cognitive Behaviour Therapy* 41, no. 3 (2012): 203–211.

Beck, Aaron T. *Cognitive Therapies and Emotional Disorders*. New York: New American Library, 1976

Burns, D. D. *Feeling Good: The New Mood Therapy*. New York: William Morrow & Company, 1980.

Hayes, S. C., K. D. Strosahl, and K. G. Wilson. *Acceptance and Commitment Therapy: An Experiential Approach to Behavior Change*. New York: Guilford Press, 1999.

Hyman, Bruce, and Christina Pedrick. *The OCD Workbook: Your Guide to Breaking Free from Obsessive Compulsive Disorder*, 3rd ed. Oakland, CA: New Harbinger Publications, 2010.

Jakubowski, Patricia, and Arthur J. Lange. *The Assertive Option: Your Rights and Responsibilities*. Champaign, IL: Research Press, 1978.

Linehan, Marsha. *Cognitive-Behavioral Treatment of Borderline Personality Disorder*. New York: The Guilford Press, 1993.

Obsessive Compulsive Cognitions Working Group. "Cognitive Assessment of Obsessive-Compulsive Disorder." *Behaviour Research and Therapy* 35, no. 7 (1997): 667–681.

O'Flaherty, V. M. S. J. "Therapy for Scrupulosity." Chap. 8 in *Direct Psychotherapy: Twenty-Eight American Originals*, ed. Ratibor-Ray M. Jurievich, p. 221–243. Miami, FL: Miami University Press, 1973.

Öst, Lars-Göran "The Efficacy of Acceptance and Commitment Therapy: An Updated Systematic Review and Meta-Analysis." *Behaviour Research and Therapy* 61 (October 2014): 105–121.

Part IV

Other Guiding
Considerations

11

It's *Impulsive*, Not Compulsive

nervous habit   compulsive   impulsive   self-injurious

FIGURE 11.1   Repetitive behaviors range of severity.

The writing of this chapter coincides with a major change in the classifica-
tion of disorders that were considered as problems with impulse control.
The *Diagnostic and Statistical Manual of Mental Disorders–Fifth Edition*
(*DSM-5*) has moved hair pulling (trichotillomania), skin-picking (excoria-
tion), body-focused repetitive behaviors, and pathological jealousy into the
Obsessive–Compulsive and Related Disorders section. Pathological gambling,
once classified as, is now its own disorder.

Nevertheless, the goal of this chapter is to help readers understand that
behaviors described largely in popular culture as compulsive have impulsive
qualities that require a different treatment approach. We know that ERP is the
behavioral treatment of choice for OCD. The primary behavioral treatment
for impulse control disorders is habit reversal. Some people have both types of
urges and behaviors.

The distinguishing difference with impulsivity is: guilty pleasure. This is
why acting on impulses is so hard to stop. Impulsivity is reinforced by the
experience of pleasure, and increased adrenaline that can lead to euphoria.
These rewarding feelings reinforce people to keep seeking it out. Compulsivity
is rewarded by a temporary decrease in anxiety. There is a brief sense of relief,
but none of the pleasure experienced by those acting on impulses.

What's the Difference?

Pleasure, reward, and gratification experienced from impulsive behaviors
reinforce their repetition. Getting a "rush" from doing something makes us

TABLE 11.1   Differences between Compulsive and Impulsive Urges and Behaviors

	Compulsive	Impulsive
Experience of Resisting Urges	Decrease through habituation	Increase over time until completion
Subjective Experience	Fear Guilt	Building tension Urge Incompleteness
Function of behavior	Decrease of Fear Decrease of guilt	Pleasant sensation
Maintained by	Negative reinforcement (ending aversive sensation)	Positive reinforcement (engaging in the behavior is strengthened by occurrence of a sense of reward)

want to keep doing it, which is why impulsive behaviors are difficult to control. Impulsivity is different from spontaneity, because there is a lack of good judgment that leads to negative consequences can be aggressive and can also lead to feelings of loss of control. Spontaneity, on the other hand, is healthy, because it's driven by creativity and self-expression. Impulsivity drives thrill-seeking and risky behaviors, whereas compulsivity is risk-averse and functions to keep things safe.

Research has shown an increased level of frontal lobe activity in compulsivity and a decrease in the same area in impulsivity.[1] Similarly, there is an increase of the neurotransmitter serotonin in compulsivity, whereas there is a decrease of serotonin in impulsive disorders.[2] With regard to instincts, dopamine and opioid neurotransmitters provide "natural rewards" such as pleasure for behaviors that are critical for survival and necessary, such as eating, loving, and reproducing. These same neurotransmitters can also produce "unnatural rewards" from the pleasure experienced from behaviors such as taking illicit drugs, among other destructive impulsive behaviors.[3]

Table 11.1 shows some other ways to understand the difference.

Nervous Habits

Everyone has nervous habits. We act on these impulses without much awareness. Nervous habits are often provoked by anxiety, boredom, and other negative feelings. They are presumed to be soothing in nature, but they actually maintain anxiety (when people are calm, they don't do them). If you are studying for a test and feel anxious, you might display repetitive behaviors, such as biting your nails, chewing your lips, pacing, jiggling your leg, twirling your hair, and the like. These are, more or less, harmless body-focused behaviors.[4]

What makes these behaviors habits and not clinically problematic is your ability to stop them when you notice them. There is an assumption of control in being able to stop them, and they typically don't cause significant harm. But, like other normal behavioral manifestations described in this book, normal behaviors can become excessive and cause functional impairment.

Body-Focused Repetitive Behaviors

Although some nervous habits can be mildly self-injurious, such as finger-nail/cuticle biting, skin/scalp picking, and the like, others can lead to self-injury. Body-focused repetitive behavior disorders (RBD) refer to a group of behaviors that includes skin picking, hair pulling, skin biting, nail biting, lip/cheek biting or chewing, and nose picking that result in physical and psychological difficulties.[5, 6] Interestingly, a similar function of compulsive behaviors that are born out of survival needs, such as health, hygiene, and procreation, occurs with some impulsive grooming and preening behaviors. Hair and skin are two common self-care behaviors that can turn into RBDs. What reinforces these behaviors is an elevated level of opiates in people who perform them. Endogenous opiates (endorphins) are released in the bloodstream, reduce the experience of pain, and also can lead to a feeling of euphoria during these episodes of self-injury.[7] When the episodes are over, people feel pain and remorse for what they have done, but the cycle repeats itself in only a short matter of time.

Trichotillomania: Although trichotillomania has recently been reclassified as an OCD-related disorder, hair pulling resembles impulsive behaviors because it is self-soothing and pleasurable.[8, 9] Anywhere there is hair on the body is fair game for pulling: head, face, eyebrows, eyelashes, armpits, legs, and pubic hair. Some hair-pullers have ritualistic behaviors such as feeling for hairs that have a bumpy texture, inspecting the hair and the follicle, biting/chewing the follicle, and sometimes eating the hair. The latter can lead to health problems, such as hair balls (trichobezoars) that can cause severe digestive and pancreatic problems. Other consequences of trichotillomania are causing bald spots that are covered by wigs or scarves, feeling shame and guilt because of the self-inflicted nature of the behavior, and having something to hide. Five percent of trichotillomania patients have OCD.[10]

Behavioral Addictions and Non–Body-Focused Repetitive Behaviors

Examples of addictive behaviors and non–body-focused impulsive behaviors are shopping, gambling, eating, excessive computer/gaming use, sexual impulsivity, and pornography. They have similar characteristics of addictions but differ in that no substances are ingested to produce the reinforcing high. There are also common brain functions and neurotransmitter activity between substance and behavioral addictive behaviors.[11]

Compulsive Buying/Shopping

Who doesn't love the feeling of buying something new? We are constantly bombarded with marketing strategies intended to make us buy things we never knew we needed. Shopping easily becomes impulsive, because stores are around every corner. Malls try to provide an atmosphere of ease and stimulation at the same time. Shopping is also a social activity—during an excursion, people can forget about reality for a while. The problem is that people often buy things they can't afford, go into debt, shop as an avoidance behavior, and accumulate material items that take up unavailable space at home. Eight percent of compulsive shoppers also meet criteria for OCD.[12]

Pathological Gambling

Casinos and lottery tickets have become more convenient, available, and socially acceptable as private and public money-generating ventures. People who have gambling problems experience euphoric highs when they win and remorseful, even suicidal, lows when they lose. They may steal time away from work and family and try to hide their behavior by lying. They can get caught in a vicious cycle of taking their winnings to chase even more thrills and money by "reinvesting" the money in more gambling—and inevitably losing. The need arises to at least get their initial money back. They may go into more debt in the process and leave themselves and families in financial ruin. Two percent of pathological gamblers have OCD.[13]

Compulsive Stealing/Kleptomania

Shoplifting and stealing also have differing functions. Those who steal "compulsively" experience similar precursive urges as other impulsive behaviors in that there is a buildup of tension that is relieved by acting on those urges. A plan is usually made ahead of time and carried out. There is an experience of pleasure and gratification during the episode, there is relief of stress, and there may even be an acting out of anger as a component of reinforcement. acting out anger. Kleptomaniacs give much less thought to their behavior and act on spontaneous urges in the moment. Little or no negative emotions are experienced, and they may even throw the item(s) away. Kleptomania has a very low prevalence rate of 0.3 to 0.6 percent within the general population.[14]

Hypersexuality, Sexual Impulsivity, and Sexual Addiction

No longer considered an impulse control disorder, sexual impulsivity and addiction share the same traits as the other impulsive addictive behaviors. Previously, excessive sexual behavior was classified as sexual impulsivity because of its similarity to disorders of impulse control. It was also called sexual compulsivity because of its similar behavioral pattern and some neurobiolological similarity to OCD. It was also referred to as sexual addiction because of the repetitive and escalating patterns of sexual behavior resulting in negative consequences to self and others.[15] Research continues to sort out the biological, psychological, and social causes of behavior addictions in general.[16] Again, it is important to distinguish the behavior as impulsive, compulsive, or addictive to select the best treatment approach.

Obsessional Jealousy

Once considered pathological or morbid, obsessional jealousy is reclassified as an unspecified obsessive-compulsive and related disorder. People who have obsessional jealousy suspect that their partner is being unfaithful. They may project their insecurities onto their partner's innocent or unintended behaviors that provoke their jealousy. Jealous thoughts are experienced as intrusive and excessive, and behaviors such as trying to control or checking up on the partner's behavior and whereabouts, asking repetitive reassuring questions, checking electronic communications, and so forth may follow.

Somewhat different than impulsivity, the obsessions and behaviors are not pleasurable, but they are destructive. Insight ranges from obsessional to delusional.[17] The morbidly jealous person commonly experiences relationship impairments and extreme difficulty in suppressing thoughts about these concerns. Obsessional jealousy can also lead to abuse and violence. The prevalence rate for obsessional jealousy is based on psychiatric chart reviews. A study of 8,134 psychiatric in-patients found 1.1 percent, whereas another study of 398 case histories from 1940 to 2002 reported a rate of 4 percent.[18, 19]

What Helps? Habit Reversal

Habit reversal consists of doing the opposite behavior than your repetitive impulsive urges. Habit reversal is a process that requires good motivation on the patient's part, because it takes effort, practice, and the results of progress generally tend to be slow. Lapses and relapses are not uncommon, but the best predictor of success is continued effort. Some people have trouble giving up their behaviors, because nothing healthy will replace the pleasure and gratification experienced during the episodes. There is sometimes a phase of high frustration and "mourning" the loss of what had been immediate and soothing relief from stress.

There are four components to habit reversal: awareness training, developing a variety of competing physical responses, building motivation, and generalization of skills.[20, 21]

Awareness training starts with the person's making a conscious effort to recognize urges that precede the action. The person can log the frequency, sensations, and situations that provoke the urges. Sometimes awareness training actually has a natural effect in reducing the urges acted upon. When this happens, the person can gain more confidence, motivation, and belief that he or she can gain control over the behavior.

Competing response training sees behavior performed in the physically opposite manner and direction of the repetitive behavior. Body-focused repetitive behaviors can be resisted or interrupted by the person keeping the hands down on the lap or grabbing onto or holding an item in whatever hand performs the behavior. The person should be able to hold onto the opposite behavior for several minutes, then, with practice, for longer durations. People with non–body-focused behaviors go in the opposite direction, ideally and literally, of their tempted location and use stress management techniques to help the urges pass. The competing behavior should also be discreet and socially appropriate. At the OCD Institute, the behavior may be so severe that use of stress or squishy balls, bubble wrap, needlework, wearing gloves, or using items with rough textures such as fabric and yarn are allowed in any situation in which the person is vulnerable. Gradually, their use in the open is phased out.

Another intervention that is helpful is called the habit inconvenience review. An inventory is compiled of situations in which the behavior caused inconvenience, embarrassment, and suffering. At some point, conduct a review of situations in which the behavior has significantly decreased or of other positive aspects of eliminating the behaviors.

To keep the impulsive behaviors from coming back, keeping a list of all of the problems that were caused by their behavior is recommended. Parents and friends are also asked to provide support and feedback to the person for his or her accomplishments in getting his or her life back in better control.

When the person is feeling more confident, he or she is encouraged to resume enjoyable activities once avoided for fear of embarrassment or shame. People can practice new skills in a variety of situations, not just those specifically addressed as part of the behavioral plan.

With regard to some BFRPs, accepting that complete abstinence of the behavior will help reduce guilt and shame for when lapses, or even relapses, occur. People always have skin and hair on their bodies. Some non-BFRPs are somewhat easier to avoid, since being more situationally based and susceptible to avoidance, such as casinos, stores, porn websites, and the like.

Notes

1. Comings and Blum, "Reward Deficiency Syndrome.".
2. Hollander and Cohen, "Psychobiology and Psychopharmacology of Compulsive Spectrum Disorders."
3. Comings and Blum, "Reward Deficiency Syndrome."
4. Croyle and Waltz, "Subclinical Self-Harm."
5. Hollander and Evers, "Review of Obsessive–Compulsive Spectrum Disorders."
6. Bohne et al., "Pathologic Hairpulling, Skin Picking, and Nail Biting."
7. Nock et al., "Revealing the Form and Function."
8. American Psychiatric Association, *Diagnostic and Statistical Manual of Mental Disorders, 5th Edition.*
9. Swedo and Leonard, "Trichotillomania."
10. Lochner et al., "Comorbidity in Obsessive–Compulsive Disorder."
11. Leeman and Potenza, "Targeted Review."
12. Mitchell et al., "Cognitive Behavioral Therapy."
13. el-Guebaly et al., "Compulsive Features in Behavioral Addictions."
14. American Psychiatric Association, *Diagnostic and Statistical Manual of Mental Disorders, 5th Edition.*
15. Jhanjee et al., "Sexual Addiction in Association with Obsessive–Compulsive Disorder."
16. Leeman and Potenza, "Targeted Review."
17. Insel and Akiskal, "Obsessive–Compulsive Disorder with Psychotic Features."
18. Soyka, Naber, and Volcker, "Prevalence of Delusional Jealousy."
19. Easton, Shackelford, and Schipper, "Delusional Disorder–Jealous Type."
20. Azrin and Nunn, "Habit-Reversal."
21. Woods and Miltenberger, "Habit Reversal."

Bibliography

American Psychiatric Association. *Diagnostic and Statistical Manual of Mental Disorders, 5th Edition: DSM-5*. Arlington, VA: American Psychiatric Association, 2013.

Azrin, N. H., and R. G. Nunn. "Habit-Reversal: A Method of Eliminating Nervous Habits and Tics." *Behaviour Research and Therapy* 11, no. 4 (1973): 619–628.

Bohne, Antje, Nancy Keuthen, and Sabine Wilhelm. "Pathologic Hairpulling, Skin Picking, and Nail Biting." *Annals of Clinical Psychiatry* 17 (2005): 227–232.

Comings, David E., and Kenneth Blum. "Reward Deficiency Syndrome: Genetic Aspects of Behavioral Disorders." *Progress in Brain Research* 126 (2000): 325–341.

Croyle, Kristin L., and Jennifer Waltz. "Subclinical Self-Harm: Range of Behaviors, Extent, and Associated Characteristics." *American Journal of Orthopsychiatry* 77, no. 2 (2007): 332–342.

Easton, J. A., T. K. Shackelford, and L. D. Schipper. "Delusional Disorder-Jealous Type: How Inclusive Are the *DSM-IV* Diagnostic Criteria?" *Journal of Clinical Psychology* 64, no. 3 (2008): 264–275.

el-Guebaly, Nady, Tanya Mudry, Joseph Zohar, Hermano Tavares, and Marc N. Potenza. "Compulsive Features in Behavioral Addictions: The Case of Pathological Gambling." *Addiction* 107, no. 10 (2012): 1726–1734.

Hollander, E., and M. Evers. "Review of Obsessive–Compulsive Spectrum Disorders: What Do We Know? Where Are We Going?" *Clinical Neuropsychiatry* 1, no. 1 (2004): 32–51.

Hollander, Eric, and Lisa J. Cohen. "Psychobiology and Psychopharmacology of Compulsive Spectrum Disorders." In *Impulsivity and Compulsivity*, eds. Eric Hollander, John M. Oldham, and Andrew E. Sokol, pp. 143–166. Washington, DC: American Psychiatric Press, Inc., 1996.

Insel, T. R., and H. S. Akiskal. "Obsessive–Compulsive Disorder with Psychotic Features: A Phenomenologic Analysis." *American Journal of Psychiatry* 143 (1986): 1527–1533.

Jhanjee, Anurag, Manjeet S. Bhatia, Pankaj Kumar, and Amit Jindal. "Sexual Addiction in Association with Obsessive–Compulsive Disorder." *German Journal of Psychiatry* 13, no. 4 (2010): 171–174.

Leeman, R. F., and M. N. Potenza. "A Targeted Review of the Neurobiology and Genetics of Behavioural Addictions: An Emerging Area of Research." *Canadian Journal of Psychiatry* 58, no. 5 (2013): 260–273.

Lochner, Christine, Naomi A. Fineberg, Joseph Zohar, Michael van Ameringen, Alzbeta Juven-Wetzler, Alfredo Carlo Altamura, Natalie L. Cuzen, et al., "Comorbidity in Obsessive–Compulsive Disorder (OCD): A Report from the International College of Obsessive–Compulsive Spectrum Disorders (ICOCS)." *Comprehensive Psychiatry* 55, no. 7 (2014): 1513–1519.

Mitchell, James E., Melissa Burgard, Ron Faber, Ross D. Crosby, and Martina de Zwaan. "Cognitive Behavioral Therapy for Compulsive Buying Disorder." *Behaviour Research and Therapy* 44, no. 12 (2006): 1859–1865.

Nock, Matthew K., Mitchell J. Prinstein, and Sonya K. Sterba. "Revealing the Form and Function of Self-Injurious Thoughts and Behaviors: A Real-Time Ecological Assessment Study among Adolescents and Young Adults." *Journal of Abnormal Psychology* 118, no. 4 (2009): 816–827.

Soyka, M., G. Naber, and A. Volcker. "Prevalence of Delusional Jealousy in Different Psychiatric Disorders. An Analysis of 93 Cases." *British Journal of Psychiatry* 158 (1991): 549–553.

Swedo, S. E., and H. L. Leonard. "Trichotillomania: An Obsessive–Compulsive Disorder?" *Psychiatric Clinics of North America* 15 (1992): 777–790.

Woods, D. W., and R. G. Miltenberger. "Habit Reversal: A Review of Applications and Variations." *Journal of Behavior Therapy and Experimental Psychiatry* 26 (1995): 123–131.

12

A Word about Countertransference

"One minute we're talking about germs, then the next, about God," my colleague lamented, to which I replied, "That's what I find so fascinating."

One therapist's bane is another's blessing. This interaction between my colleague and myself about OCD and treatment was an honest expression of how some therapists feel when religion makes an appearance in therapy. Therapists have private reactions to favored and dreaded issues brought into treatment by their patients, because therapists are humans, too. Just like OCD sufferers, those who are called to be therapists are also from "all walks of life." When the issues patients are telling us about trigger our own sensitivities, it is always best to realize it right in the moment when it's happening. Sometimes our subjective reactions are clinically useful and effective. When they aren't, we must make note of them, then give our full attention to what our patients are telling us. As the third part of the serenity prayer says, the wisdom is in knowing the difference between the two.

Countertransference is the clinical term for failing at this. But first, what is the transference in countertransference? Schwartz says that "our experience of people in the present is colored by how we have experienced important figures in our past. The more problematic past relationships have been and the less successful we have been in seeing them clearly, the more likely they are to color our present responses in ways of which we are unaware."[1] In this way, transference is a manner through which patients communicate how they are still affected and controlled by their past experiences and relationships. We know it when it happens, because the patient is interacting with us in a way that is disconnected from the relationship we have formulated with the patient.

Countertransference is the same thing, but with the tables turned. "The narrowest definition of countertransference is transference in the therapist; that is, a distorted and inappropriate response derived from unconscious conflicts in the therapist's past [and] all the therapist's emotional responses to the patient."[2] Hayes identifies self-insight, self-integration, anxiety management, empathy, and conceptualizing ability as important attributes for successful management of countertransference reactions.[3]

Religion is one of those topics that evoke countertransference consciously or unconsciously, because we may be vulnerable to our own histories and experiences we've had with it. I have found this to be an especially sensitive issue for many, but not all, cognitive behavior therapists and other mental health professionals. Notwithstanding the value of evidence-based treatment, historically "some of the foremost CBT thinkers espoused the position that adhering to religious beliefs and/or practice constituted irrational and even pathological behavior."[4] Another viewpoint on religion and psychotherapy states that it becomes problematic "if . . . many therapists have unresolved religious conflicts . . . [they may] either avoid this material or deal with their patients' religious beliefs as though they were pathological."[5]

Why is this important? Along with the therapist's skill, the quality of the relationship built between the patient and therapist is considered to be an important factor in reaching the best treatment outcome. CBT therapist characteristics that have been found to be conducive to treatment are empathy, unconditional positive regard and acceptance, warmth, genuineness, confidence, being directive,[6] verbal fluency, interpersonal perception, emotional responsiveness, expressiveness, and the sustained focus on the other.[7] A few others I consider helpful are appropriate use of humor, keeping the big picture in mind, and being kind while being firm.

So what is the problem? Because progress in OCD treatment is measured by symptom reduction through behavioral change, dynamic issues are considered to the extent that they interfere with treatment compliance. This is the appropriate contract between the OCD sufferer and the CBT therapist, but it has not seemed sufficient for many sufferers who have underlying conscience-related symptoms. Although people are happy when they experience symptom relief, relapses do occur. My experience in treating OCD has taught me that religious issues are in a special category of countertransference and may be a factor that interferes with some treatment outcome.

Religious countertransference is characterized as an emotional response by a clinician toward a patient's religious language, beliefs, practices, rituals, or community that can diminish the effectiveness of treatment. Religious countertransference can be a serious impediment when it influences a clinician to avoid a religious patient or to engage only superficially. . . . Under the influence of religious countertransference, an otherwise competent clinician can begin reacting . . . as if the patient only consists of his or her religious expressions.[8]

Conscience is a product of community life and experience and is designed to keep the individual *in community*—i.e., "good." Sin, in its most broadly defensible definition, is a rupture of this relationship, as well as the personal "condition" thus created. It has been the thesis of this entire paper that "scrupulosity" is the forlorn and inevitable outcome of the effort to devise a private solution to the problem of personal guilt and alienation in a religious context, just as "transference" is the equally unfortunate and confused expression of the effort to find, through psychoanalysis, a private solution in a secular context.[9]

Some suggestions follow:

- Be self-aware when religious issues arise, and keep being a detective to better understand whether the patient has a healthy or unhealthy relationship with them.
- During assessment, take time to address the role religion plays, or doesn't play, in a person's life—it may help the treatment process later.
- Accept that religion may play a healthy role that can help support treatment and recovery.
- Accept that even if it's unhealthy, a person may not be ready to let it go.
- Remember that what religion means to you might not be what it means to the patient.
- Arrange for pastoral consultation, with or without the patient, to process interfering factors.
- Understand the relational aspect of the person to God to better understand the need God fills in the person's life (perfectionism and the ideal are qualities inextricably linked in OCD).

Notes

1. Schwartz, "A Psychiatrist's View of Transference and Countertransference": 42.
2. Ibid.
3. Hayes et al., "Managing Countertransference": 89.
4. Rosmarin et al., "Attitudes toward Spirituality/Religion": 425.
5. Robinson, *Psychiatry and Religion*, 25.
6. Keijsers et al., "The Impact of Interpersonal Patient and Therapist Behavior."
7. Wampold, "Qualities and Actions of Effective Therapists": 3.
8. Griffith, "Managing Religious Countertransference in Clinical Settings."
9. Mowrer, "Transference and Scrupulosity": 337.

Bibliography

Griffith, James L. "Managing Religious Countertransference in Clinical Settings." *Psychiatric Annals* 36, no. 3 (March 2006).

Hayes, Jeffrey A., Charles J. Gelso, and Ann M. Hummel. "Managing Countertransference." *Psychotherapy* 48, no. 1 (2011): 88–97.

Keijsers, G. P. J., C. P. D. R. Schaap, and C. A. L. Hoogduin. "The Impact of Interpersonal Patient and Therapist Behavior on Outcome in Cognitive–Behavior Therapy: A Review of Empirical Studies." *Behavior Modification* 24, no. 2 (2000): 264–297.

Mowrer, O. Hobart. "Transference and Scrupulosity." *Journal of Religion and Health* 2, no. 4 (1963): 313–343.

Robinson, Lillian H. *Psychiatry and Religion: Overlapping Concerns.* Ed. Lillian H. Robinson Washington, DC: American Psychiatric Press, Inc., 1986.

Rosmarin, David H., Dovid Green, Steven Pirutinsky, and Dean McKay. "Attitudes toward Spirituality/Religion among Members of the Association for the Behavioral and Cognitive Therapies." *Professional Psychology: Research and Practice* 44, no. 6 (2013): 424–433.

Schwartz, Richard S. "A Psychiatrist's View of Transference and Countertransference in the Pastoral Relationship." *The Journal of Pastoral Care* Spring 1989, Vol. No. 1. XLIII, no. 1 (spring 1989): 41–46.

Wampold, Bruce E. "Qualities and Actions of Effective Therapists." *Continuing Education in Psychology* (2011): American Psychological Association.

Appendix A: Glossary

Accommodation—When others (family, coworkers, friends, etc.) help a person who has OCD to ritualize (for example, by purchasing toilet paper and paper towels, by completing rituals, or by waiting while he or she ritualizes). Accommodation, although usually well intended, actually makes a person's OCD worse. Family members can be helped by a therapist to learn different ways of being supportive without helping an individual to ritualize.

Automatic Thoughts—Thoughts that "pop" into one's mind during a certain situation. These thoughts, although sometimes very simple, can represent attitudes or beliefs that fuel feelings.

Avoidance Behavior—Any behavior that is done with the intention of avoiding a trigger to avoid anxiety. Avoidance behaviors are treated as a ritual.

Behavior Therapist—The therapist (or social worker or psychologist) who is in charge of a treatment plan for OCD using behavior therapy, most often exposure and response prevention.

Behavior Therapy—A type of therapy that applies learning theory principles to current problem behaviors that need changing. As the name implies, the point of intervention is at the behavioral level.

Checking Compulsions—Repetitive checking behaviors in order to reduce the probability that someone will be harmed, or to reduce the probability of a mistake. The checking can be behavioral (e.g., physically returning to a room to check if an appliance is turned off) or can take the form of a mental ritual (e.g., a mental review in which a person imagines in detail each step he or she took to complete a task).

Competing Alternative Behaviors—Someone trying to stop a bad habit can engage in a competing alternative behavior, an activity that inhibits the ability of the person who has OCD to engage in the habit that he or she is trying to break. For example, knitting prevents the pulling of one's own hair. *See also* Habit Reversal Treatment.

Compulsions—Compulsions, also known as rituals, are repetitive behaviors or thoughts that conform to rigid rules of number, order, and the like that function as an attempt to reduce anxiety brought on by intrusive thoughts.

Contamination Compulsions—Washing and cleaning behaviors performed in a particular order or at a particular frequency in an attempt to reduce chronic worry about being exposed to germs or becoming ill. This can also be done in response to emotional contamination, whereby a person washes and cleans to reduce the chances of taking on the characteristics of another person.

Contamination Obsessions—Excessive worries about germs, bodily functions, and illness. The risk is overestimated, considering the chances of actually getting sick.

Distraction—A strategy used primarily outside ERP to enhance the ability to resist rituals. A person performs another activity (e.g., playing a board game, watching television, taking a walk) while triggered to cope with anxiety without ritualizing.

Emotional Contamination Obsessions—Worry about being contaminated by the characteristics of another person. The worrier believes that the risk of "catching" the other person's personality is much like when one is exposed to germs. The spread of the "emotional germs" can be through touching, or can even be airborne. This usually includes magical thinking and superstitious behaviors.

Exposure and Response Prevention (ERP)—The behavioral treatment of choice for OCD, wherein a person who has OCD purposefully triggers an obsession and blocks his or her rituals to create habituation. ERP is initially done with the aid of a behavioral coach, who helps the person who has OCD resist rituals. Eventually the coaching is phased out as the person with OCD becomes more able to resist rituals without help.

Generalization—The transfer of learning from one environment to another, or from one stimulus to a broader range of stimuli in the same category.

Habit Reversal Treatment—The behavioral treatment of choice for Trichotillomania. In this treatment, the patient becomes more aware of patterns of picking or pulling, identifies the behaviors that bring on the picking or pulling, and then works on developing alternative behaviors to block the destructive habit. For instance, when feeling high levels of anxiety, a hair puller can knit, which keeps both hands occupied and keeps the individual engaged in a relaxing activity when he or she is at a high risk to pull.

Habituation—The process whereby a person stops responding to a stimulus because it is no longer new. For example, after jumping into a cold swimming pool, one might initially feel that the water is too cold; however, after splashing around for a few minutes, the water begins to feel warmer (even though the water temperature has not changed at all), because the swimmer has gotten used to the water temperature. An example of this in OCD would be when someone who worries about germs touches a doorknob without a barrier for at least 1.5 hours. As time passes without the person ritualizing, the person can no longer maintain an anxious response.

Harm Obsessions—Excessive worries that one will be harmed, or that others will be harmed, as a result of intentional or accidental behavior on the part of the person who has OCD.

Hierarchy—A list of situations or triggers that are ranked in order from easier to more difficult according to the patient's estimated SUDS ratings. Consider the hierarchy as a map or outline of future ERPs.

Hoarding Compulsions—Saving unreasonable quantities of an item "in case someone else might need it," even though space is no longer available to contain it. Objects are saved even when they are a health hazard.

Hoarding Obsessions—Worry that one must save more than is necessary to feel secure. The hoarder is not as disturbed by his or her saving and accumulation patterns as those around him or her are.

Insight—For someone with OCD, the understanding (when not triggered by an obsession) that one's worry is not realistic, nor does the logic applied to the person's ritual make any sense. Usually when one is triggered or experiencing high anxiety about an obsession, the level of insight decreases dramatically.

Mental Ritual—A mental act, done in response to an unwanted obsession, completed to reduce anxiety. Often a mental ritual must be repeated multiple times. It can be a prayer, a repeated phrase, a review of steps taken, a self-reassurance, or the like. Often a mental ritual is repeated so often that the individual barely has any awareness of the thought.

Mindfulness—A focus on the present. This is a skill that takes a considerable amount of practice.

Negative Reinforcement—When a reinforcement is removed, the behavior increases. When a person's headache is eased after taking an aspirin, that experience will increase the likelihood that the person will take an aspirin the next time he has a headache.

Neutralization—Refers to when an individual with OCD "undoes" a behavior or thought that is believed to be "dangerous" by neutralizing it with another behavior or thought. This behavior is also considered a ritual.

Not Just Right Experiences (NJREs)—Involves being stuck in the performance of a behavior until it "feels right." One might fear that something bad might happen, "but typically" there is no feared obsession. The experience is reported as a physiological feeling.

Obsessions—Obsessions are repetitive intrusive thoughts or images that dramatically increase anxiety. The obsessions are so unpleasant that the person who has OCD tries to control or suppress the fear. The more the person attempts to suppress the fear, the more entrenched and ever-present it becomes.

Obsessive Compulsive Disorder (OCD)—People who are diagnosed with OCD spend over an hour daily struggling with repetitive intrusive thoughts, impulses, or behavioral urges that increase their anxiety. They try to control their obsessions with compulsive behaviors (rituals) that function as an attempt to reduce their anxiety. Over time, the rituals become less and less effective in controlling the obsessions.

Overvalued Ideation—When the person who has OCD has great difficulty understanding that his or her worry is senseless.

Perfectionism—Unrealistically high expectations about performance on any task. Failure is catastrophic and unbearable. Anything less than absolute perfection is considered a failure. Consequently, perfectionists are paralyzed and sometimes unable to begin a task until the last minute, or sometimes unable to complete a task at all.

Praying Compulsions—Can include repetitive praying for forgiveness or asking God to protect a person perceived to be at risk, reading the Bible or watching religious television programming for hours daily, and repeatedly confessing possible sins.

Reassurance Seeking—When a person with OCD asks others questions repetitively to reduce his or her anxiety (for example, "Do you think this food is spoiled?" or "Do you think I will get sick?"). Sometimes a person with OCD can get reassurance merely from watching another's facial expression or body posture. All reassurance seeking is considered a ritual.

Relapse Prevention—A set of skills, both cognitive and behavioral, aimed at preventing an individual who has OCD from slipping back into old compulsive behaviors.

Retrigger—A thought or behavior completed by the individual who has OCD to undo the negative effects of the rituals. The person may feel relieved by a reassuring thought such as "I will be okay," but then must say to himself or herself, "Well, maybe I won't be okay—anything is possible."

Ritual—Another word for compulsive behavior, which can be a behavior that others can see or a hidden or unseen mental behavior. Many mental health professionals will identify anything that reduces one's anxiety as a ritual. For example, although avoidance behavior is done to avoid the trigger altogether, it still is the same as an outright ritual, in that it is an attempt to reduce anxiety.

Scrupulosity (Religious) Obsessions—Excessive worry about being moral, or worry about blasphemy.

Self-Reassurance—A thought or phrase said out loud or silently to lower one's anxiety (for example, "I'm not going to get sick," or "I would never hurt a child"). Considered a ritualistic behavior.

Sexual Obsessions—Unwanted, inappropriate sexual thoughts repulsive to the person affected. Often sexually aggressive toward a vulnerable population (children, the elderly, family, strangers).

Somatic Obsessions—Unrealistic worry about catching a particular illness (for example, HIV or hepatitis).

Subjective Units of Distress (SUDS)—A scale from either 1 to 10 or 1 to 100 against which the person with OCD rates his or her anxiety, with 1 being the least anxious. The scale indicates each individual person's sense of his or her own anxiety.

Superstitious Behavior—Behavior accidentally reinforced by coincidence. The behavior increases but does not have the influence that the person imagines it does.

Trigger—An external event or object or an internal thought that sets off an obsession.

Y-BOCS—Yale–Brown Obsessive Compulsive Scale. Includes a symptom checklist of OCD obsessions and compulsions and a rating scale to measure the severity of the OCD. Usually, people who score higher than 16 also meet the *DSM–TR* criteria for OCD.

Carol Hevia, PsyD
Behavior Therapist
OCD Institute, McLean Hospital

Appendix B: Types of Guilt Found in Western Literature

These are the types of guilt I've learned about over the years. Do any sound familiar?

Alien guilt: Humans die because they are born with and guilty of the sin of Adam.

Anticipated guilt: People will avoid actions that they anticipate will make them feel guilty.

Anticipatory guilt: Avoidance of transgressing; if an opportunity is neglected, an unwanted outcome will occur that the person could have prevented.

Deontological/Altruistic Guilt: Evolutionary traits that function to promote personal and moral values (deontological) and concern for interpersonal relationships (altrusitic).

Dobby Effect: When opportunities for compensation are not present, guilt may evoke self-punishment. Self-punishment was demonstrated through self-denied pleasure in a scenario study and by self-enforced penalties in an experimental study. The authors call this tendency for self-punishment the Dobby Effect and discuss it as an explanation for the widely held conviction that atonement absolves sins as well as its contribution to some types of psychopathology as and its possible functional relevance.

Emotional/subjective guilt: Requires a judgment (in the sense of a belief) that one actually is guilty, a judgment of "objective" guilt of the sort that implies moral responsibility.

Empathy-based guilt: Becomes pathogenic when it provokes cognitive errors in understanding causality.

Excessive guilt: Reflects a sense of cosmic disproportion between what is and what ought to be; unending remorse about past mistakes.

Existential guilt: Reflects a sense of cosmic disproportion between what is and what ought to be; a free-floating, non-specific internal sense that does not arise from personal failures or misbehavior.

Habitual/empathic guilt: The feeling of sympathy, with the feeling of sadness also present but with less force.

Inordinate guilt: Someone trying to serve God but always thinking about past sins is like a driver who is always looking in his or her rear-view mirror, putting himself or herself at greater risk of a crash.

Interpersonal guilt: Guilt was positively related to reported dissatisfaction with relationship among friends and in a work or school setting. Guilt was strongly related to such interpersonal variables as loneliness and shyness.

Maladaptive guilt: Chronic self-blame and an obsessive rumination over some objectionable or harmful behavior.

Misassigned guilt: When (abuse/trauma) victims blame themselves, introject their oppressors, and identify with their abusers.

Moral guilt: One reason for the frequent urge of human beings to accept guilt and responsibility where they have none is a deep-seated need to feel power over their lives, whether by influencing fate or by authoring events. It suggests, in other words, that accepting guilt may, on occasion, be the only way of attributing efficacy to oneself—and, as a corollary, that the pain of guilt may, in such circumstances, be less than the pain of irrelevance.

Neurotic guilt: Generally follows the mere thought or fantasy about wrongdoing; If the religious conflict becomes the conscious scene onto which an unconscious psychic conflict has been transposed—as is the case with neurotic guilt—it then becomes necessary to work it out on a specifically psychological level.

Normal/healthy guilt: Feeling anxious and disturbed about real and specific wrongful behaviors and feeling a desire to make reparation; violation of personal standards of right and wrong.

Obsessive emotional guilt: Serves as a drive that motivates compulsive responses, much as do fear and anxiety; whether OCD is guilt- or anxiety-determined disorder depends on whether the patient's early history emphasized the evil or the fearful nature of the impulses.

Omnipotent responsibility guilt: This guilt involves an exaggerated sense of responsibility and concern for the happiness and well being of others. Omnipotent responsibility guilt may be seen as an exaggeration of adaptive guilt, which concerns feeling anxious and disturbed about real and specific wrongful behaviors and the desire to make reparation.

Pathological guilt: Intent, even unconscious, is equated with deed, and the person reacts to the unconscious intent as if it were an already accomplished misdeed. Often the neurotic person of the obsessive–compulsive type unconsciously considers wrong what he unconsciously wishes to do. The endless rituals and gyrations to atone are understandable, but they are endless and relief seems never to come.

Reciprocal altruism: Evolutionary biology describes guilt as a component of reciprocal altruism selected for in humans to regulate opportunism in service of maintaining social relationships.

Religious guilt: Stifles the very life of faith and, by a surreptitious reemergence of passions that have been disregarded, ultimately alters the fundamental attitudes that govern faith. Even according to religious criteria, an exaggerated sense of guilt represents a distortion.

State guilt: Transitory feeling of the moment within a situation.

Survivor guilt: Mental condition that occurs when a person perceives himself or herself to have done wrong by surviving a traumatic event; a specific form of empathy-based guilt that tends to become pathogenic when based on a false belief that one's own success, happiness, or well-being is a source of unhappiness for others, simply by comparison. People who have high survivor guilt may falsely believe they are cheaters.

Trait guilt: An acquired disposition to avoid guilt-inducing behaviors.

Trauma-related guilt: Perceived responsibility for causing the event, perceived lack of justification for actions taken, and false beliefs about pre-outcome knowledge/hindsight bias.

Bibliography

Basile, B., F. Mancini, E. Macaluso, C. Caltagirone, R. S. Frackowiak, and M. Bozzali. "Deontological and Altruistic Guilt: Evidence for Distinct Neurobiological Substrates." *Human Brain Mapping* (April 2010).

Hampton, Simon J. "Can Evolutionary Psychology Learn from the Instinct Debate?" *History of the Human Sciences* 19, no. 4 (November 1, 2006): 57–74.

Jones, Warren H., and Karen Kugler. "Interpersonal Correlates of the Guilt Inventory." *Journal of Personality Assessment* 61, no. 2 (1993): 246–258.

Appendix C: Harder Personal Feelings Questionnaire

This test measures guilt and shame. For each of the following listed feelings, to the left of the item number, please write down a number from 0 to 4, reflecting how common the feeling is for you.

4 = Continuously or almost continuously
3 = Frequently but not continuously
2 = Some of the time
1 = Rarely
0 = Never

____ 1. Embarrassment

____ 2. Mild guilt

____ 3. Feeling ridiculous

____ 4. Worry about hurting or injuring someone

____ 5. Sadness

____ 6. Self-consciousness

____ 7. Humiliation

____ 8. Intense guilt

____ 9. Euphoria

____ 10. Feeling "stupid"

____ 11. Regret

____ 12. Feeling "childish"

____ 13. Mild happiness

____ 14. Feeling helpless, paralyzed

____ 15. Depression

_____ 16. Feelings of blushing

_____ 17. Feelings of deserving criticism for something you did

_____ 18. Feeling laughable

_____ 19. Rage

_____ 20. Enjoyment

_____ 21. Feeling disgusting to others

_____ 22. Remorse

To see your guilt score, add item numbers 2, 4, 8, 11, 17, and 22. The range is 0–24. If your score is 10 or more, then you have a higher level of guilt than most people.

To see your shame score, add item numbers 1, 3, 6, 7, 10, 13, 14, 16, 18, and 21. The range is 0–40. If your score was more than 16, then you have a higher level of shame than most people.

Source: D. W. Harder and A. Zalma, "Two Promising Shame and Guilt Scales: A Construct Validity Comparison," *Journal of Personality Assessment* 55 (1990): 729–745.

Appendix D: Rate Your OCD

To assess your OCD symptoms and the severity of your episode, please visit http://psychology-tools.com/yale-brown-obsessive-compulsive-scale/ to find out your score and the range of your OCD's severity. If you are in the moderate level and beyond, your OCD is interfering in your life more than necessary. Even if your severity level is on the lower end, you will still benefit from treatment.

Appendix E: Pennsylvania Inventory of Scrupulosity

Please circle your religious affiliation:

If yours is not listed, please circle "other" and write your religious group in the space provided.

Please use the space provided to rate how strongly you hold your religious beliefs:

1. not at all
2. somewhat
3. strongly
4. very strongly
5. extremely

Roman Catholic

Orthodox Christianity

Episcopalian

Lutheran

Methodist

Evangelical

Protestant

Baptist

Presbyterian

Fundamentalist Christian

Pentecostal

Jewish Orthodox

Jewish Conservative

Jewish Other

Christian

Jehovah's Witness

Mormon

Unitarian

Muslim

(Continued)

Buddhist
Hindu
Agnostic
Atheist
Other religion

Directions: The statements below refer to experiences that people sometimes have. Please indicate how often you have these experiences using the following key:

0--------------------1--------------------2--------------------3--------------------4
Never   Almost Never   Sometimes   Often   Almost Always

Fear of Sin: add numbers 1, 3, 4, 7, 8, 11, 12, 14, 16, and 18

1. _____ I worry that I might have dishonest thoughts.
2. _____ I fear I will act immorally.
3. _____ I feel urges to confess sins over and over again.
4. _____ I worry about heaven and hell.
5. _____ Feeling guilty interferes with my ability to enjoy things I would like to enjoy.
6. _____ Immoral thoughts come into my head, and I can't get rid of them.
7. _____ I am afraid my behavior is unacceptable to God.
8. _____ I must try hard to avoid having certain immoral thoughts.
9. _____ I am very worried that things I did may have been dishonest.
10. _____ I am afraid I will disobey God's rules/laws.
11. _____ I am afraid of having sexual thoughts.
12. _____ I feel guilty about immoral thoughts I have had.
13. _____ I worry that God is upset with me.
14. _____ I am afraid of having immoral thoughts.
15. _____ I am afraid my thoughts are unacceptable to God.

Fear of God: add numbers 5, 9, 13, 17, and 19

Total Score: _____

The total possible score is 60. If you scored below 24, you have subclinical scrupulosity. If your score was 24 or above, your scrupulosity warrants discussion with a mental health professional or a clergy member who has a background in psychology.

Source: Olatunji, B., J. Abramowitz, et al. (2007). "Scrupulosity and Obsessive–Compulsive Symptoms: Confirmatory Factor Analysis and Validity of the Penn Inventory of Scrupulosity." *Journal of Anxiety Disorders* 21, no. 6: 771–787.

Appendix F: The Loyola Religious Obsession and Compulsion Checklist

This checklist identifies some typical religious obsessions and compulsions. Under the following conditions, referral to a qualified mental health professional is necessary:

- *The symptoms are not improved with standard pastoral guidance.*
- *The symptoms interfere with important life activities.*
- *The symptoms generate significant emotional upset.*
- *The person has thoughts of harming self or others.*

Obsessions: Unwanted thoughts, impulses, or images that cause anxiety

Aggressive
Physically harming someone

- Fear of hitting someone with a car when driving
- Worry about harming someone with objects (e.g., knives, belts, cords, hot water, blankets)
- Images of people dying or being killed
- Worry about contamination of germs and poisons

Religious Obsessions
Blasphemous thoughts, urges impulses; doubts that one has fulfilled religious obligation faithfully

- Cursing God
- Making obscene gestures at religious figures, taking clothes off in church
- Obscene thoughts about religious figures or symbols
- Distractions during prayer or religious service

Moral Concerns
Excessive concern about honesty, or being charitable

- Counting change from sales transactions
- Checking income tax returns repeatedly

- Trivial concerns about being charitable to others—e.g., need to greet everyone passed on the street, donate to every homeless person, worry that a harmless statement injured someone, any negative statement "defames" a person

Unwanted Sexual Impulses
Sexual impulses, images, or thoughts

- Pedophilic thoughts
- Homosexual thoughts
- Thoughts about sexual perversions
- Belief that sexual feelings are sinful in themselves

Compulsions: Repetitive behaviors or mental acts in response to obsessions to reduce stress or prevent dreaded event. Any repeated behavior to "correct" for an unwanted obsession

Purification
Acts or behaviors meant to purify oneself to relieve guilt—not part of religious practice

- Showering after sexual activity for anxiety relief
- Cleaning the table carefully so as not to poison family

Repeating
Repeating religious acts

- Repeating prayers, religious rituals, confessing over and over, asking for forgiveness, seeking constant reassurance that one has not sinned

Joseph Ciarrocchi, PhD

Appendix G: Family Accommodation Scale for Obsessive–Compulsive Disorder

FAMILY ACCOMMODATION SCALE FOR OCD

Self-Rated Version (FAS-SR)

Today's Date: ____/____/____

Your Gender: *(circle one)*

1 = female 2 = male

I am the patient's _____. **[What is your relation to the patient?]** *(circle one)*

1 = parent 2 = spouse 3 = partner 4 = adult child 5 = sibling 6 = other

Introduction for the Family Member

You have been asked to complete this questionnaire because you have a relative or significant other who has been diagnosed with obsessive–compulsive disorder (OCD) and who has identified you as the family member who is most involved with him/her and the OCD. Throughout this questionnaire, your relative/significant other with OCD is referred to as "your relative" and you are referred to as the "family member."

Part I of this questionnaire describes obsessions and compulsions and asks you to identify your relative's current OCD symptoms to the best of your knowledge. Part II of this questionnaire asks you to identify possible ways in which you may be modifying your behavior or routines in response to your relative's OCD.

Part I: Report of Relative's OCD Symptoms Obsessions

Obsessions are distressing ideas, thoughts, images or impulses that repeatedly enter a person's mind and may seem to occur against his or her will. The thoughts may be repugnant or frightening or may seem senseless to the person who is experiencing them. Below is a list of different types of obsessions common in OCD. Please place a check mark by each type of obsession that your relative experienced (to the best of your knowledge) **during the past week**.

Obsessions

____ HARMING OBSESSIONS
Examples: fears of harming oneself or others, stealing things, blurting out obscenities or insults, acting on unwanted or embarrassing impulses; being responsible for something terrible happening (e.g., a fire or burglary); experiencing violent or horrific images.

____ CONTAMINATION OBSESSIONS
Examples: excessive concerns about or disgust with bodily waste, secretions, blood, germs; excessive concerns about being contaminated by environmental toxins (e.g., asbestos, radiation, or toxic waste), household cleansers/solvents, or animals (e.g., insects); discomfort with sticky substances or residues; fears of contaminating others.

____ SEXUAL OBSESSIONS
Examples: unwanted, repeated thoughts with forbidden or perverse sexual themes (e.g., sexual involvement with children).

____ HOARDING/SAVING OBSESSIONS
Examples: worries about throwing out seemingly unimportant things, resulting in accumulation of possessions that fill up or clutter active living areas or the workplace.

____ RELIGIOUS OBSESSIONS
Examples: intrusive blasphemous thoughts; excessive concerns about right and wrong/morality.

____ OBSESSION WITH NEED FOR SYMMETRY OR EXACTNESS
Examples: worries about whether items have been moved; worries that possessions are not properly aligned; worries about calculations or handwriting being perfect.

____ SOMATIC OBSESSIONS
Examples: excessive concerns about having an illness like AIDS or cancer, despite reassurance to the contrary; excessive concerns about a part of the body or aspect of appearance.

____ MISCELLANEOUS OBSESSIONS
Examples: an excessive need to know or remember unimportant details; a fear of losing things; a fear of saying certain words; a fear of not saying just the right thing; a discomfort with certain sounds or noises; or repeated thoughts of lucky or unlucky numbers.

Compulsions

Compulsions (also called rituals) are defined as behaviors or mental acts that a person feels driven to perform, although s/he may recognize them as senseless or excessive. It may be difficult or anxiety provoking for a person to resist performing these behaviors.

Below is a list of different types of compulsions common in OCD. Please place a check mark by each type of compulsion that your relative experienced (to the best of your knowledge) **during the past week**.

_____ CLEANING/WASHING COMPULSIONS

Examples: excessive or ritualized hand washing, showering, bathing, tooth brushing, grooming, or toilet routine; excessive cleaning of household items; efforts to prevent contact with contaminants.

_____ CHECKING COMPULSIONS

Examples: excessively checking locks, stove, appliances; checking to ensure that nothing terrible did or will happen, or that s/he did not make a mistake; checking tied to fears of illness.

_____ REPEATING RITUALS

Examples: rereading and/or rewriting things; repeating routine activities (e.g., going in/out of door, getting up/down from chair).

_____ COUNTING COMPULSIONS

Examples: counting floor tiles, books on a shelf, or words in a sentence.

_____ ORDERING/ARRANGING COMPULSIONS

Examples: excessive straightening of papers on a desk, adjusting furniture or picture frames.

_____ HOARDING/SAVING/COLLECTING COMPULSIONS

Examples: saving old newspapers, junk mail, wrappers, broken tools since they may be needed one day; picking up useless objects from the street or garbage cans.

_____ MISCELLANEOUS COMPULSIONS

Examples: seeking reassurance (e.g., by repeatedly asking the same question); excessive list making; taking measures to prevent harm to self or others, or to prevent terrible consequences; mental rituals other than checking or counting (e.g., reviewing, ritualized praying); need to touch or tap things; ritualized eating behaviors.

Part II: Report of Family Member's Responses to OCD

INSTRUCTIONS: Keeping in mind your relative's OCD symptoms that you identified in Part I, the next set of items describe possible ways that you may have responded to those symptoms during the past week. For each item, please indicate the **number of days during the past week** that you responded to your relative in the way specified. For each item, rate the NUMBER OF DAYS from 0–4 on the blank. If an item refers to something you did not do at all in the last week, fill in the circle for "none/never happened."

NUMBER OF DAYS THIS PAST WEEK

0 = None/Never

1 = 1 day

2 = 2–3 days

3 = 4–6 days

4 = every day

_____ 1. I reassured my relative that there were no grounds for his/her OCD-related worries. *Examples: reassuring my relative that s/he is not contaminated or that s/he is not terminally ill.*

_____ 2. I reassured my relative that the rituals he/she already performed took care of the OCD-related concern. *Examples: reassuring my relative that s/he did enough ritualized cleaning or checking.*

_____ 3. I waited for my relative while s/he completed compulsive behaviors.

_____ 4. I directly participated in my relative's compulsions. *Examples: doing repeated washing or checking at my relative's request.*

_____ 5. I did things that made it possible for my relative to complete compulsions. *Examples: driving back home so my relative can check if the doors are locked; creating extra space in the house for my relative's saved items.*

_____ 6. I provided my relative with OCD with items s/he needs to perform rituals or compulsions. *Examples: shopping for excessive quantities of soap or cleaning products for my relative.*

_____ 7. I did things that allowed my relative to avoid situations that might trigger obsessions or compulsions. *Examples: touching public door knobs for my relative so s/he wouldn't have to.*

_____ 8. I helped my relative make simple decisions when s/he couldn't do so because of OCD. *Examples: deciding which clothes my relative should put on in the morning or what brand of cereal s/he should buy.*

_____ 9. I helped my relative with personal tasks, such as washing, grooming, toileting, or dressing, when his/her ability to function was impaired by OCD.

_____ 10. I helped my relative prepare food when s/he couldn't do so because of OCD.

_____ 11. I took on family or household responsibilities that my relative couldn't adequately perform due to OCD. *Examples: doing bills, shopping, and/or taking care of children for my relative (when, except for OCD, I wouldn't have done so).*

_____ 12. I avoided talking about things that might trigger my relative's obsessions or compulsions.

_____ 13. I stopped myself from doing things that could have led my relative to have obsessions or compulsions. *Examples: not moving items that my relative has carefully lined up.*

_____ 14. I made excuses or lied for my relative when s/he missed work or a social activity because of his/her OCD.

_____ 15. I didn't do anything to stop unusual OCD-related behaviors by my relative. *Examples: tolerating my relative's repetitive actions such as going in and out of a doorway or touching/tapping objects a certain number of times.*

_____ 16. I put up with unusual conditions in my home because of my relative's OCD. *Examples: leaving the home cluttered with papers that my relative won't throw away.*

_____ 17. I cut back on leisure activities because of my relative's OCD. *Examples: spending less time socializing, doing hobbies, exercising.*

_____ 18. I changed my work or school schedule because of my relative's OCD.

_____ 19. I put off some of my family responsibilities because of my relative's OCD. *Examples: I spent less time than I would have liked with other relatives; I neglected my household chores.*

TOTAL SCORE *(sum of responses to items 1–19)* _____
A higher score indicates higher family accommodation of OCD.

Self-Rated Version (FAS-SR)

Developed by Anthony Pinto, PhD, Barbara Van Noppen, PhD, & Lisa Calvocoressi, PhD.

Copyright and Permissions

The Family Accommodation Scale for Obsessive Compulsive Disorder—Self-Rated Version (FAS–SR) copyright © 2012 by Anthony Pinto, PhD, Barbara Van Noppen, PhD, & Lisa Calvocoressi, PhD. The Family Accommodation Scale for Obsessive Compulsive Disorder—Self-Rated Version (FAS-SR) includes a modified version of the Yale Brown Obsessive Compulsive Scale (YBOCS) Checklist, copyright © 1986, 1989, with permission.

Bibliography

Pinto, A., B. Van Noppen, and L. Calvocoressi. "Development and Preliminary Psychometric Evaluation of a Self-rated Version of the Family Accommodation Scale for Obsessive–Compulsive Disorder. *Journal of Obsessive–Compulsive and Related Disorders* 2, no. 4 (October 1, 2013): 457–465.

Correspondence

For permission to use or adapt this instrument for clinical or research purposes, please contact

Lisa Calvocoressi, PhD
Yale University School of Public Health
Yale University School of Medicine
lisa.calvocoressi@yale.edu
Used by permission.

Index

Brain (*continued*)
  orbito-frontal, 25, 107; prefrontal
  cortex, 11, 44; striatum, 6
Bunyan, John, 51

Catholic(ism), 17, 48, 62, 67, 111, 160;
  Church, 47; fasting, 64, 71; mindset for
  prayer, 75
Clairvaux, Bernard, Saint, 49
Cleaning. *See* Behaviors
Clergy, 47, 112, 115, 116, 151, 160–161
Climacus, John, 48
Cognitive, 6, 110; bias, 30; considerations,
  42–44; defusion, 154; developmental
  stage, 82; domains specific to OCD,
  146–147; expressions, 29–31;
  restructuring, 149–150
Cognitive-behavior(al) therapy, 42, 81, 145,
  160–161, 174; treatment plan, 161
Compulsions. *See* Rituals
Compulsive, 69, 165, 166, 182; apologies,
  120; apologizers, 94; apologizing,
  119, 155–156; behaviors, 29, 167, 179,
  180; buying, 168; checking, 29; hand
  washer, 120; shoppers, 168; stealing,
  168; urges, 52
Confess, 13, 49, 66, 110, 190
Confessed, 48, 58
Confessing, 60, 113, 131, 143, 179, 192
Confession, 4, 49, 51, 67, 74, 87, 117, 161
Confessor, 49
Conscience, 3–16, 13, 79, 142, 174;
  conscience-related, 7, 79, 98, 112, 151,
  155; examination of, 67; examine, 116;
  examining, 113; guilty, 13, 74; obsessive
  4, 47–55, 60, 79, 84, 102, 108, 113, 122,
  146, 154; social, 30
Contamination, 24, 41, 53, 69, 93, 97, 101,
  108, 119, 140, 145, 177, 178; emotional,
  29, 80, 178; germ, 70, 121; moral, 138;
  spiritual, 122–123

de Ligouri, Alphonsus Maria, Saint, 50
de Pazzi, Mary Magdalene, Saint, 50

Dialectical Behavior Therapy (DBT),
  154, 155
Diaz, Cameron, 54
DiCaprio, Leonardo, 54
Donatus, Saint, 49
Doubt(s), 3; doubt, 3, 12, 24, 50, 52,
  54, 59, 73, 74, 75, 90, 93, 99, 122,
  126, 142, 152, 153, 158, 160, 191;
  nagging, 12; obsessive, 38, 39, 89,118;
  pathological, 24
Doubting disease, 61, 146
Dulaney, Siri, 27

Emotion(s), 26, 99, 126, 168; anger, 13, 101,
  102, 114, 149, 153, 154, 159, 168; moral,
  4, 5; negative, 4, 13, 38, 101, 102, 148,
  154; regulation, 153, 155
Emotional, avoidance, 154; contamination,
  29, 80, 178; dysregulation, 154; guilt,
  181, 182; response, 174
Empathy, 4
Epidemiology, 21
Erasmus, 51
Evolution, 5, 6, 14
Evolutionary: adaptations, 16; advantages,
  13; biologists, 17; biology, 11, 182;
  grounds, 14; pressures, 8; social,
  14; social function, 17; traits, 181;
  viewpoint, 15
Exactness, 13, 69, 142; obsession, 194
Exposure and response prevention (ERP),
  4, 7, 82, 94, 107–142

Foligno, Angela, Saint, 49
Forgiveness, 68
Fox, Megan, 54
Functional magnetic resolution imaging
  (fMRI). *See* Neuroimaging

Genoa, Catherine, Saint, 50
Generalized Anxiety Disorder, 42
Golden Rule, 15, 84–85
Greed. *See* Seven Deadly Sins
Greediness, 115

About the Author

Leslie J. Shapiro, LICSW, is a behavior therapist who has been treating OCD and related disorders since 1989 and who continues to provide treatment for patients at the OCD Institute, where she has worked since its inception in 1997. Early in her career, Shapiro developed expertise in addressing the conscience-related aspects that underlie almost all types of OCD symptoms. She was awarded the first Interdisciplinary Career Development Research Grant at McLean Hospital in Belmont, Massachusetts, to support her project "A Psychoeducational Group to Address Pathological Guilt in Obsessive Compulsive Disorder." She also received support from the David Judah Fund of Massachusetts General Hospital in Boston for her research on OCD, scrupulosity, and pathological guilt. Along with having made dozens of clinical and research presentations on scrupulosity and obsessive guilt, she has several professional publications, including L. J. Shapiro, J. W. Krominger, C. M. Gironda, & J. A. Elias, "Development of a Scrupulosity Severity Scale Using the Pennsylvania Inventory of Scrupulosity–Revised," *Journal of Obsessive–Compulsive and Related Disorders*, 2 (2013): 420–424, and L. J. Shapiro & S. E. Stewart, "Pathological Guilt: A Persistent Yet Overlooked Treatment Factor in Obsessive–Compulsive Disorder," *Annals of Clinical Psychiatry*, 23 (2011): 63–70. She is a committee member of the Partners for Research Advancement in Nursing and Social Work. Her other roles involve teaching, supervising, and training students and staff at the OCD Institute. She was invited to be an expert content editor for a continuing education course titled "Obsessive–Compulsive Disorder: Signs, Symptoms, and Treatment." She is a graduate of the Boston University School of Social Work, where she has also been an adjunct professor, and has been a lecturer at Harvard Medical School.